Greatness and Goodness:

BARBARO

AND HIS LEGACY

April 29, 2003 – January 29, 2007

2006 KENTUCKY DERBY WINNER

ALEX BROWN

Illustrated by Lynden Godsoe

First Edition
First Printing

Copyright © 2011 by Alex Brown

Published by Glen View Media
308 Baker Drive
Lincoln University, PA 19352
302.750.0468
info@glenviewmedia.com
www.glenviewmedia.com

Cover and Interior Design: Gwyn Kennedy Snider
Front Cover Photo: Barbara Livingston
Back Cover Photo: Matt Wooley/Equisport Photos
Barbaro Foxhound Photo: Rai Phelan
Back Cover Quote: Eric Liddell as portrayed in *Chariots of Fire*

ISBN 978-0-9832139-0-1

Printed in Canada

Praise for *Greatness and Goodness: Barbaro and His Legacy*

"For over eight months, people all over the world became immersed in Barbaro's battle for survival, turning to Alex Brown's website for the latest information, as reported to him by New Bolton Medical Center. In his new book, Brown has crafted an engrossing behind-the-scenes look at those unforgettable eight months, during which the racing world and mainstream America came together in hope and prayer, while in constant admiration of Barbaro's courage and determination. Brown takes the reader through every touching moment of Barbaro's plight, from the setbacks to the days of progress when it appeared the story would have a miracle ending. Brown also branches off into other aspects of Barbaro's story, including the positive effect it had on veterinary medicine and the emergence of horse rescue organizations all over the country. And it is all displayed with beautiful, never-before-seen photos that tell the entire story, from Barbaro's birth to his death. Even if you weren't part of the Barbaro saga, you will relish every page of this unique and enlightening chronicle of a very special horse."

-STEVE HASKIN, Senior Correspondent, *The Blood-Horse*

"Alex Brown's *Greatness and Goodness: Barbaro and His Legacy* doubtless will remain the most comprehensive biography of this brilliant racehorse. For that reason, it is an important reference for racing historians and fans. What makes Greatness and Goodness even more than that is its careful examination how and why Barbaro inspired people around the globe to create his real legacy: the salvation of countless horses from disease and slaughter."

-GLENYE CAIN OAKFORD, writer, *Daily Racing Form*, and author of *The Home Run Horse*

"Alex Brown brings a horseman's inside knowledge, an intrepid journalist's persistence and, just as important, a fine writing touch to the story of Barbaro. Nobody is more qualified to get his arms around the whole saga. In fact, nobody wrote more words about Barbaro when he was alive, or got to know all the parties involved like Alex did. He did all that while getting up before dawn to exercise horses every morning. Read the first chapter and you'll be hooked."

-MIKE JENSEN, writer, *Philadelphia Inquirer* and winner of an Eclipse Award for a story on Dr. Dean Richardson.

"Alex Brown, who kept Barbaro's story going throughout his life, has done even more to heighten this amazing horse's legacy. Through extraordinary details and interviews with virtually everyone connected with Barbaro's remarkable life, Alex has created a non-fiction work of art that stands as a monument to everyone connected with Barbaro and everything he's come to represent. If you thought you knew everything about this remarkable Thoroughbred, think again. Alex Brown has risen to the occasion by writing a Grade 1 tribute to the Jacksons and their amazing athlete."

-MICHAEL BLOWEN, President, Old Friends

"Drawing many voices into a compelling chorus, Alex Brown's work celebrates a remarkable life while welcoming us into stories that still are unfolding. Through powerful words and pictures, we feel Barbaro's presence, revel in his triumphs, and yearn for what might have been. But this book also is devoted to what still can be. Understanding the perils that injured and unwanted horses face, and seeing how a community rallied to confront those challenges when Barbaro stirred their souls, new audiences may feel moved to join those who continue to support horse research and rescue in Barbaro's name."

-DOROTHY OURS, Author, *Man o' War: A Legend Like Lightning*

"Alex Brown garnered a reputation as a true trailblazer and leading-edge thinker during his fifteen year tenure as an MBA Admissions officer at the University of Delaware and the University of Pennsylvania's Wharton School. He brings that same sense of adventure to his story of Barbaro. His access to the people who really knew Barbaro and the racing industry as well as the 164-photo essay sets this book apart. Barbaro has a tremendous advocate in Alex Brown."

-JENNIFER CHIZUK, Chief Operating Officer /Senior Assistant Dean, Haas School of Business, UC Berkeley

This book is dedicated to Dicky and Ralph.

Acknowledgments

Many, many people made this book what it is. If the book is successful, then these people are why.

This book would not have come to pass without the support of Barbaro's owners, Roy and Gretchen Jackson. Their support for my work as I managed TimWoolleyRacing.com during Barbaro's time at New Bolton Center was critical. Their support for this book project has also been critical. Without their support, I would not have embarked on either endeavor, and without their support, I am sure I would not have been able to conduct the number of interviews I was able to for this book.

I also need to thank all those associated with Barbaro during his life, specifically Michael Matz and his team, and Dean Richardson and his team. They were instrumental in the success of TimWoolleyRacing.com and thus the formation of Fans of Barbaro and the work that has followed. On that note, I should also thank Tim and Penny Woolley, for allowing me to borrow their website for a few months!

In December 2009 Carolyn Karlson met with me when I returned from my more-than-two-year travel experience, and really encouraged me to write this book. I had already made a few false starts along the way, and Carolyn persuaded me to continue and offered to help with putting the work together. Carolyn put in hundreds of hours helping put shape to the content, while also helping with the editing.

Kim Gatto also put in hundreds of hours. Kim would take the content that Carolyn and I had developed, and then would provide detailed feedback. I would work with that feedback, and then Kim would take another look, and then another. Kim also wrote a little content, when I was tired and had run out of energy.

Carolyn and Kim have been amazing. It makes you wonder what I did really! Well, I did do a lot of interviews, and this book would not be what it is without the insights from the nearly one hundred people I interviewed and those who helped me seek out the right people to interview.

They are: Alexa King (sculptor), Dr. Amy Woodford (vet), Barbara Livingston (photographer), Dr. Barbara Dallap (New Bolton Center), Barclay Tagg (trainer), Beverly Strauss (MidAtlantic Thoroughbred Rescue), Bill Finley (*New York Times*), Bill Nack (author), Bill Sanborn (Sanborn Chase), Bruce Wagner (Pimlico), Chip Woolley (trainer), Chris Sobocinski (Delaware Park), Christine Picavet (artist), Dr. Chuck Arensberg (vet), Dr. Corinne Sweeney (New Bolton Center), Dr. Dan Dreyfuss (Pimlico), Dan Gelston (Associated Press), Dan Hendricks (trainer), Dave Johnson (race caller), Dave Rodman (race caller), Dr. David Zipf (Pimlico), Dr. Dean Richardson (New Bolton Center), Debby Oxley (owner), Debbye Turner Bell (ABC), Dick Jerardi (*Philadelphia Daily News*), Dorothy Ours (author), Ed Bowen (Jockey Club-Grayson Foundation), Ed Fountaine (*New York Post*), Ed Madden (Matz's team), Edgar Prado (jockey), Fran Jurga (*Hoofcare and Lameness Magazine*), Fred Stone (artist), Gary Stevens (jockey), Gladys McHargue (Pimlico), Glen Kozak (Pimlico), Glenye Oakford (*Daily Racing Form*), Graham Motion (trainer), Dr. Hanna Galantino-Homer (New Bolton Center), Headley Bell (Mill Ridge Farm), Henry Heymering (farrier), Dr. Hollie Stillwell (vet), Jack Ireland (*News Journal*), Dr. James Orsini (New Bolton Center), Jane Simone (New Bolton Center), Javier Castellano (jockey), Jay Hovdey (*Daily Racing Form*), Jay Privman (ESPN), Jeannine Edwards (ESPN), Jennie Rees (*Courier-Journal*), Jennifer Morrison (*Toronto Star*), Jennifer Rench (New Bolton Center), Jennifer

Roytz (Three Chimneys), Jill Baffert, Jill Stephens (Stephens Thoroughbreds), John Asher (Churchill Downs), John Hennegan (*First Saturday in May*), Kathee Rengert (Fair Hill), Kathleen Fallon (Breyer), Dr. Kathy Anderson (Fair Hill), Kathy Freeborn (New Bolton Center), Kim Brette (Matz's team), Dr. Laura Richardson (vet), Laurie McDowell (Pimlico), Dr. Liberty Getman (New Bolton Center), Lou Raffetto (Pimlico), Matt Hartmann (Pimlico), Michael Blowen (Old Friends Equine), Michael Dickinson (trainer), Michael Gathagan (Pimlico), Michael Matz (trainer), Michael Jensen (*Philadelphia Inquirer*), Michael Schuh (WJZ), Michael Trombetta (trainer), Michael Welsch (*Daily Racing Form*), Michelle Hyland (Matz's team), Pat Forde (ESPN), Dr. Patricia Hogan (vet), Peter Brette (Matz's team), Peter Rotondo (NTRA), Dr. Rachel Beard (Pimlico), Ramon Dominguez (jockey), Randy Moss (ESPN), Ray Paulick (*Blood-Horse*), Richard Rosenblatt (Associated Press), Richard Bozich (*Courier-Journal*), Russell Jones, Sabina Louise Pierce (photographer), Sandy McKee (*Baltimore Sun*), Sarah Baker (New Bolton Center), Dr. Scott Palmer (vet), Sean Clancy (author), Sharon Greenberg (Pimlico), Sid Fernando (pedigree expert), Staci Hancock (Stone Farm), Steve Haskin (*Blood-Horse*), Sue McMullen (*Scottish Herald*), Tom Albertrani (trainer), Tom Durkin (race caller), Tom Law (*Thoroughbred Times*), Tom Pedulla (*USA Today*), Tom Zungailia (Jacksons), Vic Stauffer (race caller), Victoria DeMore (photographer), Vic Zast (author), and Wendy Treinan (Kentucky Derby Museum).

Many of the photographers for this book provided me photographs either for free or for a fee once the book has been sold. I am especially thankful for Adam Coglianese, Barbara Livingston, Brandon Benson, Chad Harmon, Cindy Dulay, Lydia Williams, Matt Wooley, Rai Phelan, Sabina Louise Pierce, Sarah Andrew, Shawn Foley, and Terence Dulay.

Lynden Godsoe did the illustrations for this book. I just love them, and am very grateful for her work and dedication.

Others who helped with providing feedback, printing, and other tasks that were necessary for me to keep moving forward are: Alyssa Hernandez, Claudette Lemesurier, Corinne Phillips, Gary Littlewood, Jayne Lornie, Jennifer Duffy, Nancy Sanderson, Priscilla Godsoe, and Sanjay Modi.

This book would not have happened without the support I received from those who helped develop, run, and manage both TimWoolleyRacing.com and AlexBrownRacing.com. They include Eliza James (web design), Brad Garrison (web development and support), Wendy Wooley, Mary Locarumo, Katarina Villaneuva, and Amy Spear. Prospero, which was acquired by mZinga, provided a free license for our discussion board. I will always be grateful for that generosity. I should also acknowledge the co-hosts of our ABR radio show, Andy Durnin and Bob Hatfield. Thanks also to Lisa Grimm and Sue McMullen, who provided original content for our website. And finally, the support I received from Kelly Colgan, who facilitated my two year travel experience by making sure my bills were paid.

This book has been truly a team effort. I sincerely thank everyone I have mentioned, and no doubt a few I neglected to mention, for making this book what it is.

Contents

Foreword

Perhaps once or twice in a lifetime, an event or encounter leaves a mark upon our soul and changes us forever. While at times the impact or meaning may not be evident for years to come, these experiences have a way of leaving us better, more enlightened people. For many, Barbaro's struggle for survival was one of those events.

The dramatic moments in Barbaro's life have been chronicled and reflected upon, but never in the manner of this book. Alex Brown doesn't just detail Barbaro's improbable journey, he takes us inside the journey with him. Alex is a horseman who shared Barbaro's home base of Fair Hill and was close to several people connected with the horse. His background in Internet marketing afforded Alex the unique ability to chronicle the horse's meteoric rise and ultimate demise in a fashion that kept followers riveted on a daily basis. Alex later became an integral part of Barbaro's saga, earning the trust of Gretchen and Roy Jackson, and becoming one of only a select few to tend to the horse during his hospitalization.

This book will take you beyond the news reports, inside Barbaro's formative years as a youngster, and later, inside a voyage—heartache and all—that would leave its mark on followers around the globe. From the perspective of someone in the media, it was the most emotional story I've ever covered.

At Pimlico, some of us were standing in the infield, right on the finish line, near the Preakness winner's circle as Barbaro burst through the starting gate early. It was rather alarming, but Edgar Prado and the outrider quickly pulled him up. As the race began, all I remember was the blurred image of a horse being passed quickly by others, followed by gasps from the crowd, and then silence. Barbaro was struggling to come to a halt on three legs, not far from where we were standing. The race continued on, virtually meaningless at that point. The air had literally been sucked out of Pimlico. You could hear a pin drop. It was like being kicked in the stomach.

We ran across the track and up into the jocks' room to attempt an interview with Edgar, but he was too distraught to speak on camera. I then ran back down and interviewed Dr. Larry Bramlage, one of the foremost equine orthopedic surgeons and the "AAEP Vet On Call" for our TV shows. He gave me a very preliminary briefing. It appeared to be a catastrophic injury and the situation was critical.

A long and challenging surgical repair took place the next day at the University of Pennsylvania's New Bolton Center. We spent eleven hours there, keeping the viewers informed of Barbaro's tenuous battle for life.

Ten days later, I was privileged to be part of ABC's and ESPN's access to Edgar's visit with Barbaro. It was the first time Edgar had seen Barbaro since the Preakness, and we were in the ICU with our cameras, all done up in scrubs, as the reunion took place. I loved how Barbaro tried to push people around and wanted to march right out of his stall. It was heartwarming to say the least. Edgar told me it was comforting to see how bright and well his partner looked. But the pendulum was about to swing.

In early July, some of those "bad things" that Barbaro's surgeon, Dr. Dean Richardson, kept warning us about, started to happen. Barbaro wasn't comfortable, had an infection, and underwent several cast changes. I was sent to cover these developments as ESPN took a genuine interest in the horse's welfare and wanted to follow the story every step of the way. The network felt Barbaro was important to their audience. (As it turned out, Barbaro was important to *every* audience.) Viewers were horrified and saddened, as were we, when Dr. Richardson told us Barbaro had foundered severely in his left hind foot, and his chances for survival were poor. He could not have been more direct. Barbaro had as bad a case of laminitis as you could get. But somehow Barbaro plugged on. The pendulum was swinging again.

In mid-November, we were hearing talk of Barbaro possibly being well enough to move on to a new home. ESPN told me they wanted to cover it, whenever that day arrived. Little did we know, it never would.

Three days before Barbaro's death, I spoke to Dr. Richardson and asked how Barbaro was. He said, "He's not where I'd like him to be. It's terribly disappointing. He's up and eating his grass, but he's not where I want him to be. It's been a rough few weeks." Dr. Richardson sounded dejected. Two days later, Richardson applied an external fixator to Barbaro's leg, to literally hold it together and bear weight for him. I spoke to Michael Matz about the horse's deteriorating condition. Michael was subdued and seemed ill at ease. He told me, "How many times can you get punched in the nose and keep getting back up?"

I got the news two days later that a press conference was coming, and that Barbaro had been put down. I rushed up to New Bolton Center and did several live reports upon arriving. Once again, as we had done many times before, the media gathered in the amphitheatre. Back on May 21, the mood was one of foreboding, anticipation, and the unknown. Over the next eight months, it would swing from cautious optimism to grim reality and back again. But always there was a glimmer of hope. On Monday, January 29, 2007, it was over.

But Barbaro's story didn't end there. In fact, it was still evolving in a wonderful, heartwarming, positive way. Let Alex take you on this implausible journey . . . you too will most certainly emerge with a profound mark upon your soul.

JEANNINE EDWARDS
ESPN REPORTER

PART ONE

BARBARO

Christmas Day, 2006

TODAY I WAS HELPING OUT WITH BARBARO in the absence of Tom Mehrtens, the Jacksons' farm manager. The idea was for me to go over to New Bolton Center, groom Barbaro, and take him out to walk and graze. While I had planned to arrive at 1:00 p.m., I decided to go earlier after surveying the clouds. I also had another poster to hang on the outside fence (likely the first from overseas), so I arrived around 12:15 p.m. to hang the poster and to visit Barbaro.

Upon arriving at the ICU, I noticed that a few people were already there. On hand were Lucy and Tom (Mr. and Mrs. Jackson's daughter and son-in-law) and their four children (the Jacksons' grandchildren, who visit quite often). I had met Tom before, so it was nice to be able to meet their entire family, who seem to be very nice people (no surprise there). On duty in the ICU was Kathleen Gardner. Ray Gonzalez was also helping out.

I set to work as I chatted away with Barbaro's visitors. I entered Barbaro's stall, put on his halter, and tied him up in preparation for grooming. I planned to give him a quick groom before he went out, and then a more thorough job once he had been outside. I started by picking out his front feet, then I gave Barbaro a quick once over with a body brush. He seemed to really enjoy it as I was brushing his forelock, something I would not have entirely anticipated. Anyway, it did not take me long to get him ready.

I put a blanket and shank on him, and led him outside. Barbaro's visitors then left, and I was one-on-one with Barbaro for the first time while we were outside. It was very cool. He was so well behaved when he was outside, just very happy to be in a different environment. In his stall, you had better keep an eye on him, and make

purposeful moves. Outside he was just much more relaxed.

After grazing for five minutes, it started raining very lightly. I thought I would have to bring him in quickly so I decided to have him do his walking, just to make sure he got his exercise. Barbaro was so intent on eating that it took me a little while to convince him to walk on, but once walking we did our five minutes pretty easily. By that time, the drizzle had eased off and Barbaro went back to grazing. He was very happy. It was peaceful. After about forty-five minutes in total, I decided to bring him in. The drizzle had returned and there was no need to get wet.

Once he was back in his stall and tied up, I went to work grooming Barbaro. This time I used a curry comb and body brush. Because his disposition changed slightly in the stall, I was more careful with him, spending most of the brushing time with one hand on his halter, my eyes locked on his eyes. Barbaro cleaned up very well. I then picked out his feet for a second time, and finally attended to his head with a light sponging out of his nostrils and eyes, followed by a wipe over with a rag. I then let him loose in his stall. Along the way, I fed him a couple of carrots.

All in all, it was another very pleasant visit. I chatted with Kathleen and Ray a little. I left the ICU at 1:45 p.m., so I shared a peaceful hour and a half with Barbaro on Christmas Day.

The above was written shortly after my Christmas Day visit with Barbaro, and posted to TimWoolleyRacing.com

The Early Years

LA VILLE ROUGE

Kathee Rengert was sitting at her home in Pennsylvania, feeling somewhat sorry for herself. It was the Keeneland October sales of 1998, and because of health issues, Rengert was unable to attend. This situation is less than ideal for a bloodstock agent, whose business is recommending horse purchases for clients. Especially since Rengert's friends and clients, Roy and Gretchen Jackson, were there looking at weanlings with another friend and bloodstock agent, Russell Jones.

Rengert opened up the *Daily Racing Form,* the horse racing industry's trade paper. As she browsed the pages, her attention was drawn to a lightly raced two-year-old filly in New York that had "good numbers." The horse's name was La Ville Rouge. Rengert wondered if this filly would suit the Jacksons. And more importantly, would she be for sale?

As an outsider, the world of thoroughbred racing can seem very complex, but upon closer inspection it is obvious that most horses are for sale. Rengert knew the trainer of the filly—another friend, Philip Serpe. She made the call. She asked Serpe about the two-year-old and learned that indeed, the filly was for sale; however, another prospective purchaser had planned to inspect her. Rengert asked Serpe whether she could get first option on the filly if she had someone look at her first thing the next day. This type of aggressive negotiation was very unlike Rengert, but in this case, it worked and her friend agreed.

Rengert's next call was to Russell Jones at Keeneland. She mentioned La Ville Rouge, noting that she had not seen the filly. Rengert explained that La Ville Rouge had a decent pedigree and a good, albeit short, race record. Rengert expected Russell to go to New York to see the filly. She was surprised when the Jacksons themselves headed up to New York the next morning.

They looked at La Ville Rouge, and made a deal based on a clean vet exam.

La Ville Rouge had three trainers in her career: Phil Serpe, Graham Motion, and finally Phil Johnson. During the time Johnson trained La Ville Rouge, Debra Cedano was an assistant trainer. Cedano remembered, "La Ville was one of the toughest racehorses that I have been around. The more she trained the better she got. She hated her mane being pulled, but she loved sugar cubes. I think sugar cubes saved her groom's life on numerous occasions. She loved to pin him in the back of the stall and he would yell for help. I really loved her! She had so much character."

La Ville Rouge never did win a stakes race. She ran twenty-five times over a three-year period, demonstrating her durability in a series of very creditable races. She was second in the Grade 3 Tempted Stakes at Aqueduct as a two-year-old. As a four-year-old, she placed three times in graded stakes. Coincidentally, jockey Edgar Prado rode her on six occasions, winning once, an allowance race. In total, La Ville Rouge bankrolled a little more than $250,000 in a racing career that spanned three years.

Once La Ville Rouge's career was over, she had residual value as a broodmare. At the time, that was one of the focuses of the Jacksons' bloodstock strategy: buying fillies with decent pedigrees that would have value as both potential racehorses and as breeding stock.

Now retired, La Ville Rouge was sent to Saint Ballado for her first mating. This match produced Holy Ground, a good-looking chestnut colt that also had a decent race record. In 2005, he won the Stanton Stakes at Delaware Park by thirteen lengths. He also demonstrated versatility by winning on dirt, turf, and a sloppy racetrack in his abbreviated career.

Headley Bell became the Jacksons' bloodstock advisor in 2001. It was in Bell's first year working for the Jacksons that La Ville Rouge was sent to Dynaformer for her second mating. It was an auspicious beginning to their working relationship, but Bell will admit that Dynaformer was not initially his first choice. He had created a list of three stallions for this La Ville Rouge mating to recommend to the Jacksons. Capote and Saint Ballado were above Dynaformer on that list. The recommendations were designed not only to suit La Ville Rouge, but also the Jacksons' other mares. Mating decisions were made in terms of how they would affect the entire broodmare band. Bell and the Jacksons discussed the three options for La Ville Rouge and ultimately selected Dynaformer.

"La Ville Rouge ran her best races from six furlongs to a mile and an eighth, and she has classic American speed in her pedigree," explained *Daily Racing Form* writer Glenye Cain-Oakford about the match in the summer of 2010. "She is by a proven sprint sire, Carson City, who is by Mr. Prospector, one of the great American speed influences in the modern era. Dynaformer tends to get horses that prefer a distance of ground, but he had strategic speed himself. So the mating of Dynaformer and La Ville Rouge looked on paper like a nice combination of speed and distance. You are adding a good dose of stamina through Dynaformer, without giving up the tactical turn of foot that both the male and female sides of Barbaro's pedigree suggest."

Several factors helped Bell and the Jacksons select Dynaformer for La Ville Rouge, including how Dynaformer's pedigree would match with the pedigree of La Ville Rouge, the adaptability of Dynaformer runners to perform well on any surface, the compatibility of Dynaformer's conformation, and his size. La Ville Rouge was not a big mare and by mating her with Dynaformer, it was thought she would be able to produce a larger horse.

Dynaformer's initial stud fee was $5,000 in 1990. His stud fee in 2002 when he was first mated to La Ville Rouge was $50,000. His stud fee in 2010 was $150,000.

Dynaformer tends to not be commercially fashionable because his foals can be plain looking and late-maturing. Both these issues are problematic for commercial breeders who want to target the sales ring for a rapid return on their investment. However, Dynaformer's offspring tend to run and are durable in the sense that they can have long careers. Perfect Drift and Film Maker, two of Dynaformer's highest-earning progeny, competed until they were nine years old and six years old, respectively.

Sandy Hatfield, stallion manager at Three Chimneys where Dynaformer was based for most of his career, commented about Dynaformer, "First of all, let me describe Dynaformer's physical appearance—dark bay, seventeen hands, he has nice short cannon bones and pasterns, a short back, and long underline. He is very correct with a lot of bone. He is perhaps a little plain in the handsome department, but as they say 'Pretty is as pretty does' and as a sire he does it all!

"Regarding Dynaformer's personality, let's just say that he doesn't suffer fools lightly. He is a bit on the aggressive side and is very much a creature of opportunity so you never want to take your eyes off him while you are handling him. One thing nice about him that I can't say about all the tough horses I have handled is that he will usually let you know when he has had enough and you better start doing something else! Most of the time, if you are paying attention, he is all right but if he is in a bad mood the best way to handle it is just do what needs to be done and leave him alone. He kind of reminds me of a neighbor's pit bull: he's all right with the owner and he looks fairly nice but you wouldn't want to go in the house uninvited!"

The fact that La Ville Rouge was first sent to Saint Ballado indicates that there was no divine understanding that the Dynaformer/La Ville Rouge mating would create the greatness that we were to witness in Barbaro. After La Ville Rouge was mated to Dynaformer for the first time, which produced Barbaro, she was sent to

Quiet American for her third mating. Man in Havana, the subsequent foal, never raced. For her fourth mating, she was sent to Deputy Minister. Sadly, she did not carry that foal to term. When it appeared that Barbaro was a very nice yearling, it was decided that La Ville Rouge would return to Dynaformer. Of course, once Barbaro started running, the decision was repeated each year through to 2010.

The dam plays a very strong part in any mating decision. Not only does she represent half of the pedigree, but she also nurtures the subsequent foal for the first few months of its life.

"Of course, once they produce a baby like Barbaro you take notice," said Bell about La Ville Rouge. "But she has so much class, much like the Jacksons in that regard. She clocks everything. She's very attentive to her offspring. She's the boss, but she is also very feminine and independent. In terms of conformation she is short-coupled and average size, but a bit bigger than the typical Carson City stock."

SANBORN CHASE: BIRTH
"La Ville" Baby — 0–17 Months

Barbaro spent more time—seventeen months—with Bill Sanborn at Sanborn Chase than he did with anyone else.

Barbaro was born on April 29, 2003, at Sanborn Chase in Nicholasville, Kentucky. Bill Sanborn and night watchman Irvin White assisted with the foaling. Even at birth, Barbaro was large. La Ville Rouge, a light-framed and well-balanced mare, was not big. As La Ville Rouge pushed, Sanborn pulled on Barbaro's front legs. Hold, push, and pull. Once Barbaro's shoulders were clear he came out with ease. Sanborn remembers that Barbaro was a leggy foal, somewhat narrow compared to his older half brother Holy Ground, but taller. Barbaro was soon on his feet, remarkably quickly for a foal with so much leg—a strong indication of athleticism and balance.

One of about 34,000 registered thoroughbred foals born that year with aspirations for greatness, Barbaro impressed Sanborn even in the early days. Sanborn

Barbaro at six weeks

had also foaled Holy Ground who, like Barbaro, had a terrific attitude when around people. Where they differed, however, was Barbaro's attitude when he was outside with his herd-mates. When he was young, Holy Ground was laid-back when outside, only really doing just enough and quite content with doing very little. Barbaro, on the other hand, was a player. He would race around with his friends and try to dominate. One foal in particular, Last Best Place (by Gone West), was Barbaro's close companion. The two would spend hours outside running around, challenging each other, and basically just being horses, albeit young horses.

Sanborn suggests three attributes that are critical for a young horse with aspirations to be a great racehorse: mind and attitude; interaction in the field; and physical presence. Barbaro, from the beginning, clearly exhibited all three.

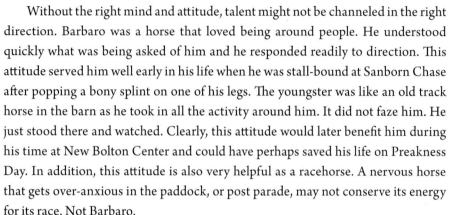

Mind and Attitude

Without the right mind and attitude, talent might not be channeled in the right direction. Barbaro was a horse that loved being around people. He understood quickly what was being asked of him and he responded readily to direction. This attitude served him well early in his life when he was stall-bound at Sanborn Chase after popping a bony splint on one of his legs. The youngster was like an old track horse in the barn as he took in all the activity around him. It did not faze him. He just stood there and watched. Clearly, this attitude would later benefit him during his time at New Bolton Center and could have perhaps saved his life on Preakness Day. In addition, this attitude is also very helpful as a racehorse. A nervous horse that gets over-anxious in the paddock, or post parade, may not conserve its energy for its race. Not Barbaro.

Interaction in the Field

Known as "hell raisers," Barbaro and Last Best Place often played with each other in the field. They would run, play, jump, and race each other from the time they were foals. In fact, they were only separated when Last Best Place became too much of a handful in the early summer of 2004.

Nearly 34,000 registered thoroughbred foals were born in 2003. Of those foals, 441 were nominated to the 2006 Triple Crown. Twenty were entered to race in the Kentucky Derby. One won.

Physical Presence

From the time he was born, Barbaro was a big horse relative to his peers. Sometimes size can result in clumsiness. This was clearly not the case with Barbaro, who displayed his athleticism and balance very early on.

Headley Bell visited the Jacksons' foals and yearlings at Sanborn Chase and created reports to send to the Jacksons. Here are three of those reports about Barbaro:

THE BEGINNING OF JULY 2003, BARBARO WAS TWO MONTHS OLD: *"A very big colt who is quite strong and has very good use. Considering he is a Dynaformer, he has good quality and hopefully won't be too big."*

EARLY JANUARY 2004, BARBARO HAD JUST TURNED ONE AT THE TIME (all thoroughbreds in the Northern Hemisphere celebrate their birthday on January 1): *"Also a very nice individual especially for being a Dynaformer. He has good scope and balance with scope. He is also a natural mover and has very good presence."*

AND FINALLY, EARLY APRIL 2004: *"I am very pleased with this colt as well. When you breed to Dynaformer you never quite know what you are going to get. But he is an excellent stallion as demonstrated by his ever-increasing stud fee. This is a strong colt that is quite athletic and a racehorse."*

In all, Barbaro spent seventeen months in the care of Bill Sanborn at Sanborn Chase. He spent about six months with his mother, La Ville Rouge. Then he was weaned and joined the herd of other weanlings. He would spend another year simply growing up before he was ready for stage two of his young life.

Aside from a brief recovery period in a stall following the splint injury, and weather permitting, Barbaro was outside for much of the time while at Sanborn Chase. In winter months, he would spend the nights inside, and be turned out during the day. As the climate changed, he would spend the nights outside and some of each day inside, in order to eat and rest a little. This routine did not waver, even when other yearlings were being prepared for the sales and were required to spend more time inside under careful supervision. Yearlings like Barbaro, that were going to race for their breeders, were able to remain outside and simply continue to develop naturally.

THE STEPHENS: EARLY EDUCATION
"Dynaformer Colt" — 17–24 Months

Barbaro arrived in the care of Jill and John Stephens on September 17, 2004. As yet unnamed, he was simply known as "the Dynaformer colt." He was now ready for his early education. He would spend seven months with the Stephenses in Florida, transforming from a yearling that had never been ridden, to a young racehorse that was working slow three-eights-of-a-mile workouts.

The Stephens Thoroughbreds training facility is located in Marion County, Florida. It is approximately 160 acres, and includes a three-quarter mile irrigated racetrack, 68 stalls, 31 turnout paddocks, a swimming pond, and wooded riding trails.

Upon arrival, it was discovered that Barbaro had two new small bony splints on his front legs. This meant that there would be a delay in terms of when to start his education. Time was needed to make sure the small injuries could fully recover. Barbaro was stall-bound during this time rather than turned out in the paddocks, and he was hand-walked daily for a little controlled exercise. This routine lasted two months. In mid-November, Jill Stephens began working with him, and later in November, Barbaro was able to be turned out in the paddocks when he was not working with Jill.

The first few days of Barbaro's education involved plenty of one-on-one interaction with a rider, in this case Jill Stephens, who actually spent most of the time on the ground with the horse. Trust was built. Barbaro was first lunged in circles, eventually moving to larger circles and then tighter circles while responding to voice commands from the center. After a couple of days, Barbaro was equipped with long lines. This allowed Stephens to "drive" Barbaro from behind. The lines in her hands were attached to a bit in Barbaro's mouth. Always using comforting yet assertive voice commands, Stephens helped Barbaro become accustomed to the instructions of a person. In addition, long lining Barbaro introduced him to the rest of the farm. As he was driven, he became familiar with the trails he would later see when he was being ridden.

After a few days, Stephens began to get on his back, which was a several day process. First, she "bellied up" over the saddle, lying across the saddle on her stomach. Stephens bellied up in his stall, then bellied up outside in the round pen, which is a slightly larger area allowing for more movement (yet still more restricted than an open paddock).

Barbaro was named after a foxhound from a lithograph owned by the Jacksons. Barbaro's full siblings, Nicanor, Lentenor, and Margano, are also named after foxhounds from the same lithograph. In Spanish, Barbaro can mean "great" or "fantastic." When Michael Matz asked Peter Brette what Barbaro meant, Peter replied, "Kentucky Derby winner."

When Stephens was ready, she swung her right leg all the way over and suddenly, Barbaro was being ridden for the first time, albeit back in his stall. It was not a predetermined moment; it occurred when she felt the time was right. Barbaro was ready, and after getting on him in the round pen, it was time for him to be ridden around the farm. Eddie Villicana took over the reins for this first ride around.

Exercise riders Eddie Villicana and Martin Miranda were both employed by the Stephenses and shared the riding duties of Barbaro once he got going. Barbaro was an easy ride and thus did not require one person's complete attention.

"Barbaro was a very nice horse to gallop," said Miranda. "He did everything you asked him to do. The first time I open galloped him he was a little tentative; the second time he understood and he went very nicely. He was sometimes a playful horse, but he was always very manageable. He went well when he was on his own, and he went well when he was in the company of other horses. He was also very comfortable to ride."

Barbaro was playful, kind, fun to be around, and very smart. He picked things up quickly and, because he was so smart, it was important to keep altering his routine to keep him mentally focused and interested. In addition, Barbaro was very light on his feet—meaning he was well-balanced and moved efficiently across the ground.

Of course, the Stephenses did not know at the time that they had a superstar as a pupil; Barbaro was simply "the Dynaformer colt." Nonetheless, he did leave lasting impressions as being a pleasure to be around. John Stephens told the Jacksons that they would have fun with Barbaro. Jill wrote, on papers that left

Michael Matz

with Barbaro, "This horse is a lovely ride."

Barbaro left the Stephenses' care on April 28, 2005. Next stop—trainer Michael Matz's barn at the Fair Hill Training Center, Maryland.

SUMMER 2005 AT FAIR HILL

Fair Hill Training Center is a private facility that comprises eighteen barns, a mile dirt track, a seven-eighths of a mile all-weather track (at the time it was a woodchip surface; as of this writing, it is a Tapeta synthetic track), and three thousand acres of fields and woods. Each barn includes its own paddocks and round pens. The access to training in fields and up and down hills, and the ability to turn horses out in paddocks, make Fair Hill a very different training environment than a typical racetrack in North America.

Barbaro arrived at Matz's barn to the care of groom Marcus Torres and head assistant trainer Peter Brette. Brette would become Barbaro's partner in most of his gallops and breezes. Brette remembers that he was a big horse that was physically a little "backward" when he arrived. Essentially, Barbaro needed a little more time to grow into himself. While they did begin breezing Barbaro at the end of May, Matz gave him a break of about three weeks toward the end of July to allow Barbaro some time to mature. During this break, Barbaro remained at Fair Hill. Instead of going to the tracks to train, he was ridden out back along the trails and up and down the hills. Peter's wife, Kim Brette, remembers riding Barbaro out in the fields.

"I rode him when he was two, before he had run his first race, out back at Fair Hill," said Kim. "I remember galloping him up the hill behind Tim's barn [trainer Tim Woolley] and he was really well-balanced and beautiful to gallop. He was so smooth you could drink a cup of tea while you were galloping and not spill a drop."

After his July break, Barbaro came back stronger. Peter Brette remembers that while he was a good horse to ride right from the beginning, it was not until they breezed Barbaro that they realized he was special. Breezing is exercising at racing pace, which is generally around twelve seconds per eighth of a mile.

Regular gallops are conducted at about eighteen to twenty seconds per eighth of a mile. It was a gradual process with Barbaro's breezes. Each time he breezed, he tended to impress everyone a little bit more.

While Peter Brette rode Barbaro the majority of the time, others also had the opportunity to ride him: Alex Stevens, Teresa Thomas, Anne Kelly, Adam Davison, Kim Brette, and Georgina Baxter-Roberts all sat on Barbaro at one time or another while he was in Matz's care. No one fell off, although Brette said there were a few close moments, as is always the case with young horses.

"I rode him a bit at Fair Hill and then a bit in Florida," said Baxter-Roberts, who rode Barbaro fifteen to twenty times. "Galloping Barbaro made the hairs on the back of your neck stand up. I have never had a feeling like that riding a horse ever, and I have ridden some other real good ones. I never breezed him but led him in his breezes on many occasions. Barbaro was never ever beaten—on the racetrack or at home."

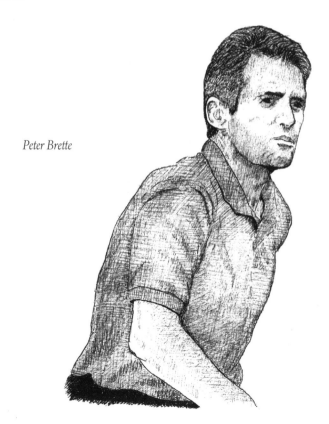

Peter Brette

Exercise rider Adam Davison rode Barbaro about half a dozen times in Florida, on Brette's days off.

"I first saw Barbaro as he was being unloaded off the van when he shipped in to run at Delaware Park for his first race," Davison recalled. "I was galloping for Michael at Delaware Park at the time. When I saw him being unloaded, I asked, 'Wow, who's that, Jimmy?' [Jimmy Herring was a Matz assistant trainer who was traveling with Barbaro.] I got to ride Barbaro a little in the winter. He was an athlete. That best describes him. Very well-mannered, Barbaro would do exactly as you wanted. He switched leads without being asked, he covered a lot of ground, perhaps more than you thought when on him."

Teresa Thomas rode Barbaro more frequently in the early days. "He had many gears," she remembered. "He was like driving an eighteen-wheeler truck. He would always have another gear available to shift into if he needed to demonstrate more power. Limitless."

A couple of Barbaro's breezes signaled what was to come. Brette noted to Thomas one morning after a work-out that if Barbaro had one more gear, he would be a good horse. Brette discovered later that he actually had two or three more gears. Also, Barbaro had a regular breeze partner, Pegasus by Storm, another highly regarded two-year-old in Matz's barn. Pegasus by Storm was by the 2000 Kentucky Derby winner, Fusaichi Pegasus. He had the pedigree to be any kind of horse. With Thomas on Pegasus by Storm and Brette on Barbaro, they worked together and stayed together in the work. How easily Barbaro worked and compared to Pegasus by Storm impressed Brette.

Barbaro's final breeze before his first start was with an older filly that was also a stakes winner. Thomas was aboard the filly and Brette, as usual, was aboard Barbaro. Matz asked Brette not to give the filly too much of a head start. Brette smiled. Barbaro—an unraced two-year-old—set off two lengths behind the older and experienced filly and, for the first time, Brette let Barbaro stretch out and lengthen his stride. Barbaro moved easily past his work companion to draw away by ten lengths.

Twelve people rode Barbaro: Adam Davison, Anne Kelly, Alex Stevens, Eddie Villicana, Edgar Prado, Georgina Baxter-Roberts, Jill Stephens, Jose Caraballo, Kim Brette, Martin Miranda, Peter Brette, and Teresa Thomas.

He went from two lengths behind his accomplished work companion to ten lengths in front. This was the first time they had tested Barbaro, but still Brette had not pushed him for effort. Brette just let the horse do what he could while remaining comfortably within himself.

While Barbaro worked well on both the dirt track and the all-weather track, (which tends to favor turf horses), Brette was adamant that Barbaro would be better suited to the turf. Barbaro's half brother, Holy Ground, had performed well on the turf. Barbaro had high knee-action— indicative of a turf runner—although Brette noted that Barbaro was so powerful his action really was undetectable when you rode him. Barbaro's pedigree also suggested that turf would not be a problem. In addition, it was decided to run Barbaro in a longer route race rather than a shorter sprint race. And if nothing else, the timing of a turf maiden race, going long, at Delaware Park was ideal. If they had opted for a dirt maiden race, they would have had to wait another three weeks. A turf maiden race would be Barbaro's introduction to racing.

Race Day

FIRST RACE: OCTOBER 4, 2005

One-mile maiden race on the turf at Delaware Park.

The Barbaro team thought they had a good horse. Barbaro had been working well leading up to his first race. He also had a good mind that would be important in allowing him to handle the new experience of racing. And, finally, Barbaro was developing into a terrific physical specimen. But until a horse races, you can never really tell. Even if a horse does develop into a great horse, its first race is not always a good one. For example, Chelokee, another Matz trainee, was training very well as he prepared for his first race at Delaware Park the following year. But he was well beaten. Chelokee then won his second start and turned into a good stakes horse, winning the Barbaro Stakes on the Preakness undercard in 2007.

Matz asked Brette if he would ride Barbaro in his first race. Peter had ridden races in his native England and had been a champion jockey during his time working in Dubai. He thought about it, but in the end decided against it. Riding in the race would have meant a total commitment to becoming a jockey again, something that Brette had put behind him at this stage of his career. Jose Caraballo, who at the time was Matz's main jockey in the Mid-Atlantic region, was given the mount on Barbaro for his first start. Caraballo had never ridden Barbaro, but had been out to Fair Hill and had seen him work under Brette. Caraballo had also ridden Holy Ground. Many times jockeys will work a horse in the morning before riding the horse in the afternoon, but this was not the case with Barbaro.

Brette did decide to go to Delaware Park to watch the race. Going to the races is unusual for him, as he typically stays back at the barn at Fair Hill during the afternoons. But Brette wanted to see how Barbaro would perform, knowing how well he had been training.

Kathee Rengert was standing with Gretchen Jackson in the paddock at Delaware Park when Barbaro headed toward the track after Caraballo had been given the leg up.

"Suddenly I shivered and the hair on my arms stood straight up," remembered Rengert. "I said to Gretchen, 'The hairs on my arms are standing straight up; I'd rather not tell you the other two times I have experienced the same reaction to a horse.' I never did tell Gretchen that the other two times were during one Saratoga meet when Seattle Slew's groom pulled him out of the stall to show him off to Mikey Smithwick and me; the electricity just ran through me. The other time was one winter in Camden, South Carolina. I walked behind the barn to see Forego staring between the slats of his custom-built round pen. The electricity surged through me in just that same fashion."

Barbaro, or "Barbarrow" as John Curran (the race caller) pronounced his name, was as impressive as a horse can be in his first start. Prior to the race, Curran saw Barbaro coming out of the paddock and warming up. To Curran, Barbaro looked outstanding and appeared to have all the ingredients of a runner. Because he was a first-time starter and the race was a mile, Curran had overlooked Barbaro from a handicapping standpoint. He quickly corrected that error and played Barbaro on the top of his exactas. But Barbaro was only the fourth choice at post time. New York invader Police Chief, with Delaware Park's leading jockey Ramon Dominguez aboard, was sent off as the favorite.

A little fussy entering the starting gate, Barbaro broke sharply and was soon forwardly placed by Caraballo. He appeared to just be galloping in hand down the backside as he had the measure of his rivals. But once Caraballo shook him loose a little, Barbaro ran away from the field. Jose took one look behind him, and likely saw his rivals shrinking from his vision. Curran noted in his race call, "This could be a nice one," inside the sixteenth pole. Curran reserves remarks like that for perhaps four or five horses each year. Barbaro won the race by an impressive eight-and-a-half lengths.

"I knew he was decent—I had seen him work at Fair Hill and I had ridden his older half brother Holy Ground," Caraballo said after the race. "Peter and Michael also seemed to be quietly confident. But I did not expect that. It was unreal when I looked behind and we were simply galloping away from the field."

Barbaro had won so easily that one could really start to think he was a good horse in development. The final time for the race was good as well—Barbaro had completed the mile in 1:35.87. The last quarter of a mile was his fastest quarter, at 23.66 seconds.

Despite Barbaro's success, people wondered what horses he had beaten, and if he really learned anything from the experience, because part of racing for the first time is the education it provides. When a horse wins so easily, how can it really learn that much?

. . . .

"We sure did not think much beyond the moment. It was a nice, exciting win, but who knows? We were celebrating after the win, but it was for that nice win. We got a little more excited when Michael [Matz] brought up the Laurel Futurity (for his next race). We take each race at a time, first it was his maiden, then a listed stake, and another stake, and each is a step up, and you get more excited with each step. We were amazed when Michael thought about the Kentucky Derby, which was mentioned maybe before the Holy Bull Stakes. We really needed to switch to dirt to see what we had."

—GRETCHEN JACKSON

. . . .

Later in the year, Curran was vacationing in Las Vegas. He bet Barbaro to win the Kentucky Derby in the futures wagering. He got 85–1.

LAUREL FUTURITY: NOVEMBER 19, 2005
A mile and a sixteenth, on the turf.

Obviously, Team Barbaro was very impressed with Barbaro's first race. As such, Matz opted for the Laurel Futurity, a stakes race, for his second start. This is the same stakes race won by some of racing's greats, including Affirmed, Secretariat, and Spectacular Bid. Sadly, along with a downturn in Maryland racing, this race has lost some of its prestige in recent years. Nevertheless, it was a stakes race and only Barbaro's second start.

> Jose Caraballo rode Barbaro in his first two victories, winning by a combined sixteen lengths.

Entering in a stakes race for a horse that had only won his maiden race is unusual for a conservative horseman like Matz. Because it was unusual, Dick Jerardi, who covers horse racing for the *Philadelphia Daily News*, took note. Typically, after a horse breaks its maiden, it runs in a conditioned race—reserved for horses that have only won one race. By opting for a stakes race, Barbaro could be meeting horses that had won a number of races. The only restriction was that the horses in the race would be two-year-olds. Barbaro had only won one race and in doing so, had beaten other maiden horses. By opting for the Laurel Futurity for their second start, Team Barbaro was sending a strong message that they thought they had a horse with a lot of potential.

The message echoed throughout the Matz barn. Shortly after his first win, Barbaro's veterinarian, Kathy Anderson, had long-time friends from Massachusetts, Josselyn Shaughnessy and her daughter Coleen, visiting her. Introducing them to Barbaro, Anderson stated, matter-of-factly, that he was next year's Kentucky Derby winner. These were high hopes indeed for a horse that had just won his first race—another example of the lofty expectations Team Barbaro had for their budding star.

The week prior to the Laurel Futurity, I was gate schooling at Fair Hill on a horse for trainer Klobia Carroll. Matz was also gate schooling horses. Carroll asked Matz if he had any derby horses among his two-year-olds. He responded that he had a Fusaichi Pegasus colt (Pegasus by Storm) and a horse running at Laurel that upcoming weekend. Matz was, of course, referring to Barbaro. While I listened to the conversation, I dismissed the notion, with a quick smile, as wishful thinking.

Aside from Barbaro's Kentucky Derby win, many consider that his victory in the Laurel Futurity, in only his second start, was his most impressive race. Barbaro's performance certainly indicated that he was a two-year-old with a lot of upside. He again dominated this race, winning by a little over eight lengths in a sharp time, 1:40, for the mile-and sixteenth-event—a course record. Barbaro completed the last eighth of a mile in less than twelve seconds. Considering that this was only his second start, he still really did not know what he was doing.

Again, Barbaro was not the favorite for this race—he was the second choice to Wedding Singer under Johnny Velasquez.

Caraballo was back in the saddle for the race.

"It was like riding a four-year-old stakes winner against two-year-olds. He was in his own class," said Caraballo. Ironically, there was a very interested observer also riding in the Laurel Futurity—Edgar Prado, fourteen lengths in arrears aboard Creve Couer.

• •

"I did ride against Barbaro a few times. For example in the race at Laurel [Futurity on the grass] I rode Diabolical, who was second to Barbaro. Barbaro was as cool on the grass as he was on the dirt. He had a very quick turn of foot. He would pick up the bit like a sprinter would. He is a very good horse."

—RAMON DOMINGUEZ,
Summer 2006

• •

Laurel Futurity

Matz's daughter Michelle Hyland was in attendance at the Laurel Futurity. Her father had told her that Barbaro was a nice horse. He does not use those words liberally, so Hyland was excited to see him run. She assumed he was going to run a decent race, but when he grabbed the lead and took off, it all seemed surreal.

"We were excited for the future. Not just for the race, but the future that seemed to be available for Barbaro," said Hyland, who soon after began a year-and-a-half stint working for her father.

As soon as Barbaro captured the Laurel Futurity, Matz's phone began to ring. Jockeys' agents were calling to try to get the mount on Barbaro, who, after only two starts, had demonstrated that he was a very legitimate horse. The first to call was Angel Cordero, agent for Johnny Velasquez.

It was now nearing the end of the year and many East Coast trainers were relocating their horses to warmer weather in Florida and the Carolinas. Barbaro, along with Matz's string, headed down to Palm Meadows in Florida to his winter quarters. Barbaro would leave the care of his groom Marcus Torres; Eduardo Hernandez would now become his caregiver.

Peter Brette was an apprentice jockey in England, and worked for noted trainers including Sir Michael Stoute. Brette then worked in Dubai and became a champion jockey in 1990. Once he retired from being a jockey, Brette trained in Dubai for ten years. He then relocated to the U.S. with his wife and young son and, after a short stint in Kentucky, began working for Michael Matz in early 2005.

It was from Palm Meadows that Barbaro would begin the second part of his campaign. His first race would be on New Year's Day 2006, the first derby of the year, the Tropical Park Derby.

TROPICAL PARK DERBY: JANUARY 1, 2006
A mile and an eighth on the turf.

The Tropical Park Derby (Grade 3) at Calder was selected as Barbaro's first race in Florida because the timing of the race was ideal. He had shipped down to Florida two weeks earlier, and had plenty of time to settle in. It was Barbaro's third race on the turf. It was also a graded stakes race, Barbaro's first test in graded stakes company. If Barbaro was to be pointed for the Kentucky Derby, earnings from this race would help him in terms of qualifying for the Derby. Gaining graded stakes earnings early in the year would also allow Team Barbaro more flexibility in planning their pre-Derby campaign if he was to move forward. Other Derby candidates had already competed in, and won, Grade 1 stakes races.

While Barbaro had been piloted in his first two starts by Caraballo, this would be Edgar Prado's first mount on the colt. Caraballo typically stays north in the winters and now Barbaro had moved to another racing circuit. Caraballo's job was well done. He was two-for-two on Barbaro, and both wins were very convincing. Prado is a favorite of Matz's as far as leading jockeys are concerned, but Matz knew Prado would only commit to Barbaro on a race-by-race basis. Prado was seeking out his best option to take him to the Kentucky Derby. Barbaro was just one of a number of top class three-year-olds he had the opportunity to ride.

Barbaro was the favorite for this race, the first time he was the betting choice. The public was now starting to get behind this horse. Barbaro sat close to the lead, and took command coming around the final turn. He won this Grade 3 event with the same ease with which he had won his first two turf races, although the winning margin was a shorter three and three-quarters lengths. The final time of the race was 1:46.6—which was good for a mile and an eighth. And like his two previous turf starts, he completed the final eighth of a mile in under twelve seconds. He also continued to demonstrate a similar race strategy—stalk and pounce.

Prado was impressed. "I first rode him in the Tropical Park Derby. I was very impressed with the way he handled himself on the track, and when he came back after the race he was not even blowing, he could not even blow out a match," he recalled. "I had not ridden a horse with such a turn of foot since Kitten's Joy, a really nice turf horse."

Questions were now being asked—would Matz try Barbaro on the dirt and consider the marquee race of the year, the Kentucky Derby? The *Blood-Horse* senior correspondent Steve Haskin was among the reporters to call Matz soon after this third win to see what plans he had for Barbaro. During the conversation, Haskin asked Matz what the name "Barbaro" meant. Matz turned to Brette, who replied, "Kentucky Derby winner." It is unknown whether Brette was displaying his British sense of humor or if he really was that confident.

Barbaro completed the last quarter of each of his turf races in less than 24 seconds. This was faster than any of his dirt races.

Matz understood that if he did not try Barbaro on the dirt, the more traditional racing surface in North America, he would never know if Barbaro could adapt to the different surface. What he did know was that Barbaro had worked on dirt, and worked well on dirt. It was now time to find out how he would run on the dirt.

The Holy Bull Stakes (Grade 3) at Gulfstream Park was selected as Barbaro's next start, and his first start on the dirt. They would see how Barbaro ran in the Holy Bull Stakes, before making any further decisions in terms of his future campaign.

HOLY BULL: FEBRUARY 4, 2006
A mile and an eighth on the dirt (sloppy).

Unfortunately for Team Barbaro, the track conditions for the Holy Bull Stakes were not ideal. Bad weather had rendered the track surface very sloppy. A decision had to be made whether to run Barbaro over the sloppy racing surface, or scratch him and wait for the Fountain of Youth Stakes, which would be the next logical Derby prep race in Florida. Brette encouraged Matz to go ahead and run Barbaro. Brette's logic was simple—would Matz scratch Barbaro if the track came up sloppy at Churchill Downs, home of the Kentucky Derby? By running in the Holy Bull Stakes on an off-track, they would find out if Barbaro could handle that surface, if it did prevail again. If Barbaro ran poorly in the Holy Bull Stakes, they could still run him back in the Fountain of Youth Stakes in the hopes of racing on a fast dirt surface. Matz agreed, Barbaro would run.

The problems with an off-track are threefold. First, by winning over the sloppy conditions you are not really proving that a horse will like a fast dirt surface, one that will more likely be experienced in the Kentucky Derby. Second, many believe that turf runners handle a sloppy track better than traditional dirt horses. Like the turf, a sloppy track does not break away from underneath a horse's stride, as does a fast dirt track. And finally, sloppy tracks can be less safe for the runners as they can be hard and sometimes uneven.

Barbaro did win the Holy Bull Stakes, adopting his now predictable stalking style, but his winning margin was diminishing close to the end with a closing Great Point. Barbaro's final eighth of a mile was a little over thirteen seconds. For the first time, he did not finish his race with a flourish. Simply put, his win was not spectacular, the kind we had witnessed on the turf, but it was a win nonetheless and Barbaro

remained unbeaten. Vic Stauffer, who was the race caller that day for Gulfstream Park, noted that Barbaro had a big, long stride and did not look entirely comfortable in the poor conditions. Stauffer's assessment was that Barbaro won the Holy Bull Stakes on raw talent alone.

> The three races in which Barbaro posted his largest winning margins were also the three races in which he did not start as the favorite.

Barbaro had passed his first dirt test and his stock was beginning to climb as a real Kentucky Derby prospect. The matter of securing a jockey would need to be addressed. A top class jockey such as Prado would have a choice of horses at this stage of the Derby trail. First Samurai, who won the Hopeful Stakes (Grade 1) and Champagne Stakes (Grade 1) as a two-year-old and was an early Derby favorite, was among Prado's options, as were Keyed Entry and Strong Contender. Prado—like Matz and the Jacksons—had never won the Kentucky Derby. But unlike Matz and the Jacksons, Prado had already been to the Kentucky Derby six times. At this point, Prado's commitment to Barbaro remained one race at a time.

FLORIDA DERBY: APRIL 1, 2006
A mile and an eighth on the dirt.

Matz's racing plan for Barbaro was to point him toward the Florida Derby (Grade 1) for his next start. Traditionally, a horse of Barbaro's caliber would have returned in the Fountain of Youth Stakes, on March 4, and then the Florida Derby. But Matz was not going to do things as they were typically done—he was going to do things that he felt were best for the development of his horse. Matz wanted a fresh horse ahead of the rigors of the Triple Crown. He had learned his lesson, from his show-jumping days many years earlier, while competing in the 1976 Montreal Olympics. By the time Matz had got to the big event, his horse was tired and ineffectual. He vowed never to repeat that experience. This meant that Barbaro would get close to a two-month break between his Holy Bull win and his start in the Florida

Derby. He would sit on the sidelines while other Derby preps were run and contenders developed—or disappeared.

First Samurai, with Prado in the irons, won the Fountain of Youth, upon the disqualification of Corinthian. The latter had bothered First Samurai during the running of the race on more than one occasion. Despite gaining the win, it was a subpar performance for First Samurai, who would have to step it up in his next start—the Blue Grass Stakes at Keeneland—to be a legitimate contender for the Kentucky Derby. In third place was Great Point, the horse that had finished second to Barbaro in the Holy Bull Stakes.

"Barbaro was a creature of habit. He enjoyed his routine, especially when he was being turned out in the round pen, both at Fair Hill and at Palm Meadows. He would dance around, buck a little, and then drop down on his knees and roll. He would get up, buck and squeal a little bit, and go back down again. And then finally he would settle down. He was a horse that just enjoyed life.

"He was the kind of horse that if you wanted to play with him, when he reached the point when he had had enough, he would let you know. He was like having a good friend, a playmate. He was unique in his whole mannerism. He knew who he was, where he was, and where he was going to go. And he proved that. He won on every kind of racing surface, he proved himself. His post position did not make any difference. Number 10 in the Florida Derby, number 8 in the Kentucky Derby. You just knew you were associated with a winner all the way around, a winning team, Michael, Peter, and Barbaro.

"I represented Michael and Peter for the Florida Derby draw. After I drew post position 10, I returned to the barn to let Michael and Peter know. They said not to worry about representing them again at a draw. I told them not to worry—he was going to win and nothing could make any difference. I was right..."

—ED MADDEN,
Michael Matz's assistant, 2005–2008

Jill Stephens attended the Florida Derby as a guest of the Jacksons and saw Barbaro for the first time since he had left her farm to head to Fair Hill Training Center. She was literally taken aback when Barbaro walked into the paddock. He had changed so much physically.

"Holy cow, he was like a train!" Stephens exclaimed. Barbaro looked much more powerful than the young colt they had dispatched north a little under a year earlier.

Barbaro had unfortunately drawn post 10 of 11, for his first race on a fast dirt surface. No horse had won a mile-and-an-eighth race from a post position wider than the 9 hole in the two years since they had reconfigured the racetrack at Gulfstream Park. Because the starting gate is relatively close to the first turn, there is a distinct bias against horses breaking from the outside. They either have to race fast early to get a good position going into the first turn, or drop back deliberately coming out of the gate to avoid being carried wide around the first turn.

Final sixteenth

"Breaking from that post made it like an obstacle course," said Vic Stauffer, who was again calling Barbaro's race for the Gulfstream Park patrons. "Like he had to scale a twenty-foot wall right after the start."

Prado decided to use Barbaro early to get a good position going into the first turn of the Florida Derby. Barbaro was at or on the lead for the entire race, and when it looked like he was going to draw away comfortably down the lane, he was instead fully tested by Sharp Humor. It was only well inside the final sixteenth of a mile that Barbaro appeared to have the full measure of his foe.

Was this the real Barbaro on a fast dirt surface? Only a little bit better than his peers? And some considered the horses he beat in the Florida Derby subpar for a Grade 1 race. Since the timing of the race, five weeks before the Kentucky Derby, was not considered ideal by many horsemen as a prep race for the Kentucky Derby, horses that might have been considered for the race were waiting for alternatives a week or two closer to the major prize.

The final eighth of a mile was completed in only a little under thirteen seconds. Did it take something out of him having to be used early? Was he really paying attention down the lane or was he goofing off, an assertion of his jockey Prado?

Stauffer noted that for the first time Barbaro had a battle on his hands. Yet despite winning by only a neck, Stauffer thought that if they had run around ten more laps Barbaro still would have won. Barbaro struck Stauffer as a horse that would do whatever it took to pull out the win. If he had to run five lengths faster, he would simply have found a way to do so.

Steve Haskin thought the race was excellent and just what Barbaro needed to set him up for his five-week break between the Florida Derby and the Kentucky Derby. Haskin's thoughts were that if he had won the race too easily, he would not have gotten what he needed out of the race and the five-week gap would have made it harder for Barbaro to be fully prepared for the Kentucky Derby. Haskin thought Barbaro's head-to-head battle with Sharp Humor was not only educational, but also toughening.

Barbaro was now undefeated in five races leading up to the biggest race in North America, the Kentucky Derby. Edgar Prado had yet to commit to Barbaro as his Derby horse, however. More Derby preps were to be run and Prado had other horses to test.

Run for the Roses

KENTUCKY DERBY: MAY 6, 2006

A mile and a quarter on the dirt.

The Kentucky Derby (Grade 1) is the one race that all horsemen aspire to win. Literally all the top three-year-olds are pointed for this one race. And since this race is only open to three-year-olds, there is only one chance at it. No do-overs. It is not simply a question of discovering that you have the best horse among its peers, but also making sure that your horse is able to perform at its best on that first Saturday in May.

Established in 1875, the Kentucky Derby is the oldest continuously held sporting event in America. It is the one time of year that our sport is showcased on the national stage as the best two minutes in sports. To have a horse compete in the Kentucky Derby is quite an accomplishment. Gaining a coveted spot in the starting line-up for the race (there is a maximum of twenty allowed) is a result of graded stakes earnings from prior starts. Horses with the most graded stakes earnings get priority. Barbaro had accumulated more than enough earnings from his wins in the Tropical Park Derby (Grade 3), the Holy Bull Stakes (Grade 3), and the Florida Derby (Grade 1) to run in the Kentucky Derby. Additionally, he was clearly one of the major contenders for the race.

No sooner had Barbaro won the Florida Derby, he was off to Kentucky. He arrived at Lexington's Keeneland Race Course two days later. Keeneland was chosen as his base for the next three and a half weeks because of the Polytrack surface (a synthetic surface) on the training track (this was prior to the switch to the Polytrack surface on the main track, which was still dirt at the time). Having access to the Polytrack meant that the weather would not interrupt training as they prepared Barbaro for the biggest test of his career.

Sean Clancy, author of *Barbaro: The Horse Who Captured America's Heart*, was at Keeneland writing for the *Keeneland Special*, and observed Barbaro's training throughout the time he was there.

"I was at Keeneland for the whole month. Barbaro trained late," said Clancy. "I saw him about five days a week. Anybody who was on the rail that month, when seeing him, would say, 'Who's that?' and then the next day, 'Oh, that's Barbaro.' It was his presence, physical stature, and great style. Just the way he handled himself. Even the antics, jumping up in the air in the paddock, it just seemed as if he was establishing his ground."

Barbaro breezed twice at Keeneland. He worked an easy half mile as his first work after the Florida Derby. His next breeze started with a half-speed gallop and finished up with a decent half mile work. Both were easy works on the main dirt track at Keeneland. Barbaro needed no more than that; he was already fit and was now thriving.

"Every time I took him to the track he was a monster," said Brette. "The penny dropped." Brette noted that Barbaro had improved twenty pounds since the Florida Derby. A twenty-pound improvement refers to the European way of handicapping horses. It essentially means that he was a better horse by about five lengths. (Four pounds is considered the equivalent of a horse's body length.)

One of the final Derby prep races was run at Keeneland, the Blue Grass Stakes. For Team Barbaro, the significance of this race was that it was Prado's final Derby prep race and this time he was aboard Strong Contender. The pair finished third and soon afterwards, Prado committed to Barbaro for the big race. Barbaro moved from Keeneland to Churchill Downs on Thursday, April 27, nine days before the Kentucky Derby. He would turn three years old in two days.

Matz, a "rookie" Kentucky Derby trainer, had the audacity to throw out the rule book written by veteran Derby winning trainers such as D. Wayne Lukas (four wins), Bob Baffert (three wins), and Nick Zito (two wins). A Derby horse needed to be seasoned, battle-tested. He needed to have had a series of prep races to get him ready for the biggest test of his life. Or so we were led to believe. Matz was running Barbaro off a five-week break from his Florida Derby win. No horse had won the Kentucky Derby after such a long layoff since Needles did it in 1956. In fact, Barbaro had only run once in the previous thirteen weeks dating back to February 5. The Kentucky Derby was to be only his sixth lifetime start, his third start on the dirt.

Tom Pedulla, of *USA Today*, had this to say about the five-week break: "I am a traditionalist, I believed in a certain path to the Derby. There are certain ways to get things done. It goes against conventional history. And history exists for a reason. Things that had not worked for years tend not to work. I have to admit now that model I had in my mind does not apply anymore."

Hall of Fame trainer Bobby Frankel, who had won the Florida Derby with Empire Maker in 2003, had wanted to take Empire Maker to the Kentucky Derby off a six-week break. He was dissuaded and Empire Maker bruised his foot in the Wood Memorial. This may have hampered his preparation for the Kentucky Derby, which was ultimately won by Funny Cide. Empire Maker beat Funny Cide in the Belmont Stakes to upset Funny Cide's Triple Crown bid.

Matz's logic was that he was preparing Barbaro for three races, the Triple Crown series of the Kentucky Derby, the Preakness Stakes, and the Belmont Stakes. He wanted a fresh horse that could handle the rigors of three races, all within a short span of each other. The question of the five-week break—as if Barbaro went on vacation rather than being trained up to the Derby—persisted

via media briefings each morning outside Barn 42 at Churchill Downs. While Matz justified his decision by wanting a fresh horse for the rigors of the Triple Crown, he also noted that the sample size, the number of legitimate Derby contenders that had come into the Derby off such a gap between races, was small—too small to draw conclusions. Mike Welsch of the *Daily Racing Form* determined that media were more concerned than fellow horsemen about the five-week gap.

"Everybody looks for a hole in the game plan," explained Sandy McKee of the *Baltimore Sun*. "Horse racing is a very traditional sport. Certainly Michael and the Jacksons did not do that and they stuck to the game plan for what was best for the horse in the long run."

Fellow horsemen were thinking, rather *hoping*, that Barbaro was really a terrific turf horse that was only adequate on the dirt. While he had won his last two starts on the dirt, those dirt wins were simply not as visually impressive as his turf scores. Barbaro was also considered to have the type of stride that was better suited to the turf. As mentioned previously, he had high knee-action, which is typically less effective on the dirt. Most horsemen will tell you this. But ask them why a horse with high knee-action prefers the turf and you will get as many different answers as the horsemen you ask. The reality is, very few horses can run at the very top level on all types of surfaces. Fellow horsemen were hoping this was the case for Barbaro also.

Barbaro had flourished since he arrived in Kentucky from his winter quarters in Florida. He literally mesmerized everyone at Churchill Downs. Steve Haskin, John Asher, Barbara Livingston, Tom Law, Rick Bozich, and Jill Baffert—all veterans of the racehorse industry who are not easily impressed—were amazed when they saw Barbaro for the first time in the flesh.

Barbara Livingston, perhaps the most noted horse racing photographer, was "thunderstruck" when she first saw Barbaro and insisted on telling everyone who would listen that he was the horse for this Kentucky Derby. John Asher, vice president of communications at Churchill Downs, was "in awe" when he first saw Barbaro out training at Churchill Downs, specifically citing Barbaro's commanding presence, glow, and physique.

Barbaro turned three on April 29, the day of his most impressive pre-Derby workout. Barbaro was the third youngest starter in the 2006 Kentucky Derby.

On the Saturday before the Derby, Barbaro's workout was one for the record books. Haskin noted how strong he was going around the turn after the work in the gallop out. Barbaro worked a half mile in a little over 46 seconds, and then galloped out an additional quarter of a mile, going the three-quarters in a little over 1:12 seconds. If an ordinary horse had worked as fast as Barbaro did that morning, he would have left the race on the training track. It would simply have been too fast and taken too much out of him—further evidence that Barbaro was no ordinary horse.

As soon as the work was over, Matz's cell phone began ringing in earnest. One clocker who had timed every Derby contender for decades remarked that Barbaro's was the best work he had seen over the last five years. *Daily Racing Form*'s Jay

Training like a monster

Privman compared the work to the 2000 pre-Derby work of Fusaichi Pegasus, who became the first Derby favorite to win since Spectacular Bid in 1979. Brette, who was riding Barbaro in the work as usual, simply noted that it felt like he took three strides down the lane after he let Barbaro lengthen his stride. Jennie Rees of the *Courier-Journal* recognized that while Barbaro did display his high knee-action that had everyone concerned, he sure got across the ground effortlessly. Like many observers, Rees moved Barbaro up on her Derby list after witnessing this work.

Mike Welsch's job for the *Daily Racing Form* during Derby week was to watch each of the horses train and make observations as they prepared for the Derby. Not only was Barbaro's pre-Derby work one that had everyone talking, but Barbaro continued to train with a lot of energy right up to the Derby. On more than one occasion during Derby week, Welsch clocked Barbaro and found him galloping faster than a "two-minute clip," which is fifteen seconds per eighth of a mile—a very fast gallop. Barbaro was simply training in a superior fashion as contrasted with his rivals. He loved his training and appeared thrilled to be in Kentucky.

On Derby morning, the Barbaro team was exuding confidence. They knew their horse, and others were just catching on. Brette, Matz, and Gretchen Jackson thought they would win the Run for the Roses because he was training so well and he had improved considerably since the Florida Derby. In Brette's words, Barbaro had become a man. He had been a boy but "the penny had dropped" and Barbaro was a different horse now. Perhaps the stretch duel in the Florida Derby triggered the change; it was the first time he had a fight on his hands, and the first time he was really asked to run. Perhaps it was the five-week break that allowed Matz to work Barbaro three times leading up to the Kentucky Derby. Perhaps it was the combination of the five weeks and the toughening stretch duel. Barbaro also went through one of his growth spurts during this time. Barbaro was, after all, a late foal and only celebrated his third birthday on April 29, one week before the Kentucky Derby. Universally, people agreed that Barbaro looked fantastic in Kentucky—both at Keeneland and Churchill Downs.

"I was very comfortable after he won his races on the dirt, and I could tell he still had room to improve," said Prado. "I was very confident he was training so well coming up to the Derby, he was handling the racetrack so well, and his pre-Derby breeze (under Brette) was exceptional."

Brette took Barbaro out for a gallop Derby morning. Barbaro and his lead pony Messaging were accompanied to the track by Hyland, riding one of Matz's fillies. Hyland jogged around the track with Brette and Barbaro. While it is not always typical to gallop the morning of a race, the start time for the Derby is very late in the day. It would be a long day, so a little early exercise would help Barbaro mentally settle in for the afternoon. Barbaro was keen in his gallop. In fact, Brette struggled for a few strides to keep Barbaro keyed down, as there was a horse galloping right behind them. Brette tried to slow Barbaro down to let the other horse by. The rider on the other horse, realizing who was in front of him, also tried to slow down to get out of the way. Fortunately, all worked out in the end. Barbaro was sharp. He was ready. Thirty minutes later, he was out grazing, in front of his barn, looking majestic.

And the morning could not have started better for Barbaro's owners. From their hotel room, the Jacksons watched another horse they bred—George Washington—win the biggest race of his budding career. He won the first leg of the English Triple Crown, the 2,000 Guineas at Newmarket. A good omen for the rest of the day, perhaps?

This was not supposed to be an easy Derby win for Barbaro. He was not even the betting public's favorite—that honor went to Illinois Derby winner Sweetnorthernsaint. Barclay Tagg, trainer of the undefeated and Jackson-owned Showing Up, figured this was one of the toughest Derby fields assembled in a long time. And Tagg should know—he won the race with the popular Funny Cide in 2003. Brother Derek had looked awesome preparing for the Derby with easy wins in California. But perhaps his front-running style would expose him (it turned out it was a bad trip and a lost shoe that hindered him). Lawyer Ron looked very good after winning the Arkansas Derby and would go on to become Champion Older Male in 2007, but he looked very average in Barbaro's Derby. Bluegrass Cat would go on to win the Haskell Stakes.

And if nothing else, Barbaro's Derby was a twenty horse field. It would be the only time these horses would face nineteen other runners. This provides a lot of opportunity for things to go wrong, unless you have the tactical speed to avoid anxious moments. Team Barbaro was confident.

Jack Ireland of the *News Journal* was given the rare opportunity to walk over from the backstretch to the paddock area with the Derby runners prior to the race. He walked immediately behind Barbaro and Gretchen Jackson, an experience he later described as "the thrill of a lifetime." While Barbaro had not yet won the Derby, Ireland felt that something was going to happen that day— something extra special.

Trainer Bob Baffert had three runners in the Derby, including Wood Memorial winner Bob and John. When Barbaro entered the paddock for the Kentucky Derby, Bob's wife Jill turned to him, in awe of Barbaro. This was the first time she had seen Barbaro up close. Jill noted that he was by far the standout that day—head and shoulders above the rest. He was big, muscular, and there was grandness about his presence. After Jill expressed her opinion of Barbaro to her husband, he suggested that Barbaro was a turf horse. Jill responded, "You'd better hope so."

Rick Bozich, who also covered the Derby for the *Courier-Journal*, was in the paddock that day. "I have covered the Derby since 1979. I have heard people say that a horse looks the part, that a horse looks great, but sometimes they just don't run well," said Bozich. "In the paddock that day it was chaotic with too many people and horses moving around. I took one look at Barbaro; I had never seen a horse look like that. He was much more athletic, his coat was magnificent—he just looked like he was going to dominate. It was weird, it had never happened to me before. I had not picked him to win, I had no affinity for the horse, but when I looked at Barbaro, he just blew me away. Not before, nor since, had that happened to me. I told a few people around me."

Thoroughbred Times's managing editor Tom Law shared Jill's and Rick's assessments.

"I was standing underneath the grandstand, inside the tunnel, with Jeff Lowe just before Barbaro's Derby," Law said. "I turned and said to Jeff, 'Let's hurry up and get down to the rail, we're about to see something really awesome.'" Law was referring to Barbaro.

And we know what happened in the 2006 Kentucky Derby. Law was right, Barbaro won, and it was no ordinary performance. Barbaro sat close to the pace, and it was a strong pace early—22 seconds and change for the first quarter, 46 seconds for the half mile. Barbaro floated wide down the backside, and looked like he was going well within himself just galloping along. Ramon Dominguez, on Bluegrass Cat, thought he had a chance until about the three-eighths pole. He then saw Prado simply let Barbaro lengthen his stride. The race was over.

∙∙

Michelle Hyland, on watching the Derby with her father: "I was worried until they got in the gate. Watching the race was really exciting. Barbaro was in the perfect position the whole race. We knew he would win a long way out, but it was like the race was in slow motion. It was easy. Oh my God! We were all jumping up and down. I nearly fell over. I yelled to my dad, 'You just won the Kentucky Derby!'… [My younger brother] Alex said, 'You're going crazy, Michelle, you're going crazy.' I don't think he quite got the significance."

∙∙

Barbaro overwhelmed the field and just galloped away down the lane to win by six-and-a-half lengths under a hand-ride. This was the largest winning margin since Assault won the Derby in 1946 and the fifth largest winning margin in the 132 runnings of the Derby. (Assault went on to win the Triple Crown.) On top of that, Prado had not used his stick. Barbaro simply looked like he could have won by as many lengths as he desired. The final quarter of a mile was run in just a little over 24 seconds, a very strong closing run by Barbaro and the fastest last quarter in the Derby since Secretariat in 1973. And then, Barbaro galloped out very far in front of the field. He just looked like he had a joy for running.

Simply put, his win was phenomenal.

It was "a sublime performance" according to NBC race caller Tom Durkin. Barbaro dominated so obviously that Privman was sure he had the race won, back at the three-quarter pole.

Directly after the race, Jennie Rees of the *Courier-Journal* exclaimed, "What did we just see? Holy smokes, how good is this horse?" Ed Fountaine of the *New York Post* agreed, "Wow—did you see that?" Rich Rosenblatt of the Associated Press noted, "We were stunned into silence. When he exploded he just buried them."

Steve Haskin considered Barbaro's Derby win one of the best five he has witnessed, and that dates back to 1968. Haskin also considered that Barbaro's performance might well be the best of those five. It was the best performance Fountaine had seen since Spend a Buck's 1985 gate-to-wire Derby romp. Durkin goes one better and determined Barbaro's performance was the best he had witnessed in terms

All alone and in rhythm

KENTUCKY DERBY PARTY AT FAIR HILL

Kathy Anderson hosted a party at Fair Hill Training Center in her office suite, attached to Michael Matz's main barn. I am not entirely sure if Michael was aware of the party—although he was obviously in Kentucky, his barn was full of horses. Oh well, this was the Derby. He would have to hear about it afterwards. Fair Hill as a community was proud to have its first entrant in the Kentucky Derby, and an entrant that appeared to be one of the favorites for the race. Barbaro was undefeated, but the media had played down his chances due to his unorthodox training program. He had not run for five weeks, and no horse had won the Derby after such a long respite from racing for a very long time. I use the term respite rather than "layoff," the term more often used, yet misleading. Clearly, Barbaro had not been laid-off. His training over the preceding five weeks had been designed to have Barbaro peak on the first Saturday in May.

Regardless, the naysayers were doing us all a great favor, Barbaro was 6–1 and I thought that anything above 3–1 and he was a good bet. I bet $80 (I had originally planned to wager $100 but decided to place a $10 box exacta on Barbaro and Showing Up).

Plenty of other party attendees had also wagered on our hometown hero. About two hundred people were gathered by post time. There were plenty of upbeat conversations because most of us knew each other; we worked together in the mornings at Fair Hill, we lived in the local community, ate at our local deli Prizzio's, and worked at local farms. Can it happen? Is Barbaro the best horse? Did you ride Barbaro? What was he like? Did he look vulnerable in the Florida Derby? Was the work at Churchill a sign of a great horse, or did they get carried away and work too fast? We had each analyzed the Derby and each came up with our reasons why this was Barbaro's Derby, or why it was not to be. I saw Jose Caraballo. I asked him his thoughts. He was proud

to be a part of the Barbaro story. He rode Barbaro twice; he had had experiences because of riding Barbaro only a few had. Jose has ridden more than two thousand winners. He knew Barbaro was the most impressive horse he had ridden. He was happy to be at Fair Hill to celebrate our first runner in the Derby and hoped he would make history. If Barbaro made history, Jose was a part of that history.

The party settled down and gained focus as the horses were being loaded into the gate. Voices were heard to quiet everyone down. We did.

The gates opened and it was easy to pick out Barbaro early in the race thanks to the handy early position Edgar was able to find. It was cool for me to see Barbaro and Showing Up racing together on the backside and making a move going into the turn. I was not ready yet to count my money, but the exacta looked pretty interesting. As the field turned for home and Edgar asked Barbaro for a little more run, the atmosphere in the room was palpable. The improbable was going to happen, we knew this a quarter of a mile from home. Barbaro was running too easily as he moved to the front of the field. A Fair Hill horse was going to win the Derby in dominating fashion! As Barbaro drew clear down the lane, we were shouting and screaming. It was an amazing feeling. Everyone wanted one horse to win, even those who had decided to wager against Barbaro knew this was one for the team, for Fair Hill. Fantastic! High fives, we were amazed. This horse had done things in the Derby that had not been done for many years. Conversations switched very quickly to the likelihood of witnessing a Triple Crown winner. Elated with my gambling success (I bet about once a year) I wagered with a friend of mine $100 on Barbaro taking the Triple Crown. I got 5–1!

of a comprehensive win; he showed speed, stamina, and his ease of victory made it more remarkable than Spend a Buck's win. ESPN's Randy Moss considers Barbaro's Derby performance one of the top three he had witnessed to that point, dating back to 1980, adding: "He finished as strongly from the three-eighths to the wire as any Kentucky Derby winner I have witnessed." John Asher determined that Barbaro's Derby performance was one of the five best performances he had witnessed in all racing. And for it to happen in the Kentucky Derby simply made it all the more special. Law agreed. Privman thought that aside from Secretariat's Belmont, this performance was as good as any he had seen.

....

"Bluegrass Cat was a very cool horse, and was very easy to ride. Todd Pletcher, prior to the race, gave me little instructions. We had a great trip. He broke very sharply to gain a good position. Going into the first turn, I was able to come over to the rail to save as much ground as possible. On the backside, I was able to ease him out, and by the five-eighths pole, I was just behind Barbaro. Without question, Barbaro was traveling the easiest of all the horses. By the three-eighths pole, I tried to make my run. It was between the three-eighths pole and the quarter pole when I realized Barbaro had too much, Edgar had let him lengthen his stride . . . ."

— RAMON DOMINGUEZ

....

Hall of Fame Jockey Gary Stevens, who has won three Kentucky Derbys, with Winning Colors (1988), Thunder Gulch (1995), and Silver Charm (1997), had this to say about Barbaro's Derby performance: "His performance in the Kentucky Derby was brilliant. I was working for NBC that day. His last eighth of a mile was spectacular. He was a beautiful horse to look at. A beautiful eye. His stride was just perfect that day. Barbaro was phenomenal. It's difficult to compare horses from different eras. For the Derbys I have witnessed, and the ones I have ridden in, Barbaro's Derby performance was the best."

Seconds after his win, many pundits were thinking that this was it, finally we would witness a Triple Crown winner—the elusive Holy Grail of the horse racing world in North America. Affirmed was the last horse to take the Triple Crown in 1978.

"No sooner had Barbaro crossed the wire in the Derby than I, like most people, started thinking that this is the year we're going to see a Triple Crown winner," noted Haskin. "That performance got me as excited as any Derby performance I've ever seen. It was very much like the feeling I had after Secretariat's win. Here was the perfect racehorse. He had the looks, the temperament, the brilliance, the tactical speed, the stamina, and the closing punch. There were no chinks in his armor. He appeared limitless."

THE NEXT DAY

Sunday morning Michael Matz, Peter Brette, and Barbaro were outside Barn 42 entertaining media questions, a tradition for the Derby winning connections. Tom Pedulla was one of many media in attendance:

"The day after the Derby, Barbaro was at the barn, grazing. He looked magnificent. It did not look like he had run a race. He looked like a confident animal and he looked like he had done something special. You could use any superlative to describe him. The race had not taken any toll on him.

"Michael Matz and Peter Brette were giving interviews. They fed the enthusiasm. They were so excited themselves. Peter Brette noted, 'The world could be his oyster. We still have not seen the best of this horse.' Derby winning trainers, the next day, are always outside the barn to give media a fair amount of time. It's a big victory; they are very cooperative. In this case, Peter, who was such a part of the success, was gushing about the horse: 'What you saw was good, there is a lot more there.'"

Pedulla continued, "While his Derby win was magnificent, special, and authoritative, what struck me was the next day, after the performance, to look as good as he did. They don't always bring out the Derby winner, and you know why. It's a hard race going a mile and a quarter. In full view, Barbaro was looking special."

Barbaro was now heading back up north to his home base. The set up was perfect for him to capture the Triple Crown that had just slipped from the grasp of Smarty Jones (2004), Funny Cide (2003), and Real Quiet (1998), all of whom were beaten in the Belmont Stakes. The biggest aspect of the challenge, for Barbaro, appeared to be to race again in two weeks for the Preakness. But Barbaro was fresh and deliberately prepared for the three-race challenge of the Triple Crown. And the Kentucky Derby seemed to have hardly reached the bottom of his deep well of talent. The Belmont, which had defeated recent Triple Crown protagonists with its stamina stretching mile-and-a-half trip, was considered the easier of the two remaining Triple Crown races for Barbaro. He was expected to relish the extra distance given his pedigree and demonstrated running style.

BACK TO FAIR HILL

After being featured on the greatest stage of horse racing in Kentucky, Barbaro returned to the surroundings of bucolic Fair Hill, Maryland, arriving the following Monday. He now had a little less than two weeks to recover and prepare for the second leg of the Triple Crown: the Preakness Stakes. Things seemed to be falling into

Just being a horse

place. Barbaro appeared to have had an easy race in the Derby and, as Durkin had noted in his race call, he had saved something for his upcoming challenge.

As is normal for a horse after a race, Barbaro had three days away from training on a track. His training for those three days included walking in the shed row, grazing outside, and being turned out in either a paddock or a smaller round pen. I distinctly remember seeing Barbaro out grazing—seemingly enjoying life—only two days after his most famous victory. As Matz put it to me that day on the horse path at Fair Hill, two days prior he was excelling in front of more than 150,000 people. Now Barbaro was at peace, grazing, without a care in the world—just being a horse.

On the Wednesday following the Kentucky Derby, Barbaro returned to the track at Fair Hill. Brette was back aboard as usual, and Matz was escorting them on his pony Messaging. Barbaro looked terrific. It was almost as if he knew he was that good. He had an aura and swagger about him. Predictably, the media had followed Barbaro to Fair Hill. And of course, those of us at Fair Hill began to look forward to each morning in case we were fortunate enough to catch a glimpse of the great horse training.

Barbaro's training routine over the next few days varied between the dirt track and the all-weather track—jogging and galloping—after which Barbaro was turned out to eat grass. Life could not have been better, nor gone more smoothly, for the Kentucky Derby champion. There was now, however, an element of pressure with which the Barbaro team had to contend. Prior to the Kentucky Derby, they were excited thinking that they had a true star and sharing him with the world. Now the world knew who Barbaro was, and there was a huge expectation he now had to match. He had dominated in his Derby performance. Many observers assumed he would be our long-awaited Triple Crown winner. Matz now had to entertain more media when he would have simply preferred to focus his time on his horse, and the remainder of horses he had under his care. With the additional media, also came questions that at times bordered on the bizarre. But this was now part of the price of winning America's greatest race. And Matz handled it well. Nevertheless, the pressure had increased significantly.

The only training question appeared to be whether Matz would choose to work Barbaro before his Preakness start. Given that there is only a two-week break between the Derby and the Preakness, working a horse in between the two races is not a foregone conclusion. It was not until the middle of the second week that a decision to work Barbaro was made. He worked a quarter of a mile on the dirt at Fair Hill, two days prior to the Preakness, to allow him to get air into his lungs and stretch his legs. He completed the quarter mile work in 24 seconds.

I was able to watch the work while I was aboard a horse for trainer Paul Rowland. I was standing next to Lil Klesaris, trainer Steve Klesaris's assistant, who was on her pony Amigo. As we were watching Barbaro galloping around, I asked Lil when she thought he was going to work. She glanced down at her watch and replied that he had just worked. It was amazing to watch. He did not appear to get out of a gallop, and if you did not have a watch on him, you would not have realized that he had just breezed.

Barbaro's training over the two weeks also included a little gate schooling. It was very straightforward and he stood in the gate without a problem. It was all part of the routine preparation for another horse race. Barbaro was doing fantastically well. Certainly, there was no indication of the tragedy to come.

Training for the Preakness

Unspeakable Tragedy

PREAKNESS DAY: MAY 20, 2006

On Friday afternoon, Barbaro was loaded onto a Brookledge van, along with the Steve Klesaris–trained Diabolical, and headed to Pimlico Race Track in Baltimore, about fifty miles south. Vince Mast was responsible for getting Barbaro to Pimlico; Vince had also driven Barbaro from Keeneland to Churchill Downs, ahead of the Kentucky Derby. *Philadelphia Inquirer's* Mike Jensen was among the twenty or so people in attendance at Fair Hill for the departure: "Barbaro was walked into the van under a passing rain shower. A few minutes earlier, Michael Matz had looked at Barbaro's hind end and quietly said, just talking to himself, 'God, he's a fit horse.' Earlier that day, Peter Brette had told me, 'I can't see him getting beat at all.' These guys were quietly confident."

ESPN's Randy Moss was part of a larger crowd on hand to greet Barbaro when he arrived at Pimlico.

"When Barbaro unloaded at Pimlico, I was right there with our producer Bob Goodrich and director Steve Beim," said Moss. "Barbaro was brought out of the van, and was walking toward the barn. Beim remarked, 'Holy cow, can you believe how beautiful this horse is!' You could just see it, Barbaro knew he was superb. He had a presence; he really looked spectacular."

On Preakness morning, Barbaro was taken to the track at Pimlico for some light training, much as he had done on the Derby morning. This time it went without incident. While cooling out after the gallop, Barbaro was examined by one of the three state vets, Dr. David Zipf. This type of inspection occurs for all runners before all races. Barbaro was jogged up and down. All was well. Dr. Zipf

then examined his legs and again, all was well.

It was going to be another long day and Barbaro was now settled down in stall 40, the stall reserved for the Kentucky Derby winner.

The Preakness attracts two types of runners—those that ran in the Kentucky Derby and those that did not. Of those that ran in the Kentucky Derby, both Brother Derek and Sweetnorthernsaint were coming back for another chance to defeat Barbaro. Both had been among the leading candidates for the Derby two weeks prior, but were overmatched. Brother Derek's Derby was not without incident, given that he was not forwardly placed as usual and he lost a shoe, a combination that resulted in him finishing in a dead-heat for fourth. Derby favorite Sweetnorthernsaint proved a disappointment to trainer Mike Trombetta, who had expected to see his gelding close to the first flight of horses as they ran past the

Arriving for the Preakness

stands for the first time, not in seventeenth or eighteenth place. Trombetta knew he had already lost the race at that point, but thankfully, Sweetnorthernsaint came out of the race in good shape and had trained well coming up to the Preakness.

Of the "new shooters," Bernardini was the most intriguing. A lightly raced horse, he had most recently won the Withers Stakes in New York in very smart style. It was only his fourth race. Bernardini was the one horse other than Barbaro that was getting some attention from the public and media alike. Because he did not run in the Derby, he was not competing in the Preakness with only a two-week break—a possible advantage over Barbaro and the other Derby starters. But Barbaro had been so good in the Derby it would be hard to fathom that he could lose his form in only two weeks. And Matz had deliberately prepared Barbaro to be a fresh horse going into the Derby so he could have something left as he prepared for the Preakness.

Simply put, this was supposed to be Barbaro's Preakness. He had won the Derby in such scintillating style, and appeared not to have been asked for everything in doing so. He had trained well at Fair Hill and seemed ready for another big effort. Barbaro had not lost yet and there was no reason to think today was going to be the day. Smarty Jones and Funny Cide, two recent winners of the Kentucky Derby, had also dominated their rivals in the Preakness and, like them, it seemed that Barbaro overmatched all the other Preakness runners. Dick Jerardi assumed that Barbaro was simply going to crush the field.

A record crowd of more than 118,000 was on hand to see if Barbaro could take the next step toward the Triple Crown. Inevitably, the majority of the crowd was focused on one horse. As the horses emerged from the paddock, the crowd noise was building to a crescendo.

"The atmosphere was unbelievable," said equine veterinarian Hollie Stillwell, who was attending her first Preakness. "All day, all the talk was about Barbaro. *Only* about him. Other races were ancillary. Other competitors in the Preakness seemed to be simply along for the ride. There seemed to be an assumption that he was going to win."

The horses were on the track to warm up, a routine ten-to-twelve minute process that consists of jogging and galloping. All three state veterinarians were on

Warming up

hand to observe the horses to ensure everything was okay. Dr. Zipf was stationed by the starting gate and kept a close eye on the field. He noticed that Barbaro took a funny hop-step behind and that Prado looked around as if to note something had happened. A yellow jacket, an insect, had landed on Barbaro's back and irritated him. Dr. Zipf continued to observe him, and determined that Barbaro was perfectly fine after the incident.

Gladys McHargue and her pony Paco escorted Barbaro and Prado through the warm-up before the race.

"I ponied Barbaro for the Laurel Futurity as well as for the Preakness," said McHargue. "At the Laurel Futurity he was still a baby. At the Preakness, he had grown up. He was focused. Edgar was very serious. There was no chitchat. The crowd noise was very loud and was keyed-in on Barbaro, but it did not faze him. The only thing he would do was try to eat Paco's flowers, which were braided into his mane. Barbaro seemed ready, he warmed up perfectly. As I handed Barbaro off to the gate crew, I thought I would now be a small part of history. Only it turned out it was not the history we all wanted."

Barbaro was one of the first horses to be loaded in the gate. He stood there quietly and with focus. He appeared sharp, but not anxious. The crowd noise level remained intense; so powerful that it made it difficult for the starters to communicate. As the outside horse was being loaded, Barbaro broke early from the gate.

"The outside horse was coming in. Barbaro was looking strong and feeling good," explained starter Bruce Wagner. "His assistant starter had a hold of him, with his head slightly turned in to him. Everything was normal amid the chaos of the intense crowd noise. He might have heard something and he just went. Edgar was sitting on him nice and quietly and then he just went. The assistant starter had two choices, to try to go with him or to let him go so Barbaro could go straight. He made the right decision. Only Barbaro's head hit the front of the gate. The gates are held closed by magnets that are designed to open under force in order to avoid serious injury. Barbaro's legs never hit anything."

Jockey Javier Castellano was in a nearby post aboard Bernardini, also waiting for the race to begin. "They were still loading the horses, everyone was almost ready to go, it was just bad luck in the moment," said Castellano. "Mentally Barbaro seemed ready to go. Nothing was bothering him; he was just ready to go. He must have heard a noise and he just went and broke through the gate."

"I'm not superstitious, but most horses do not run good after they have broken through the gate like that," continued Castellano. "Barbaro was really the only horse to beat. And when this happened, I think we all thought that we really had a chance to win the race."

Once Barbaro had broken through the gate, Prado gathered him up easily with the help of outrider Sharon Greenberg. Greenberg noted that Barbaro was quite professional and laid-back once he had broken through the gate. It just seemed that he mistook a noise as a cue to begin the race and once he realized he had made a false start, he recovered his composure quickly. Prado remained intense.

Horsemen concurred with Castellano; they know that horses simply do not seem to run their race if they have broken through the gate early. It is a bad omen, according to Ed Fountaine of the *New York Post.* Perhaps the most famous example of this was when Seattle Slew did the same thing in the Jockey Club Gold Cup in 1978. He was ultimately beaten by the ill-fated Exceller after setting wicked early fractions.

The public saw Barbaro's early emergence from the gate as a sign of anxiety, rather than a function of the intense noise and a simple miscue.

"It appeared very out of character. I had never seen Barbaro rattled, he had that great style," recalled Sean Clancy. "That was not stylish; it was a weird thing for him to do. Nothing had gone wrong up to this point, nothing. It was as if everything had been choreographed. It had been flawless. Everything had been perfect, from his turf starts to his race in the Kentucky Derby, to his pre-Derby work and his month at Keeneland. Perfect…and then this."

As disappointed as many felt with this unexpected event, Barbaro was reloaded into the gate after being thoroughly examined by Dr. Zipf. He observed Barbaro jogging back to the gate for approximately fifteen to twenty yards. Dr. Zipf checked for any injuries and found nothing visible. He then asked Prado if he felt that Barbaro was okay. Both agreed that nothing appeared to be visibly wrong with Barbaro. In order for Dr. Zipf to scratch Barbaro at this point, something had to be visibly wrong. Starter Bruce Wagner concurred. He also observed Barbaro when he came back to the gate and noted that the colt looked perfectly fine.

While nothing appeared to be wrong with Barbaro, everything was wrong with what had just happened. Barbaro had gone from being a lock to win this race to a horse that was totally vulnerable simply because he broke through the gate early.

Once the race got underway, a second uncharacteristic thing occurred— Barbaro was not close to the lead. Dick Jerardi noted that Barbaro should have been second, off a moderate early pace. He had displayed a similar running style in all his races. It was very predictable. Barbaro now had half the field in front of him for the first time in his career. This race was now going to present a different challenge for Barbaro. We would now see if he was a truly great horse.

Then the worst possible scenario unfolded. Barbaro broke down in his right hind leg and was eased by Prado only an eighth of a mile into the race. To describe this as tragic would not do justice to the situation. Everyone was anticipating crowning a champion, an unbeaten horse that appeared to be just that—unbeatable.

Sadly, everyone was wrong.

Now the champion was stricken, looking anguished and puzzled at the same time, as he struggled to come to terms with his circumstances. The Preakness had now evolved into two separate events. The race was continuing, while the Kentucky Derby champion was being attended to by his handlers and Pimlico officials. The crowd was in shock. It was a devastating blow to the atmosphere built around a horse that was supposed to be the star of the day. In all other sporting events if someone gets hurt, the play stops. In a horse racing event this does not happen. Dave Rodman called the race for those in attendance that day.

"As the horses headed down the backstretch and into the far turn, it was kind of surreal," Rodman recalled. "I'll never forget it. I just felt that this was not happening. The first pack of leaders, including Like Now, Brother Derek, and Sweetnorthernsaint, appeared to be running in place, as if *they* sensed this could not be happening. I was relieved when Bernardini made his move. He snapped me out of it. I don't know whether it was psychological; I could feel the stunned feeling of the crowd through my open window, but I could not look down to see Barbaro's condition. I had to stay focused on the race. I wanted to look at Barbaro, but also needed to give Bernardini his due in winning the Preakness."

- -

"Barbaro was falling back. His jockey was pulling him up. He got off Barbaro right where I was. He was trying to soothe him, hold him still in position. It was such a frightening scene for any animal lover. Gretchen had turmoil and emotion written all over her face. Prado was just crestfallen. He was emotionally broken. It was awful. So many people who had been so joyous moments before were now heartsick because that horse was such a beautiful animal and he was hurt so badly. I just remember the sadness of that day and having to cover it for the next eight months."

—SANDY McKEE

- -

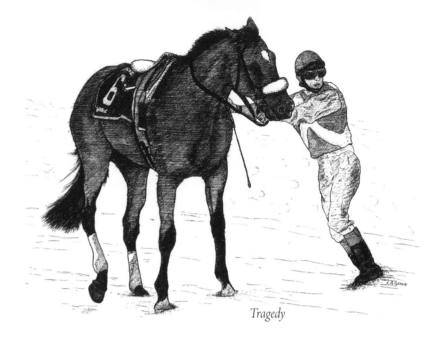

Tragedy

And Bernardini did win the Preakness in great style.

"Early in the race I was focused on getting a good position, maybe third, fourth, or fifth," recalled Castellano. "That was my goal and it fit the style of Bernardini. We all broke pretty evenly. At one point, I saw Barbaro next to me, then I did not see him anymore. I just thought Edgar was changing tactics and decided to slow down to get position."

"Turning for home I just kept riding my horse," continued Castellano. "I passed the wire, I had won the race, and then I saw Barbaro as I was galloping out. 'What happened here?' I thought. I had just figured Barbaro was behind me in the race. Seeing him there with all the people surrounding him just sucked the emotion out of me. I had never had the opportunity to win a Triple Crown race. My first emotion was I won the race, then I saw Barbaro. I was shocked. I thought I had just beaten him. It was so sad, I just did not know what to think in the moment anymore. I had wanted to celebrate but I just couldn't."

The crowd had turned its attention to the happenings right in front of it as Barbaro was now in a new race—one for his life.

First on the scene to help Edgar Prado pull up Barbaro was Rafael Orozco, a Michael Matz groom. Outrider Sharon Greenberg was also close at hand. Her job was to shield Barbaro from the runners in the race as they came past the winning post and as they returned to unsaddle. It was important the riders knew what was happening, and it was critical Barbaro did not get spooked by the other horses. Greenberg was stoic in her role, as was her thoroughbred pony DJ. As an equine, DJ's role was also important in terms of helping Barbaro to feel secure. Alongside Greenberg was assistant track manager Glen Kozak, who arrived as a visibly shaken Prado and Orozco were holding Barbaro. Eduardo Hernandez, Barbaro's groom, was also immediately on the scene, along with Peter Brette.

· ·

"I was very fortunate that day, my teller window had a TV screen just off to the side, and I would be able to see the race clearly for a change. Some local exercise riders were within earshot, hovering around the TV. The race went off and it was evident quickly that there was trouble. I watched Edgar Prado trying with everything he had in him to pull Barbaro up…my heart was in my throat at that moment. I was stunned…all I could think was noooooooooooo! My eyes were frozen on the screen. Every ounce of mental energy I have ever had went out to Prado to have the strength to get Barbaro pulled up. I glanced over at the exercise riders standing there watching the race, their faces dropped…not good. Arms crossed, focused, they were watching it happen… two of them turned and started to walk away, heads dropped, staring at the floor, then they stopped and turned back, to watch again. They knew instantly what had happened and what it usually meant for the horse. I searched their faces, looking for a glimmer of hope that maybe it wasn't that bad. The looks on their faces told it all. It wasn't about a lost bet on their faces either. It was much more than that. One of them walked by me…I said to him, 'How bad is it?'…he just shook his head and responded, 'Not good, not good, it's the leg, broke down.' They can tell…they all knew it was bad.

"It was strange, not only watching a veil of sadness and disbelief drop across the crowd, but hitting specific people at first…the horsepeople that were there that day."

—CINDY JOHNSTON,
Pari-mutuel Teller, Delaware Park Racetrack and Slots

· ·

Matt Hartmann, a vet technician, arrived, having watched the events unfold from the turf course by the wire. Dr. Dan Dreyfuss was the first vet on the scene. Matz, Ritchie Orozco (Barbaro's hot walker and son of Rafael), the Jacksons, and other Pimlico officials also quickly came to Barbaro's aid. Barclay Tagg was also in attendance: "I was not sure I should be there, but the Jacksons are lifelong friends of mine. I wanted to go and comfort Gretchen."

This type of event is entirely unplanned for, yet everyone involved seemed to know their role and did their job as necessary.

Eduardo Hernandez, Barbaro's groom, has worked for Michael Matz since Matz's show-jumping days. Eduardo is also the groom for Barbaro's brothers Nicanor and Lentenor. Preakness Day 2006 was also Eduardo's birthday.

Hernandez and Brette, the two people Barbaro knew best, were there to help reassure the stricken colt. The horse ambulance arrived with Jo Miller at the wheel and passenger Dr. Zipf. Dr. Dreyfuss had departed the scene to get his truck. Track superintendent Jamie Richardson, with the help of Hartmann, applied a Kimzey splint to quickly stabilize the injured right hind leg. A blue tarpaulin shield was erected to conceal the ongoing events from the Preakness crowd and also shield Barbaro from the crowd. Unfortunately, the shield caused Barbaro to spook. It also made the crowd more anxious due to the shield's reputation of being a precursor to euthanasia. Matz quickly asked for the shield to be taken down. Once Barbaro's leg was stabilized by the Kimzey splint, he was loaded onto the ambulance to take him to the Stakes barn for further examination. Hernandez and Hartmann were among those traveling with Barbaro. As the ambulance moved, Barbaro could be seen with his head peering out at the crowd. It provided a glimmer of hope to fans who were waiting, hoping, and pleading for their star. Voices could be heard, shouting, "Don't do it!" (referring to euthanizing Barbaro) and "Good luck, Barbaro." Fans were openly crying and leaning on each other for support.

"What I found most notable was that by the time the winner was returning to the winner's circle (his name lost to obscurity because he won on the day Barbaro broke down), you could have heard a pin drop," said Hollie Stillwell about the crowd's reaction to the tragedy. "There were tens of thousands of people in attendance and yet there was this bizarre vacuum of noise. No one was saying anything. People were visibly shocked and upset."

⋯⋯⋯⋯⋯⋯⋯⋯⋯⋯⋯⋯⋯⋯⋯⋯⋯

"The Preakness turned out to be the biggest roller coaster of emotions a lot of us have ever experienced in horse racing. I came with one of the favorites [Brother Derek] to win the race. As we waited for the race with all the buildup, first Barbaro broke through the gate early. Subsequently Brother Derek broke poorly, which took him out of our game plan. Then the devastating sight of seeing Barbaro being pulled up so soon after the start just left a big hole in my stomach. It was the biggest drop in the roller-coaster ride. I find it very difficult to explain how you feel when things like this happen. I was asked shortly after the race how my horse was. I knew he was okay, but we were all more concerned with Barbaro."

—DAN HENDRICKS

⋯⋯⋯⋯⋯⋯⋯⋯⋯⋯⋯⋯⋯⋯⋯⋯⋯

"I think because it was Barbaro it was different," she continued. "He had been so inspirational in his Derby win and now this. I won't ever forget that weird vacuum of noise in that gigantic crowd. And that crowd included some horrendous drunks in the infield. They had been rowdy and obnoxious, but even they too went silent. It was extremely sad, yet interesting to see such a gigantic group of people silenced for a horse, more so than they would perhaps have been for a human being."

John Hennegan, co-producer of *First Saturday in May*, was in the infield as events were unfolding.

"I knew something bad had happened to Barbaro, but from my position in the infield, I was not able to see him," said Hennegan. "Word spread quickly and all of a sudden you could cut the air with a knife. Pimlico had instantly become the place where you didn't want to be that day. There was something different about the anticipation with that horse. In addition to the obvious injury, that's what made it such a dark day for racing."

Dr. Scott Palmer, a veterinarian and lifelong friend of Matz, was in attendance that Preakness Day. As Matz's guest, he was looking forward to celebrating a Preakness win with the Matz family in a restaurant in downtown Baltimore. Palmer was now a part of the crowd, in shock. He was with Dr. Larry Bramlage, who served as the media on-call vet. Dr. Bramlage's role, in a crisis like this, is to relay ongoing events to the media so that the attending vets could focus on the tasks at hand.

⋯⋯⋯⋯⋯⋯⋯⋯⋯⋯⋯⋯⋯⋯⋯⋯⋯

"I was as horrified as anyone. There was a big groan in the press box, I could not watch much. They are going to put this horse down now—I am writing, I am watching, it was very emotional, tragic, one of the most horrifying things I have seen on the racetrack. And then I was amazed they vanned him off and he was still alive. You could see the horse in the van. You could see the horse was still alive. Wow, this horse has a lot of guts, I thought, he is something special."

—RICH ROSENBLATT

⋯⋯⋯⋯⋯⋯⋯⋯⋯⋯⋯⋯⋯⋯⋯⋯⋯

Matz needed Dr. Palmer to help with Barbaro but did not have his telephone number. He called Dr. Anderson at Fair Hill to get it and then tried calling Palmer's cell phone, but there was no signal. A message was relayed to Dr. Bramlage to see if he knew where Palmer was and to get him to the Stakes barn immediately. Palmer heard the message and ran.

Dr. Dreyfuss was now one of four vets in attendance at the Stakes barn.

"Barbaro was smart enough, and coordinated enough, to hop the twenty-five feet from the ambulance to his stall," said Dr. Dreyfuss.

Dr. Nick Meittinis set up the initial radiographs that showed three injuries: a condylar fracture to the cannon bone, a shattered long pastern bone, and a fractured sesamoid. Dr. Scott Palmer was now on the scene as the "consulting vet." He would advise Matz and ultimately, the Jacksons, of the reality of the situation and the best course of action going forward. Dr. Rachel Beard, who was attending the Preakness as a guest of Dr. Palmer, was assisting, as was Hartmann.

Barbaro was very calm through the entire process. After the radiographs were taken, the Kimzey splint was taken off Barbaro and he was checked for any breaks in the skin. Breaks in the skin would have increased the likelihood of infection significantly and would have meant that any necessary surgery would have to be undertaken that night. Barbaro never moved a muscle. It was almost as if he knew they were trying to help him.

"There were times when Nick, Scott, and I were resting in silly positions in order to check him over," Dr. Dreyfuss recalled. "It was idiotic, but you got the sense he understood, to whatever degree he understood."

The four vets and Hartmann proceeded to put a large Robert Jones bandage that stretched from above the hock to the ground on Barbaro's leg. The Kimzey splint was then reapplied to the lower part of the leg. Some PVC piping and other materials were applied to further stabilize the leg from both the back and the side, and prepare Barbaro for his ninety-minute trip to New Bolton Center.

The injuries were catastrophic. Dr. Palmer knew they were in serious trouble with Barbaro, and started to explain the situation to Matz. The long pastern bone was shattered. There was no strut—no intact piece that would serve as an anchor to reattach the other bone. There was a danger of telescoping—with the shattered pieces simply sinking to the bottom of the leg much like a bag of ice.

The one piece of good news was that there were no visible breaks in the skin. Other than that, this was a dire situation. Barbaro did have a chance to survive—an extremely small one, but there was a possibility that he could be saved. And even though his odds were very slim, Palmer's rationale for trying to save Barbaro was that if he had a chance, he should get the opportunity to fight; he deserved it. Euthanasia at this point was an option that was never discussed—not among the vets, between Dr. Palmer and Matz, and not with the Jacksons. Barbaro had a slim likelihood of overcoming this injury, and they would do everything they could to save his life. After all, he was the unbeaten Kentucky Derby champion. He had been nothing short of spectacular in dominating his Derby. And he was being a very pliant patient. He had the right temperament to give himself the best of opportunities.

"Barbaro was an incredible animal. I mean really, he was as wonderful a patient as you could ever imagine," remembered Hartmann. "A horse with a broken leg…letting us take X-rays like that. Putting on the Robert Jones bandage, he was an absolutely wonderful individual to work on. That was the biggest hope we had, that he was going to be a class individual."

There were two viable options to consider for Barbaro's injury, an internal fixation or an external fixation. Both required getting him out of Pimlico as swiftly as possible, to New Bolton Center, and under the care of Dr. Dean Richardson. The more viable of the two options was an internal fixation. Dr. Palmer called New Bolton Center to speak with Dr. Richardson and learned that Richardson was in Florida. Palmer made the call to Florida. Dr. Richardson had watched the catastrophe unfold on a black-and-white monitor after coming out of surgery with his friend Dr. Byron Reid. Dr. Richardson knew, as soon as he saw Barbaro being pulled up, that if the colt was going to require surgery, he would likely be involved. He had long-standing relationships with both Matz and the Jacksons. He was highly regarded as an orthopedic surgeon—one of the very best. And New Bolton Center was in reasonably close proximity to Pimlico. Richardson had called Kathy Anderson even before Barbaro had been vanned off the track.

Dr. Richardson received the radiographs via e-mail. Decisions were made, surgery would occur the next day, and Dr. Richardson would fly up the next morning to lead the surgical team. Thankfully, the intact skin on Barbaro's

PREAKNESS PARTY AT FAIR HILL

On the Preakness undercard, Better Talk Now won the Grade 2 Dixie Stakes under an inspired ride from Ramon Dominguez. Blackie, as he was known in the barn, was a Fair Hill favorite, and is the leading money winner at Fair Hill and a Breeders' Cup winner. In winning his first race of the year, he set the tone for the afternoon and raised our already lofty expectations. Today was going to be Fair Hill's day. I watched Blackie's race at home, only a five-minute drive from Fair Hill. I then headed over to the Preakness party; it was the same location as the Derby party and hosted again by Dr. Anderson. There was no need to watch the pre-race programming, we knew all the stories, and most of all we knew more about Barbaro than could be told. The atmosphere at the party was one of calm expectations. We had the horse, we had all seen him over the previous two weeks. We knew this was likely going to be the tougher of the two remaining races of the Triple Crown to win, but the way Barbaro had dominated his rivals in the Derby, and how well he looked training at Fair Hill over the last two weeks, left no doubts as to what we should expect this afternoon. Barbaro had united Fair Hill in its support for one horse.

When Barbaro broke early from the gate, we were stunned. This is not something we would expect from a horse as professional as Barbaro. And we knew that horses that break through the gate before a race starts typically do not fare well. But surely, this was Barbaro. He could even overcome this. Shortly into the race, we saw he was in serious trouble. Kathy Anderson, who sat closest to the TV screen, dropped her head into her hands. No one knew what to say, so nothing was said. Some stayed in the room to watch the race, others simply left. I exited the room even before the remainder of the field had navigated the first turn of the Preakness. It was more than three years later, when I first watched Barbaro's Preakness. I waited outside for about an hour among a small gathering of people. A little while later I spoke with Kathy Anderson to try to understand what she knew of Barbaro's status. There is truly no way to describe how devastated we all felt.

broken leg meant that the surgery could wait until the next day. And waiting a little while was actually better for the horse so that he could become accustomed to his new circumstances before coming out of anesthesia after surgery.

While Barbaro was being examined, wrapped, and prepped for ambulance transport, winner's circle ceremonies were taking place on the main side of the racetrack. But this was hardly the celebration that had been envisioned, and those in attendance appeared to be just going through the motions. They had won a major horse race, but their biggest rival was robbed of an opportunity to challenge for the Triple Crown, and they were denied the opportunity to race with Barbaro. It was a hollow victory, perhaps, but a Grade 1 victory on the national stage nonetheless.

"While happy to win a Triple Crown race, there was a bad feeling," explained Tom Albertrani, who trained Preakness winner Bernardini. "It was very upsetting to see such a great horse being put in the horse ambulance. No one wants to experience what Michael (and his team) had to experience. It definitely took away from the excitement of the victory."

Javier Castellano recalled, "After the winner's circle ceremonies I went in to the jocks' room. Everyone was offering me their congratulations. I just wanted to go up to Edgar and apologize. It has happened to me before. I apologized to him. I just did not want to see what had happened. We like horses. We love our horses.

"Edgar is a very classy guy. We all like him and respect him. He just said, something like 'things happen,' but you could see it in his eyes. He was looking down and was just so sad. Barbaro was a very special horse. He did not say much, but what could you say after something like that?

"I just wished we could have done it again, I wished I could enjoy the moment and recognize my horse's ability. But it did not work out that way."

Prado stopped by the Stakes barn after changing in the jockeys' room and was able to see Barbaro standing in his stall. It provided him some hope. Barbaro was still standing and being attended to by his caregivers. This would

be the first of many visits to Barbaro by his jockey.

Barbara Livingston had the winner's circle assignment, and went through the process of taking the mandatory photographs without letting Barbaro out of her thoughts, convincing herself that by now, he was likely euthanized. She then walked from the winner's circle to the Stakes barn to confirm her worst thought.

"I was surprised to see he was still alive when I got there," said Livingston. "I was happy to call my mum to let her know he was still alive."

Livingston looked around and observed people emerging from the racetrack and heading toward the Stakes barn area. Wearing or holding Barbaro T-shirts, many were crying as the darkness began to fall around them, and police arrived to help maneuver the record crowds through traffic patrol. "There was something about watching the van and police motorcycles," continued Livingston. "There was such a hope to it yet such hopelessness. It was like watching a movie."

When it was all over, Dr. Dreyfuss remembered, "We were completely emotionless while working with Barbaro, but when it was done and he was headed to New Bolton Center, Nick and I were like, 'What just happened?' It went by so quickly. It was not until later that I cried on my way home at the end of the night. I am not ashamed to admit it. It was heartbreaking to see that horse—he was a magnificent looking horse. He was as good as you could have ever wanted him to be, as were the Jacksons and Michael Matz."

Barbaro left for New Bolton Center in the horse ambulance pulled by a new tractor recently purchased by Pimlico's owner, Magna Entertainment. This was a godsend, as the tractor could also operate on highways and would be the safest and fastest mode of transport on Route I-95. With Jamie Richardson at the wheel and Glen Kozak as passenger, Joe Miller, Hernandez, and Barbaro began their journey to New Bolton Center. Thankfully, Karen De Francis, wife of Joe De Francis (who was Maryland Jockey Club's CEO) contacted Maryland's governor, Robert Ehrlich, who provided a police escort that comprised Baltimore police and state police. This allowed Barbaro's motorcade to exit the heavily congested area expeditiously and travel swiftly north. Dr. Palmer and his wife

Janet followed the ambulance in their vehicle, as did Brette and Matz in Brette's vehicle.

Throughout the journey, Miller was in touch with the cab via phone. Barbaro stood very quietly. Well-wishers in passing cars placed small placards on their windows expressing their good wishes. Banners were draped from overpasses with messages of goodwill. Barbaro was now a national news story, and people quickly figured out who was in the horse ambulance with the police escort. The nation was now becoming acutely aware of Barbaro.

"The most amazing aspect of this tragedy was how everyone put Barbaro first. Every decision was made in the best interest of the horse and every action was performed to give him the best chance of survival. These selfless actions are often hard to find on a racetrack or in everyday life. The memory of the 2006 Preakness will always be bittersweet for me. Barbaro's breakdown and the eventual outcome were tragic. Yet the compassion that I witnessed from every person involved will stay with me forever and gives me hope for humanity."

—DR. RACHEL BEARD,
Who, as an intern of Dr. Scott Palmer,
also attended to Barbaro at the Stakes barn

WHY?

There is no evidence from the radiographs to support one hypothesis or another that explains why Barbaro broke down. There are four theories, none of which has any conclusive proof.

One theory is that something happened as Barbaro broke through the gate early, but whatever it was remained visibly undetectable with all of the adrenaline flowing through his body. Under this scenario, when Barbaro re-broke for the race, the additional pressure caused the breakdown.

Others would argue that another horse in the race struck Barbaro; however, video evidence from the race is inconclusive.

A third theory is that Barbaro appeared agitated during the warm-up before the race indicating that something was amiss. We do know an insect bothered him, which made him appear uncomfortable for a couple of strides.

Some would simply state that he took a bad step.

Whatever the reason for Barbaro's breakdown, we will never know.

New Bolton Center

Staff at New Bolton Center, like many other fans around the nation, were waiting to watch Barbaro race in the Preakness with great anticipation after his Derby win. They were hoping he would take another step forward in his quest for the Triple Crown. Many knew Barbaro's connections personally—Barbaro was *their* horse. As the horrific events unfolded, they soon realized they would each become an integral part of the Barbaro story.

Dr. Dean Richardson travels to Florida a couple of times each year to work on cases with his friend, Dr. Byron Reid. Having just completed a very difficult case, the pair went to watch the Preakness in Reid's office on a black-and-white monitor. As a horse racing fan, Richardson had watched Barbaro's Kentucky Derby while teaching a course on equine fracture repair in Columbus, Ohio. Richardson had been following Barbaro all along because of his local connections; he had known Michael Matz and the Jacksons for years. After Barbaro's Florida Derby win, Richardson was convinced he would win the Kentucky Derby. Richardson was very impressed with his Kentucky Derby performance.

"I was super excited because it was that impressive a race [the Kentucky Derby]," said Richardson. "He won it perfectly and going away. To me he looked like the real deal. Even not being there, when you saw the post parade, you could see he had star power by just looking at him."

Richardson knew, shortly after watching the Preakness, that he would likely be involved if Barbaro was to have surgery. He proceeded to coordinate with Dr. Anderson (Fair Hill), Dr. Palmer (Pimlico), and vets from New Bolton Center, including Dr. Corinne Sweeney, Dr. Barb Dallap, and Dr. Liberty Getman, to make sure everything was prepared for his arrival the next morning, as he prepared his own journey north.

Dr. Corinne Sweeney, associate dean for New Bolton Center, lives four miles from New Bolton Center. She was watching the Preakness at her home with her husband (and fellow New Bolton Center vet) Ray and their children. Sweeney received a phone call minutes after the Preakness from a colleague at the Small Animal Hospital of the University of Pennsylvania. The caller asked her if she knew if Barbaro was coming to New Bolton Center, which is also part of the University of Pennsylvania. She did not. Soon after, Dr. Richardson called Sweeney to update her on conversations he had already had with those on hand at Pimlico. Sweeney headed over to New Bolton Center.

Dr. Barb Dallap, assistant professor for emergency medicine and critical care, would be responsible for Barbaro overnight and through to the next morning. She had listened to the Preakness on the radio, while performing emergency abdominal surgery on a pony at New Bolton Center. She had also spoken with Dr. Richardson shortly after the Preakness and started preparing for Barbaro's arrival.

Dr. Liberty Getman, large animal surgery resident, who would be part of Richardson's surgery team the next day, was at Kathy Anderson's Fair Hill Preakness party. She spoke to Richardson that night.

Jane Simone, director of development at New Bolton Center, knows the Jacksons and had followed Barbaro's career leading up to the Triple Crown challenge. Simone was in New York with her son, when she watched Barbaro dominate in the Kentucky Derby. She was at home, close to New Bolton Center, watching the Preakness. Ten minutes after the accident, she made her way to New Bolton Center, in order to help in any way she could. Simone remembered, "I just felt I needed to go there. When I arrived, people were already there, lining up along the campus fence line. People just wanted to be there to wait for the ambulance to arrive."

Jennifer Rench, who worked in the public relations department at New Bolton Center, watched the Preakness at her home, some twenty minutes from the hospital. After Barbaro broke down, she made some phone calls to see if she would be needed at New Bolton Center. She realized that if Barbaro were heading to their hospital, media would also be there.

Kathy Freeborn, who works in admissions at New Bolton Center, watched the Preakness from home with her husband. She, too, was anxious to see how Barbaro would run after watching his spectacular win in the Kentucky Derby. She headed over to New Bolton Center after the Preakness tragedy.

These are just seven of the staff at New Bolton Center who quickly realized the enormity of the situation, and that they would play an important role in the upcoming events of Barbaro's life.

Prior to Barbaro's arrival at New Bolton Center, Dr. Dallap, who was the emergency veterinarian on duty that evening, coordinated with her staff to make preparations for his arrival. The goal of Dallap's team, over the next twelve hours, was to ensure that no further damage occurred to Barbaro's injury as he awaited surgery. Dr. Dallap's team had other patients in their care that night, not the least of which was the pony in surgery. Before they could plan for Barbaro, they had to finish their tasks at hand. They also needed to continue to treat their other patients throughout the night.

Dr. Sweeney would not be involved in the direct care of Barbaro; rather, her task was to manage the overall situation that night and the following day. Sweeney oversaw the arrival of Barbaro, the media, and various well-wishers who had brought banners and posters. A situation like this had never occurred at New Bolton Center, so planning for it was not straightforward. Should the media and well-wishers be allowed on campus? If so, where should they go? Dr. Sweeney figured that working together with media was the best approach.

"They had their job, and we had our job," said Sweeney. "There was no reason we could not work well together. And the well-wishers, they were good people simply wanting to show their support for Barbaro. We could make it work."

The media and well-wishers were asked to remain in front of the hospital, as they all waited for the arrival of the horse ambulance. The driver, Jamie Richardson, had already been instructed where to unload. Around 9 p.m., one of the members of the media noted a helicopter overhead, and alerted Sweeney that the ambulance was close. The ambulance was coming from the east, but should have been approaching from the west. The driver had missed the turn off Route 1 at Toughkenamon and taken exit 82 instead. As the ambulance approached New Bolton Center, the crowd parted to let it through with no fuss. It was a very respectful scene. Dr. Dallap had developed a plan to ensure that Barbaro's arrival came off without a hitch. She had discussed it with Dr. Richardson and they were now ready to execute that plan. Barbaro was unloaded from the horse ambulance.

"He walked off the ambulance great. Barbaro was amazingly calm, he was very good," said Dallap. "That kind of behavior goes a long way in preserving himself. He got acclimated to his new surroundings very quickly."

Dallap's team had Barbaro's stall ready. Once he was settled in, they performed their usual blood work, inserted a catheter into a vein in Barbaro's neck, which would allow them to administer Barbaro's drugs, and performed other routine tasks to check and manage his health. Dr. David Nunamaker, professor of orthopedic surgery at New Bolton Center, joined Dallap as they reviewed the leg cast. They added some material to provide additional support, but that was all. They also determined not to leave Barbaro in cross-ties for the night, which is often the case for a patient awaiting surgery. Because of his professional demeanor, they decided to let him free in his stall, so he could get further used to his situation. Through the night Barbaro was able to comfortably get up and down, which was a very good sign. He also ate well that night, another very positive sign.

Others at New Bolton Center that night included Michael Matz and Peter Brette, who had arrived from Pimlico, and Dr. Anderson, along with Matz's assistant Sue Danner, who traveled from Fair Hill. Dr. Palmer and his wife Janet also arrived from Pimlico. Dr. Dallap updated Matz regarding Barbaro's situation. Matz held an impromptu briefing to share the update with the media. As nothing else was planned for that night, it would also be an opportunity to break for the evening, as they would all be back the next morning. At the conclusion of the briefing, a media representative asked Matz who he was. Matz confided with Dallap afterwards that he was very tempted to reply, "Dr. Dean Richardson." Clearly, despite the stress of the day, Matz was still able to maintain his composure and "almost" add a little humor.

It was a long day for everyone involved. Dallap continued with her duties, attending to Barbaro as well as attending to other patients that came in that night. She would go home, come back, and go home through the night. Almost everyone else left for the night, but some media representatives had nowhere to go. They slept on the campus.

The next morning, Dr. Sweeney arrived with donuts and coffee from the local Dunkin Donuts. She would convene with Jennifer Rench and others throughout the day. The media was thankful for the refreshments, and it was now time to simply wait for the arrival of Dr. Richardson, who was flying up from Florida. Dr. Getman helped prepare Barbaro for his surgery while the team waited for Dr. Richardson to arrive. He came straight from the airport, constantly in communication with his team to make sure everything was as it should be. When Richardson arrived, he held a brief press conference. Mike Jensen remembers, "As bleak as it had been late the day before at Pimlico, even after Barbaro had arrived safely, nobody left New Bolton. A few of us talked about going to grab some lunch and immediately thought better of it, figuring there could be news at any time, realizing that it wouldn't be good news. Then Dean Richardson gave his pre-surgery press conference, and you got a quick sense of the man. Asked when surgery would start, Richardson said, 'As soon as you stop asking me questions.' There were not too many questions after that."

The surgery team was comprised of Dr. Richardson, Dr. Getman, Dr. David Levine, and Dr. Steve Zedler. The anesthesia team consisted of veterinary anesthesiologist Dr. Bern Driessen, anesthesia nurse Shannon Harper, and surgery resident Dr. Sarah Dukti. There were also two operating room nurses, Kate Cole and Erin Ortell.

"A producer from New York met me there, and we were there for nearly ten hours that Sunday. Dr. Richardson arrived and addressed us in the press conference room by saying he was going to 'attempt' a surgical repair on Barbaro, but that he didn't know what he was going to find once inside the leg. You could tell Dr. Richardson had some trepidation but was pumped up for the challenge. He was blunt, assertive, and had that cocky Dr. Richardson persona that we've all come to know and love.

"When Dr. Richardson did not return to us shortly after beginning the surgery, we took it as a good sign. If he was still gone and working, that meant Barbaro must still be alive. That offered hope. For nearly seven hours, we waited, starved for information. I did frequent updates on ABC (our parent network) and ESPN TV and radio throughout the day. Later that evening we finally got the news we had waited all day with bated breath for: Barbaro was alive, his splintered leg had miraculously been reassembled, and he was back in his stall. I reported the much-anticipated news live on ESPN and finally, totally drained, I drove home around 11:00 that night. My phone never stopped ringing that day or the next with various co-workers, acquaintances, and TV and radio networks from around the country seeking updates."

—JEANNINE EDWARDS,
ESPN Reporter

The team knew this was going to be a hard surgery, but they had performed complex surgeries before. In the early afternoon, they began putting Barbaro's leg back together. Sweeney provided pizza for the media; the long wait continued. More media arrived and the well wishes kept pouring in. *USA Today*'s Tom Pedulla recalled, "When I went to New Bolton Center, the next day [Sunday], just to see banners already up, the cards coming in, the gift baskets, I was shocked by it all. It really surprised me. Thoroughbred racing is no longer high profile, the Preakness is not high profile. I was shocked by the response. I understood the public interest was massive, but I was surprised. I talked to Laura Hillenbrand and Bill Nack about the reactions to the horse. What an animal meant to people. Part of me will always be a little amazed by what followed."

Nobody at this stage knew if Barbaro would survive the surgery, or what were the conditions of the leg and blood supply to the foot. The longer the wait, however, the more optimistic the media became that the surgery might be successful. As the hours went along, the media observed Dr. Sweeney for signs of progress. She kept reassuring them regarding what was happening. Later in the afternoon, she did walk over to the surgery site for the first time, and learned that Barbaro was just being lifted from the recovery pool. She announced to the media that Dr. Richardson would soon be with them, but did not answer any questions.

. . . .

"In equine orthopedics you have a single goal, get the broken leg comfortable enough, and stable enough to walk on the leg comfortably."

—DR. DEAN RICHARDSON

. . . .

Joined at the press conference by Matz, Dr. Richardson discussed the surgery and the prognosis going forward. *Philadelphia Inquirer* columnist Bob Ford asked about Barbaro's overall survival odds. Dr. Richardson's response: "A coin toss." The "easy" part was behind them, but Richardson knew that many issues would lie ahead before they could consider his surgery a success.

Barbaro's surgery was national news, and his next eight months would become an event important to many people around the world.

Dr. Anderson recalled the weekend events later in a note to her friends. The following are excerpts from that e-mail:

"Preakness Day had dawned beautiful, crisp and sunny...and in schizophrenic style vacillated between blustery threats of rain and tranquil sunshine. Anxious anticipation prevailed at Fair Hill as people went about their work in order to be done to enjoy an afternoon of quality racing and what would be another page in the history of the quest for the Triple Crown. About two hundred Fair Hill horse people crowded into the Equine Vet Care Clinic in the late afternoon bringing their own refreshments and a pot luck array of edibles."

"We watched proudly as Fair Hill Training Center's best was brought to national television—great film footage and interviews with Matz, Brette, and Barbaro filled our hearts with pride. Post time arrived—Barbaro's premature break from the gate surprised us—with another horse that would have cost him the race but we believed that our Barbaro could overcome this altercation," said Dr. Anderson. "Surprise turned to shock as our hometown hero bobbled and hobbled not an eighth of a mile into the race—shock became horror as we realized the seriousness of

WEEK 1

MAY 21 – MAY 27

All things considered, the first week of Barbaro's recovery went very well. Barbaro received regular visits from Michael Matz, Peter Brette, and Kathy Anderson, the principal members of his Fair Hill team. He also received a visit from the president of the University of Pennsylvania, a signal of Barbaro's emerging star power.

WEEK 2

MAY 28 – JUNE 3

The second week post-surgery was another very good week for Barbaro. A cast change on the shattered right hind leg was planned for this week, and then was postponed. A good sign. The longer the reconstructed leg can remain in a cast, without the change, the better for the recovery.

WEEK 3

JUNE 4 – JUNE 10

The third week after surgery for Barbaro was another good week. The cast on the right hind leg remained unchanged as Barbaro continued to do well. Much like the previous weeks, Barbaro received regular visits from Michael Matz and others from his Fair Hill team. Either Matz or Peter Brette would visit each day and groom Barbaro and change his regular bandages as needed. Despite the

fact that New Bolton Center is an outstanding facility for the type of surgery Barbaro underwent, many horsemen still like to be involved in the aftercare of their horses as that is an important aspect of the recovery process.

Barbaro's gait. The race was run but we did not see it, for our hearts were crying out for Barbaro to stay upright and be able to leave the racecourse in one piece."

Anderson explained how those close to Barbaro's team circled together for moral support—Brette's wife Kim and two-year-old son Nicholas; Sue Danner, Matz's right-hand person for many years; Grae Kennedy, new to the team; and various grooms and riders alike not able to believe that history had taken this turn.

"My cell phone began to ring incessantly," Anderson continued. "Dr. Dean Richardson calling within minutes from Florida, Dr. Scott Palmer calling, Michael Matz calling for Dr. Palmer's cell phone number—and so it went."

"Sue Danner and I left the deflated and rapidly departing group at Fair Hill to meet the ambulance at the ICU at New Bolton," recalled Anderson. "The media had arrived before us—security wrestled with order. Barbaro's approach was signaled by the helicopter overhead. Hospital Chief Dr. Nunamaker and Dr. Barb Dallap greeted us and showed me the radiographs that had been e-mailed ahead. The fractures were catastrophic...a lateral condylar fracture that teetered on the verge of breaking the skin, a fractured sesamoid indicating significant soft tissue disruption to the attached suspensory, and a completely shattered pastern bone (P1)—clearly it would take a miracle for Barbaro, the warrior, to survive this.

"The ambulance backed right up to the ICU and Barbaro carefully maneuvered his way from the trailer to the stall—he had been bandaged and splinted from above the hock down to his foot to encase the injury in the Kimzey brace. Careful examination indicated that he could benefit from longer splints over the cannon bone region—these were promptly applied as he was hooked up to IV fluids and offered feed and water. Dr. Palmer and his wife arrived and continued their moral support and veterinary consultation. Within the hour, Barbaro had urinated, had a drink, and was eating 'voraciously' (as described by Dr. Dallap). Barbaro was alive and probably as well as could be expected under the circumstances. Matz made a release to the press regarding his condition and the evening drew to a close."

"I took Barbaro's groom Eduardo back to Fair Hill, Sue took Michael home to rejoin his family, and Peter returned to his waiting family," continued Anderson. All they could do now was wait.

"On Sunday, a call from Dr. Dallap set the hopeful tone of the day. Barbaro had been eating 'voraciously' all night and managed to lie down and get up several times without further damage to his leg. He appeared stable and ready to go to surgery. Dr. Richardson arrived late morning and the very complicated surgery commenced to repair his shattered right hind leg. A cast was placed on that leg, and a special shoe was affixed to his left hind foot, the one most susceptible to laminitis from a weight-bearing standpoint. Post surgery, Barbaro recovered in a recovery pool system. This type of recovery reduces the risk of post-surgery complications as a result of a horse waking up from anesthesia and thrashing around as he determines where he is and tries to comprehend his predicament. Sadly, that is how the great race mare Ruffian died, post surgery."

"Many hours later I get the call from Dr. Richardson that Barbaro is in the recovery pool and the surgery has been completed utilizing bone plates, screw fixation, cancellous bone implants, and a cast over the entire repair to protect and support the injured area," recalled Dr. Anderson. "I sob tears of relief that Barbaro

WEEK 4

JUNE 11 – JUNE 17

New Bolton Center had been releasing daily updates on Barbaro's condition. Because Barbaro continued to do well, they moved from daily updates to weekly updates at this stage. Barbaro did undergo his first cast change this week. This cast change went extremely well and reports on the status of the leg were very positive.

WEEK 5

JUNE 18 – JUNE 24

This was another good week for Barbaro. So far, so good in his recovery. The mood was good and all those who visited Barbaro seemed to have positive things to say.

WEEK 6

JUNE 25 – JULY 1

Barbaro was still in his second cast on the right hind leg, and a proposed cast change was postponed much like the first cast change. Barbaro's condition seemed to change from a day-to-day condition to week-to-week.

is still with us and tears of sadness for what might have been. Then I start the task of letting all his concerned human friends know the 'good' news—tomorrow is another day."

THE RECOVERY

The two main post-surgery concerns for Barbaro were infection from the surgical area, and the onset of laminitis, an extremely painful disease of the foot that is often fatal.

Three triggers could cause laminitis for Barbaro: taking weight off his injured leg and bearing additional weight on another foot, stress related to the injury and surgeries, and heavy use of medications.

The risk of infection typically lasts for fourteen days post surgery, after which time infection is much less likely. Then a third concern comes into play. Will the new bone and support structure, often referred to as hardware, be strong enough to support Barbaro in the long run? Barbaro had begun his long race against time—his bones needed to heal before the metal hardware fatigued and failed.

As the first week of Barbaro's recovery gave way to the second, the mood was upbeat, positive, and cautiously optimistic. Matz assistant Grae Kennedy described Barbaro's temperament as that of "a nine-year-old jumper," which obviously boded well for his recovery.

Because Barbaro was doing so well in his first cast, it was decided not to change the cast for the time being. Barbaro was taken off antibiotics on Tuesday, nine days after surgery, and all remained well. The fact that Barbaro remained in good shape once he was taken off antibiotics indicated that infection at this stage was not going to be a concern.

Among Barbaro's parade of visitors during his second week at New Bolton Center was Edgar Prado. Many credit Prado's quick action on Preakness Day—his ability to pull Barbaro up and keep the horse calm until others were able to help—as a key factor in saving Barbaro's life. The National Thoroughbred Racing Association (NTRA) knew Prado was anxious to visit Barbaro, and wanted to use the opportunity to illustrate compassion in the horse racing industry. The plan was to work with the TV show *Good Morning America* to broadcast the visit. ESPN's Jeannine Edwards would interview Prado for the show. NTRA provided Prado with a limousine to get him to New Bolton Center. Peter Rotondo, NTRA's vice president for television, traveled from New York with Prado for the visit. Certainly, Prado would have been more comfortable with a more private visit, but he also wanted to see his horse. Jeannine Edwards observed Prado's reaction to seeing Barbaro for the first time since that fateful Preakness Day: "Edgar didn't know what to expect when he first visited Barbaro. Would he look pitiful, or crippled, or a shell of his former self? But you could see Edgar's face visibly change from concern to relief and peace when his eyes saw the horse for the first time. Barbaro was bright-eyed, had his ears up, was munching hay, and moving around comfortably. Edgar told me afterwards, 'Now I can sleep at night.'"

After visiting with Barbaro and talking to the media, Prado and Rotondo headed to Fair Hill with Matz and the Jacksons to review the Preakness tapes. They were looking to see if there was evidence to suggest that another horse had accidently

WEEK 7		WEEK 8	WEEK 9
JULY 2 – JULY 8		JULY 9 – JULY 15	JULY 16 – JULY 22
Two cast changes in three days—on July 4 and July 6, plus the discovery of an abscess on Barbaro's left hind heel. During the first cast change, a bent screw was replaced and three more screws were added to the pastern area. Essentially, these few days were the first signs that all was not progressing perfectly for Barbaro. And then, for a couple of days things seemed to improve.	*But then Saturday night, Barbaro endured a long surgery and longer recovery. The pastern area, where the screws were replaced and added, had become infected. All the "hardware" was now replaced.*	*The left hind foot abscess was a precursor to laminitis, the foot disease that was always a considerable threat in a case like Barbaro's. This was a devastating blow to his recovery, and Barbaro's life was in grave danger. Barbaro was now using a sling for additional support. On Saturday a vigil was planned for the first time, and continued each Saturday.*	*Sunday, July 16, was Delaware Handicap Day. ESPN reporter Jeannine Edwards interviewed Michael Matz regarding Barbaro's prognosis. Jeannine noted that Michael was in a pretty emotional state. Barbaro's condition had become a roller-coaster ride and understandably, very draining. Michael explained, "All it takes is one miracle," and with tears in his eyes, added, "He's a fighter."*

struck Barbaro during the Preakness. Pimlico had sent the tapes to Matz. Upon extensive review of the tapes, the Barbaro team determined that there was nothing conclusive to suggest another horse had interfered with Barbaro. Rotondo returned to New York with Prado; fast food and a six-pack helped the two decompress on their journey home. Rotondo had this to say about the day: "Personally, it was one of the most surreal days of my life; from the long silent limo ride to New Bolton with Edgar; to putting on the scrubs to see the surprisingly alert Barbaro in his stall; to working the DVD player showing the various angles of the Preakness for Michael, the Jacksons, and Edgar."

Another highlight of the second week was a visit by two soldiers from Fort Benning, Georgia, who delivered an American flag that had allegedly flown in airspace over Iraq. The soldiers had admired Barbaro's courage and will to continue running in the Preakness, despite his obvious predicament. They noted that that is exactly what a wounded soldier does. Clearly, Barbaro had shown—and continued to show—courage in the face of adversity, as did the human connections that surrounded him.

Fair Hill trainer Mike Rea passed Matz on horseback shortly after Barbaro's surgery.

"The Lord doesn't give you anything you can't handle," Rea said to Matz—a considerable irony given that just two weeks later, Rea would face a life-threatening fate following an early morning training accident. As Rea rode away, after a couple of strides he stopped, looked back at Matz, and said, "He must think you're an awfully tough guy."

The third week after surgery was another good week for Barbaro. The cast on the right hind leg remained unchanged as Barbaro continued to do well. It was during this time that Barbaro received a visit from the governor of Pennsylvania, Ed Rendell. During the visit, Barbaro was rearing up a little, displaying his good feeling. The governor presented New Bolton Center with a check for $13.5 million. This was a gift that was in the works prior to Barbaro's injury, but it is likely that because of Barbaro the delivery date was moved forward.

The end of the third week of Barbaro's care coincided with the Belmont Stakes, the final leg of the Triple Crown. Much of the horse racing media focus on Belmont Day was on Barbaro. In fact, Barbaro was able to watch the race from a television set rolled to the outside of his stall. At Belmont Park, Prado led in the ceremonious signing of a huge get-well card dedicated to Barbaro. Jazil, who dead-heated for fourth place, with Brother Derek, in Barbaro's Kentucky Derby, won the Belmont Stakes. Bernardini did not run in the race. Jazil did not win another race.

A little over three weeks after Barbaro's tragic accident, it was time to change his original cast on the right hind leg. His temperature had elevated a little bit (one half of a degree) and the cast appeared to be causing itchiness. These symptoms necessitated the decision to make the change. However, three weeks was always considered the best-case scenario for the use of a cast, thus on Tuesday of the fourth week, the cast was changed. This also enabled the veterinarians to take a closer look at the leg's healing process. While radiographs can be taken through a cast, they work much better when the cast is taken off.

There are risks associated with a cast change. If the new cast is not an exact fit,

WEEK 10

JULY 23 – JULY 29

Michael's reports of Barbaro's condition were now getting a little more upbeat, which further suggested things were getting more on an even keel.

WEEK 11

JULY 30 – AUGUST 5

Massages were now also becoming part of Barbaro's routine. Barbaro was still getting national media exposure, more so than any other horse.

WEEK 12

AUGUST 6 – AUGUST 12

Barbaro's pain medication regimen was now being reduced as he continued to do well. Barbaro was also using the sling less often. Barbaro was beginning to regain weight, and went outside to graze for the first time on Wednesday.

WEEK 13

AUGUST 13 – AUGUST 19

Barbaro was no longer using the sling, signaling further progress in his recovery. His pain meds were further reduced. Barbaro's left hind foot bandage continued to be changed every day; Barbaro was gaining weight, and was now being walked about thirty minutes a day. He walked soundly in his right hind cast.

it can cause discomfort and rub marks, which, in turn, could result in infections. Fortunately, this cast change seemed to go without a hitch and Barbaro had another good week with a new cast in place. Radiographs were taken and all appeared well with the healing process. Barbaro had overcome a hurdle.

It seemed that, at this stage, the two major risks to Barbaro would be laminitis, which could occur at any time, and the race for the hardware to knit the bones together to support Barbaro before the hardware failed. The mood was upbeat, and Barbaro was as comfortable as could be expected. Barbaro's comfort was further illustrated by "ear-scratching episodes." He would use his good left hind leg to scratch his ear. This would require he support himself on his right hind leg—the broken leg. Barbaro was also bucking for fun, something he would not have done if it hurt him. It was also becoming clear that while the daily visits of Brette and Matz were very good for Barbaro and his routine, they were also good for the two horsemen. It helped them ease their pain and deal with the question of what could have been.

"The Kentucky Derby was just the start, not the end for him," said Brette. "He was just going to get better and better."

As the first official day of summer approached, Barbaro continued on his path of slow but steady improvement. Visitors included a second stop by Prado, who this time arrived without media fanfare, and with his family. Prado was taking advantage of the Monday's "dark day" for racing in New York (a day of non-racing) to give himself a little more time to do things other than be a jockey.

As the Independence Day holiday weekend beckoned, Barbaro continued to do well. No news really was good news, and many fans began to take for granted that complete recovery was only a matter of time. While it was obvious that Barbaro would never race again, certainly his future at stud could be discussed if he was able to bear his own weight. At this stage, we were all thinking things were simply getting better and better for Barbaro. Perhaps we had gotten a little complacent. We had no idea of the tsunami of events that lay ahead.

Barbaro's cast was changed for a second time on Monday, July 4. It had been three weeks since the second cast had been applied, so from a timing standpoint the change made sense. Dr. Richardson also acknowledged that the cast was now beginning to display signs of wear. During this procedure, a bent screw was replaced and three screws were added to the pastern area of the broken leg. Because of the fracture, everything above the pastern was now locked in place, putting additional pressure on the pastern. Replacing a screw was always considered a possibility from the outset. It was important the right hind leg was as strong as possible to avoid undue weight shifting to other legs, thus, once the screw became loose it needed to be replaced. Because the replacement and addition of screws was Barbaro's second surgery, the risk of infection had now significantly increased.

During the cast changing process, an abscess was also discovered on the heel of Barbaro's left hind foot. Abscesses are often precursors to, or symptoms of, laminitis. But at this time it was not known that this was the beginnings of laminitis, as none of the other typical symptoms were apparent. It was instead thought that the cause of this abscess was likely a shifting of weight off the right hind leg because of soreness from the bent screw in the pastern area.

Despite these two setbacks—the abscess and the need to replace and add

WEEK 14

AUGUST 20 – AUGUST 26

Barbaro's chances of survival were now back to 50-50, whereas six weeks prior they were dire. "It's exciting, he's improving," said Dr. Richardson to the New York Times. *The mood overall was good.*

WEEK 15

AUGUST 27 – SEPTEMBER 2

On Sunday, the cast was changed on Barbaro's right hind leg. The leg appeared to be excellent. A crack had appeared in the cast, necessitating the change. Dr. Richardson was also leaving New Bolton Center for a few days, signaling confidence that his star patient was making strong and steady progress.

WEEK 16

SEPTEMBER 3 – SEPTEMBER 9

Once again, Dr. Richardson was away for a few days, this time to attend a seminar. His increasing absences appeared to be another sign that Barbaro was continuing to improve.

WEEK 17

SEPTEMBER 10 – SEPTEMBER 16

Another good week. With a routine that included massages and daily hand grazing, Barbaro was beginning to blossom.

the screws—the major fracture was shown to be healing very well, so over-all, Monday was considered "a reasonably satisfactory day." There was also an observable sense of relief among Barbaro's Fair Hill team post surgery, although that did not last long. Two days later, on Wednesday, the third cast was replaced. Barbaro had shown signs of discomfort and a new cast, at a slightly different angle, was applied. At first glance, this approach worked because minor improvement was seen as Friday folded into Saturday. Sadly, that was not the case for long. As Barbaro entered his eighth week at New Bolton Center, he endured three hours of surgery on Saturday night. The pastern had become infected, most likely because of his surgery five days earlier. All the hardware was now replaced as the joint was scrubbed clean. Clearly, this was a major step backwards. Barbaro also underwent a grueling recovery, post surgery, that lasted another twelve hours. As is usual for a horse recovering from anesthesia, he had ropes tied to his head (a figure-eight-like halter) and tail. As Barbaro fought the ropes, he lost much of the hair from his tail. The long recovery period was a clear signal that Barbaro was now struggling to survive, perhaps as a consequence of the succession of procedures he had recently undergone. Dr. Richardson acknowledged that there were times during the recovery process that he thought he might lose Barbaro right then and there. Both of his hind legs were sore and as a result, Barbaro would struggle to stand. He would then be placed back in the pool, as he was exhausted. He would fight; he would quit. It was also more likely now that the left hind foot was laminitic, given his ongoing struggles. We now know that was, in fact, the case.

Barbaro received a "long" cast in order to provide additional support for his recovery process.

"I was in tears by the end of that day, at home," Dr. Richardson told the *Philadelphia Daily News*. "I almost get emotional just thinking about how upset I was about that day, because I thought we were going to lose him. Getting him up was so stressful. Getting him up out of the pool and not having him stand and then fight us."

"It's one thing for everybody else who was there, because there were tons of other people involved in this. They were all stressed," continued Richardson. "But I'm sure that on that one day, as stressed as everybody else was, that's the one day I would say I'm sure I was more stressed than anybody else because I knew that every decision that was made basically was mine—good decisions, bad decisions were my responsibility. That was an awful day. That's when he was foundering [a progressive case of laminitis]. At that point, I knew we were in trouble. You second-guess every single thing you did from the day after the Preakness."

While the new long cast might have been useful for the initial recovery, it created some discomfort, and by Monday, July 11, Barbaro received yet another cast, a shorter one. The shorter cast would make it easier for Barbaro to move around and get up and down. During this procedure, a second abscess was discovered and treated in the "good" left hind foot. Clearly, problems were beginning to add up. Media was closing in on New Bolton Center and the Jacksons canceled a trip to Africa. It was around this time that Barbaro also used a sling

WEEK 18	WEEK 19	WEEK 20	WEEK 21
SEPTEMBER 17 – SEPTEMBER 23	SEPTEMBER 24 – SEPTEMBER 30	OCTOBER 1 – OCTOBER 7	OCTOBER 8 – OCTOBER 14
It was four months now since the Preakness and Barbaro continued to do well. A massage blanket was now being used as part of Barbaro's routine.	*Another good week for Barbaro. His left hind foot now had eighteen millimeters of growth, albeit uneven, and he was outside grazing each day for thirty to forty minutes.*	*Another good week in Barbaro's long and slow recovery process.*	*Barbaro had his right hind leg cast changed under general anesthesia, and also had his feet trimmed and a new shoe put on his right hind foot. This was another good week for Barbaro.*

for the first time. The sling is designed to help a horse support itself by becoming weight-bearing when a horse rests one or more of its legs. The sling will not suspend a horse, as this would lead to other complications. Since Barbaro was an intelligent horse, he quickly figured out how best to use the sling, almost like a child in a jolly jumper.

On Tuesday, in his eighth week of treatment, the infection from the abscess in the left hind foot worsened.

Yet despite all these problems, Barbaro's attitude remained positive. It was this attitude that may well have saved his life over the next week. A crisis meeting was held at New Bolton Center that included the Jacksons, Michael Matz and his wife D.D., and Richardson. The horsemen were distressed at the recent turn of events that Barbaro had endured. Tears were flowing. A debate ensued about whether it was time to euthanize Barbaro. The meeting was held in full view of Barbaro. It was Barbaro's appearance, as if to say, "I can handle this, give me a chance," that convinced Matz that the team should continue to try to save his life. The situation was dire, but it was not yet hopeless.

New Bolton Center announced a press conference for Thursday. The press conference was designed to address Barbaro's status, all at one time for all media, rather than answering individual media requests. Mrs. Jackson made it clear that unless something drastic happened in the twenty-four hours prior to the press conference, Barbaro's euthanasia would not be a discussion topic, despite rumors to the contrary.

As the press conference drew near, Barbaro continued to hold his own.

Michael Matz was at Fair Hill on Wednesday morning. He gave me a positive update. What I thought was more positive was that he was at Fair Hill at all and not camped out at New Bolton Center with Barbaro's caregivers, the media, and everyone else who was there.

After Thursday morning's training hours at Fair Hill, I headed over to New Bolton Center for the press conference. When I arrived in the lobby, media representatives were setting up equipment, their satellite trucks aligning the fence of New Bolton Center. One look around the lobby of New Bolton Center was all it took to appreciate the support Barbaro had received since he had arrived. Most striking were the six large greeting cards that included many signatures from well-wishers from Churchill Downs, home of Barbaro's greatest triumph. Each card read, "Once a Derby winner, always a Derby winner."

The press conference began, and Dr. Richardson came straight to the point. Barbaro now had laminitis in his left hind foot. While we suspected this was the news, it was the first time this information was made public. This was the extremely painful foot disease we all dreaded. Dr. Richardson noted that the onset of laminitis had been very rapid. Barbaro's condition was dire, but they would do all they could do while his comfort level remained adequate. They would not continue if his comfort became unmanageable. Dr. Richardson appeared to be very emotional. He might be able to repair the original fracture, but it might now all be for naught with this wicked condition.

I was shell-shocked. Numb. The news was devastating for all. Barbaro's very survival was now a long shot. Two weeks earlier, Dr. Richardson really thought

WEEK 22
OCTOBER 15 – OCTOBER 21
Another good week in Barbaro's recovery, although the left hind foot's growth was now the major concern. There appeared to be no growth along the front of the hoof.

WEEK 23
OCTOBER 22 – OCTOBER 28
Peter Brette began to visit Barbaro more often as Michael Matz was now in Kentucky preparing Round Pond for a Breeders' Cup race. Growth in Barbaro's left hind foot seemed stalled, although the colt remained in good spirits and continued to gain weight.

WEEK 24
OCTOBER 29 – NOVEMBER 4
Team Barbaro was honored at the NTWA dinner at Churchill Downs ahead of the Breeders' Cup, which ran over the weekend. Round Pond won for Michael Matz. I went to the Breeders' Cup thanks to the generosity of Fans of Barbaro (FOB).

WEEK 25
NOVEMBER 5 – NOVEMBER 11
On Monday, Barbaro's right hind cast was replaced with a bandage and fiberglass splints. This was a big step forward in the recovery of the right hind leg. It took Barbaro a little time to adjust to the change in support, which included lying down more often. The left hind foot appeared to be in a status quo zone.

Barbaro had a chance; all was going so well. Then came the bent screw in his right hind pastern and things went downhill from there. Barbaro now had a cast on the left hind foot, and was using the sling regularly.

Then as quickly as it all had started just a week prior, the tumbleweed of negative reports appeared to cease. Kathy Anderson visited Barbaro shortly after the press conference and reported that Barbaro remained comfortable. She reported the same thing the next day. Matz's report on Friday morning, directly from Dr. Richardson, was similarly positive.

That was it—all reports after this press conference were positive again. Barbaro yet again demonstrated amazing fortitude. He survived another crisis and calmer waters lay ahead. His condition remained a real concern, but the management of the condition appeared to go flawlessly.

At the conclusion of this fateful eighth week—ironically, a number that had brought him his greatest luck just a few months prior in the Kentucky Derby— Edgar Prado once again visited his buddy Barbaro. This was another unannounced visit, but this time on a day when he had to return to New York to ride races that afternoon. He had left New York at about 4:30 a.m. on Friday morning in order to spend an hour with Barbaro. Edgar noted that Barbaro looked better than he had anticipated. Barbaro fell asleep, leaning against his shoulder.

The reality was that it seemed that Barbaro himself did not want to give up. And he showed this resilience each time he was faced with a major setback. Barbaro had already shown his power of recovery in the two days subsequent to the announcement of laminitis in the press conference. Barbaro wanted to win this battle as much as he had won every race in which he finished. Through the first eight weeks of Barbaro's stay at New Bolton Center, he had shown the character required to survive almost insurmountable obstacles. The legend of his heroic fight was growing.

With week nine of treatment and in the heart of summer, Barbaro's reports became more positive. That said, the recovery of Barbaro would now take much longer given that new complications were now added to the list of what he had to overcome. To treat the laminitis, 90 percent of his left hind foot had been removed. Would it grow back, and how would it grow back? Barbaro now had significant challenges in both his hind legs. One was broken; the other had very little healthy hoof remaining. While his right hind fracture was healing, problems persisted with the infection of the pastern area. Would it fuse, would the infection abate? Now much of his other hind foot had been removed, and a cast had been applied. Could his pain be managed? Two of his four legs had problems. It would be catastrophic if laminitis afflicted his front feet, which was a distinct possibility.

Barbaro was getting used to using the sling—twelve hours in and twelve hours out. Another cast change took place at the onset of week nine, this time with positive results. The pastern was stabilizing, which implied that the there was no active infection. Barbaro's front feet also were checked frequently to make sure they were normal. No heat. Barbaro was battling back; he was demonstrating his will to live. In this effort, he had the unconditional support of his owners, Roy and Gretchen Jackson.

"We have an obligation…we are their keepers," said Roy Jackson to the *New York Times* amid persistent rumors that they were only trying to save Barbaro's life

WEEK 26	WEEK 27	WEEK 28	WEEK 29
NOVEMBER 12 – NOVEMBER 18	NOVEMBER 19 – NOVEMBER 25	NOVEMBER 26 – DECEMBER 2	DECEMBER 3 – DECEMBER 9
We heard that farms in Kentucky were "checking in" to see how Barbaro was doing. If Barbaro was to recover sufficiently, he would become a very valuable stallion based on his racetrack performance. No doubt there would be competing farms interested in standing him as a stallion.	*It was now six months since the Preakness. A cast was placed on Barbaro's left hind foot to stabilize it. Edgar Prado visited for the sixth time. Barbaro was now 1,135 pounds as he continued to do well. I visited Barbaro for the first time.*	*As Michael Matz's crew headed south for the winter, Monday was Peter Brette's last visit with Barbaro. Barbaro continued to do well and Dr. Anderson noted an improvement in his disposition.*	*This was another good week for Barbaro. It had been a month since his right hind cast had been removed. Dr. Richardson announced Barbaro could soon leave New Bolton Center.*

because of financial considerations. Edgar Prado also was asked about the Jacksons' extraordinary effort to save Barbaro.

"Many, many, many people dream of standing in the winner's circle on Kentucky Derby Day," Prado said. "That horse gave those people the biggest thrill of their lives, and I think they were just trying to give something back. I mean, that's the least we can do for these horses. Give them one more chance."

The mood at New Bolton Center began to improve, and daily updates were replaced with bi-weekly updates. His pain levels were still being aggressively managed, but Barbaro was no longer in immediate danger.

Barbaro's blood work continued to improve, which illustrated that the infection on the right hind pastern was now under control. On Wednesday of week ten, Barbaro's cast was changed on his right hind leg. Growth also was starting to emerge from the coronary band of his left hind foot. Cautious optimism filled the air, as did the smell of flowers. Kennett Florist, a local florist from Kennett Square, was now a regular visitor to New Bolton Center. They would provide baskets of goodies for Barbaro and the New Bolton Center team, gifts funded by Fans of Barbaro. Kennett Florist would also report on the mood at New Bolton Center during their visits, a universal morale booster for all.

As this was the end of July, racing was in full swing at Saratoga Race Course in New York, one of the oldest, prettiest, and most prestigious tracks in North America. Preakness winner Bernardini won the Jim Dandy Stakes (Grade 2) at Saratoga the weekend of July 30—his prep race for the Travers Stakes (Grade 1) and his first race since winning the Preakness. Matz and his team were now questioned about their level of disappointment in not witnessing a duel between Barbaro and Bernardini. Matz's response was direct and to the point: "Right now, I am more worried about saving his life instead of whether he's a three-year-old champion."

. . . .

"After Bernardini's win Saturday in the Jim Dandy, Michael Matz was one of the first to congratulate me. Later in the evening, I caught up with Michael again. He gave me an update on Barbaro. We are all really rooting for him."
—TOM ALBERTRANI,
Bernardini's trainer, Summer 2006

. . . .

As August began, Barbaro's condition remained stable and the mood at New Bolton Center remained upbeat. Barbaro was still using the sling to keep his weight off his front feet, whenever needed. Matz had spent a few more days in Saratoga and returned to Fair Hill, intent on continuing the Barbaro visits that appeared to be working. Because Barbaro was out of the sling at night, Matz shifted his schedule so he could see Barbaro standing on his own. As he continued in his progression toward recovery, Barbaro's pain medication also was beginning to be reduced. Barbaro now had a bandage on his left hind foot, which was changed daily. This allowed the vets to keep a close eye on the foot's progress. Barbaro's right hind cast

WEEK 30	WEEK 31	WEEK 32	WEEK 33
DECEMBER 10 – DECEMBER 16	DECEMBER 17 – DECEMBER 23	DECEMBER 24 – DECEMBER 30	DECEMBER 31 – JANUARY 6
Barbaro continued to gain strength in his right hind leg. The left hind foot was progressing slowly, but the comfort of the foot remained acceptable.	*Dr. Scott Morrison, a vet and blacksmith from Rood & Riddle Equine Hospital in Kentucky visited on Tuesday and performed some minor work on the left hind foot. I visited Barbaro twice this week. The catheter that had been in Barbaro's neck since he came to New Bolton Center also was removed this week.*	*I visited Barbaro three times this week, including grazing him on Christmas Day. It was another good week for Barbaro.*	*My final visit with Barbaro was this week. Dr. Morrison worked on Barbaro's left hind foot to try to improve the alignment of the foot with the coffin bone. The foot was now back in a cast.*

was changed, under anesthesia. All appeared to be progressing well.

He also seemed to want out of his stall. On Wednesday, August 9, Barbaro did get to go outside, for the first time since he arrived at New Bolton Center three months prior. Barbaro looked around, trying to take in his new surroundings, and after about five minutes, dropped his head to pick at grass. Five or six people were present for the occasion, including Dr. Getman, who had this to say: "It was a purely happy moment—for Barbaro and everyone who had worked so hard to get him there. It's the most natural, basic thing that horses do, and he hadn't been able to do it for so long. To see him just being a normal horse was so fulfilling, and although I can't really put the feeling into words, it's why we do what we do."

Getting outside and picking grass was excellent therapy for Barbaro's attitude. It was also a good sign that Dr. Richardson felt he was ready for this. His right hind leg, with cast, was now strong enough for a little exercise. Weather permitting, this now became a welcomed part of Barbaro's daily routine. Mrs. Jackson, who was Barbaro's most frequent visitor, brought freshly cut grass from her farm with each visit. Even though Barbaro was able to get outside to pick his own grass, Mrs. Jackson was still determined to bring him extra. Barbaro no longer needed his sling, he was gaining weight, and he was walked for about thirty minutes a day. His attitude also appeared to have improved further with his daily trips outside.

"It is no big deal for me to visit, I live so close and usually visit twice a day. Bringing the grass gives Barbaro something to do while I visit, and of course he likes it a lot. I like to visit, he has done so much for us, it is the least I can do."
—GRETCHEN JACKSON, SUMMER 2006

The longer Barbaro was being treated at New Bolton Center, the more his caregivers were falling in love with him. His primary care veterinarian, Dr. Richardson, was no exception. This type of affection for a long-term patient was normal at New Bolton Center. And the wider the circle the patient creates, the more widely that love is felt across campus. Barbaro had a very wide circle of caregivers. It also helped that Barbaro was very smart and his charisma was highly engaging.

WEEK 34

JANUARY 7 – JANUARY 13
Barbaro became acutely uncomfortable and the left hind foot cast was removed. New separation of the hoof wall was discovered and additional tissue was removed. Barbaro was now no longer going outside to graze and was back using the sling to help keep excessive weight off his other legs.

WEEK 35

JANUARY 14 – JANUARY 20
This was a better week for Barbaro. He was taken off pain medication and was no longer using the sling. Michael Matz visited Barbaro before returning to his winter base in Florida.

WEEK 36

JANUARY 21 – JANUARY 27
Barbaro underwent a procedure and an abscess in his right hind foot was drained. New shoes were applied to Barbaro's front feet to provide additional support. A major concern at this point was whether Barbaro would develop laminitis in those front feet.

WEEK 37

JANUARY 28 – JANUARY 29
Barbaro did not have a good night on Sunday. Barbaro was euthanized at 9:30 a.m., Monday, January 29, 2007—exactly three months shy of what would have been his fourth birthday.

"Every day we come to work. We read and learn what we can about Barbaro's condition. My thoughts are for him, the Jacksons, and Michael Matz. They showed tremendous class through all of this. There are still lingering effects to this incident and we're all pulling for Barbaro. It's certainly not business as usual. We feel for horses more than people typically know. Recently we had a horse, Cozy Guy, a gelding, and we tried everything we could do to save his life after a sickness, knowing he would never run again, it was very sad when he did not pull through. Good luck to all."

—DAN HENDRICKS,
Brother Derek's trainer, Summer 2006

As he entered week fourteen at New Bolton Center, Barbaro's attitude and appetite were phenomenal and his left hind foot now had one centimeter of growth. Barbaro would remain in his right hind cast for another two weeks.

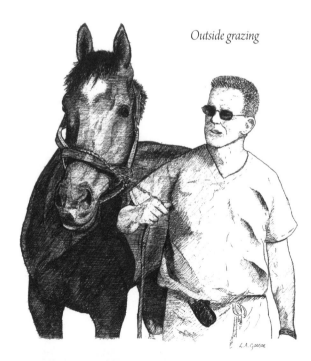

Outside grazing

During the third week of August, New Bolton Center, along with Fans of Barbaro (FOB) and Kennett Florist, celebrated Dr. Richardson's birthday with a variety of gifts and a sizable donation to the Barbaro Fund. This celebration was an indication that the overall mood of New Bolton Center and those closely following Barbaro's progress was positive. Dr. Richardson posted a message on TimWoolleyRacing.com to thank the FOBs for his birthday celebrations, stating, "It is profoundly humbling and intimidating to be responsible for a patient that has this much love going his way."

Matz also commented on the support Barbaro was receiving, "I think there are thousands of people who have been keeping the faith for him. The response, the outpouring, everything, and things are still coming in every day—fruit baskets, signs, and cards. It's really unbelievable, the support."

On August 26, Bernardini won the Travers Stakes at Saratoga, defeating Bluegrass Cat.

With the Labor Day weekend underway, yet another cast change was scheduled for Barbaro, this time due to a crack that had developed in the cast. The change gave Dr. Richardson an opportunity for closer inspection of the leg, and he liked what he saw. The leg appeared to be in excellent shape. The troublesome pastern joint had now fully fused; the left hind foot bandage would continue to be changed every day. On Monday, August 29, Barbaro did not seem to have a great night, but it was a short-lived blip in his march to recovery. Dr. Richardson left town for a few days both that week and then again the following week, a perceived sign of his confidence in Barbaro's ongoing recovery. During his absence, Brette, who had visited Barbaro on a regular basis all along, took Barbaro out for a pick of grass for the first time. Brette also took Barbaro's groom, Eduardo Hernandez, for a visit. Hernandez had not visited for many weeks but had been closely following the horse's progress. All remained upbeat in Barbaro's continued recovery.

Now that Barbaro was hand grazing daily, he began to blossom. Four months had passed since that fateful Preakness Day. The left hind foot now had eighteen millimeters of growth (one-third of the necessary growth) in the heel, however the bottom of Barbaro's foot still needed to completely heal. The cast on his right hind

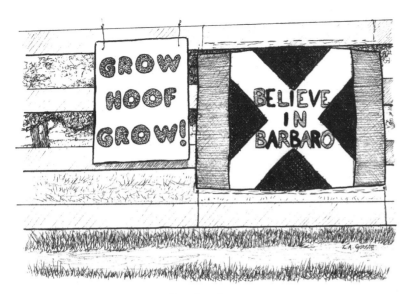

Fans show their support

leg remained simply as a precaution while the left hind foot progressed. Edgar Prado made his fourth visit and noticed positive differences in contrast to his visit in July: "He looked brighter, had gained weight, and was walking around as if nothing had happened." Barbaro even received a wedding invitation—one of the more bizarre requests received over the time he was at New Bolton Center, but another reflection of the upbeat mood for the colt and Team Barbaro.

On October 7, Bernardini easily won the Jockey Club Gold Cup defeating three overmatched rivals.

October 11 brought yet another cast change for Barbaro's right hind leg. While he was under general anesthesia, Barbaro's caregivers also were able to trim his feet and set a new shoe on his right hind foot. All seemed positive for Barbaro, who had been without pain medicine for close to six weeks at this point. If only the left hind foot would grow faster and more uniformly, a concern that became more pronounced as mid-autumn approached. Barbaro had now been at New Bolton Center for a little over five months. He had gained fifty pounds since he started his daily outside grazing in August. Barbaro still had his right hind cast, but it remained simply to help support and keep additional weight off the left hind foot, which stubbornly refused to grow uniformly.

November 4 was the Breeders' Cup, the end-of-year championship day for

horse racing. Bernardini would take on the leading older horse, Invasor, in the classic. Horse of the Year honors were on the line. A win by either horse would seal those honors, a win by another horse, and Barbaro would become a more serious contender. While Bernardini had dominated the three-year-old division in the absence of Barbaro, Invasor had excelled in the older-horse division. Invasor proved too much for Bernardini as he overpowered his rival with a quarter of a mile to race. Back in the field was the Jackson-bred George Washington, who had won the 2,000 Guineas and Queen Elizabeth II Stakes in Europe to complete his second European Championship season. This was his first time racing on a dirt surface.

In early November, Barbaro's right hind cast was replaced with a bandage and fiberglass splints. This was a big step forward in the recovery of the right hind leg. It took Barbaro a little time to adjust to the change in support, and it did affect his gait. The left hind foot remained in its stubborn state of status quo, it was all wait, wait, wait. Also eagerly awaiting progress of Barbaro's recovery were the stallion farms of Kentucky, which began contacting New Bolton Center to check on the colt's progress. If Barbaro was to recover sufficiently he would become a very valuable stallion based on his racetrack performance and his pedigree. No doubt there would be farms interested in standing him as a stallion.

It was now six months since the Preakness and yet another cast was placed on Barbaro's left hind foot to help stabilize it. Prado visited for a fifth time, and found Barbaro content, and now up to 1,135 pounds.

I also visited Barbaro for the first time.

As Matz's crew headed south for the winter, Barbaro's twenty-eighth week at New Bolton Center began with a visit from his exercise rider, Peter Brette. It would be his last visit with Barbaro. Of course, he had no way of foreseeing this, as Barbaro continued to do well, and Dr. Anderson noted an improvement in his disposition, as well. The Jacksons traveled to Santa Anita Racetrack in California to watch their Showing Up win the California Derby. Tom Mehrtens, the Jacksons' farm manager, began to visit Barbaro around this time. Coincidentally, Mehrtens's uncle, Warren Mehrtens, had ridden Assault to victory in the

MY FIRST VISIT WITH BARBARO

I was to meet Mrs. Jackson at 5 p.m. in the lobby area of New Bolton. I had not yet met Mrs. Jackson, so not only was this my first visit with Barbaro since the Preakness, but also the first time to meet his owners. I got there five minutes early, and waited a short time in the lobby area, rereading many of his get-well wishes. Mrs. Jackson arrived on time. She knew who I was and, of course, I knew her immediately. Mrs. Jackson gave me a signed win picture of the Kentucky Derby and was just effusive in her praise for our site and all that we have done (basically she put me at ease straight away).

We walked in the direction of Barbaro (with a quick hello to Kathy Freeborn) and passed by Dr. Sweeney's office. Mrs. Jackson introduced me to Dr. Sweeney and we had a very nice (albeit brief) chat. We reached the ICU and put on our ICU clothes, at which time Mr. Jackson arrived and signed my win picture. As we got ready to see Barbaro, we continued a conversation that actually went on for the entire hour. Mr. and Mrs. Jackson were just very easy to talk to and we spoke about many things, ranging from travel (I described my love of New Zealand) to horse-related issues (horse slaughter, etc.). We entered the ICU and the first thing we did was attend to a baby goat with its mother. It was tiny and precious. We then ventured over to Barbaro's stall, a well-lit area that obviously was impeccably clean. Mrs. Jackson had brought with her a large carrier-type bag full of freshly cut grass. We got to Barbaro's stall and opened the door a little; he was turned away from us and it took a little coaxing for him to turn around and come toward us. Once he did, he was very happy to see the grass. He munched away, and we stood watching him while also intermittently petting him on the head. You can imagine how he would pin his ears back and pretend to flash his teeth a little, and then resume munching on his grass. He'd then look back to us, prick his ears, and repeat the process. Visitors learned that they had to show caution around him, but when shown the respect he requires, Barbaro was very happy. He also ate a red apple (crunch, crunch, crunch, and it was gone) and a few spearmint mints (the green ones). He clearly loved those and was not happy about waiting until the wrappers were removed! We stayed with him at the front of his stall for nearly forty minutes, chatting away. He then moved to another part of his stall, and I was able to see the nearly all white markings on his left side.

Overall Barbaro looked well. His tail was still short, but this was simple cosmetic stuff that eventually would grow out. His coat was clean and shiny, his eye was clean, and his weight looked great. The bandage on his left hind leg was clean and had been recently reset. Shortly before we left, Barbaro did lay down, gingerly but conveniently close to the remainder of the grass that Mrs. Jackson had gathered. Barbaro struck me as a smart horse that seemed to understand his current predicament and what he needed to do to get through it. And so big! Simply put, I was in awe of Barbaro and all he had endured. We also spoke of Barbaro's earlier races, namely the Florida Derby. In each race for different reasons, Edgar Prado had told the Jacksons that Barbaro had not needed to put forth his best effort to win. Mr. and Mrs. Jackson were curious how I would continue Barbaro's updates once Michael Matz and Peter Brette left for winter training in Florida. They offered to help provide updates if necessary. We also discussed the relationships Michael and Peter had with Barbaro, and how things would change for him when they left for Florida. All in all, this was a wonderful experience. I met two people and a horse, each of whom seemed to represent all that is good about life.

1946 Triple Crown. Sue Danner also began to visit Barbaro more frequently to take over the duties of Matz and Brette.

During the Jacksons' travels to California, I visited Barbaro twice, finding him in apparent good spirits both times. It had been a month now since his right hind cast had been removed, and he continued to gain strength in his right hind leg, on which he now wore a special shoe. The left hind foot also was progressing slowly, and the comfort of the foot remained acceptable.

Overall, Barbaro demonstrated ongoing improvement and he continued to gain weight. His prognosis was so positive that in early December, Dr. Dean Richardson chose an opportunity (during a Breyer Products news conference) to announce that he felt that Barbaro could soon be leaving New Bolton Center. He also noted that Rood & Riddle's Dr. Morrison would be visiting New Bolton Center the following week to examine Barbaro. Sure enough, Dr. Morrison arrived the following Tuesday and performed some minor work on Barbaro's left hind foot. The catheter that had been in Barbaro's neck since he came to New Bolton Center was removed that week—further evidence of his progress.

The weather was cited as one factor in the decision to consider moving Barbaro from New Bolton Center to the warmer climate of Kentucky. Richardson made further remarks that week that Barbaro could leave in the not-too-distant future.

Three Chimneys, home of Barbaro's sire Dynaformer, was to become Barbaro's new home. Preparations were already underway to accommodate Barbaro and to ensure they could provide access for his fans. Sandy Hatfield, stallion manager at Three Chimneys, recalled, "When I learned that it was a possibility that Barbaro would come to Three Chimneys, I was ecstatic! We have worked with stallions that had physical limitations in the past, Seattle Slew being the most high profile one. I think the most important thing that we found is that we had to be prepared for any scenario and we worked toward that.

"I traveled to New Bolton Center and met Barbaro and the Jacksons, it seemed like the perfect fit. We all had the horse's well-being at the forefront of all we were doing. The Jacksons visited the farm and saw where Barbaro would live and the way we cared for our horses, especially the older ones that needed that extra special touch. The more we talked, the more at ease we all became and it seemed like it was going to happen. They knew that whether he became a breeding stallion or not he would always have a great home with us."

The holiday season had arrived at New Bolton Center. I visited Barbaro three times between December 24 and 30, including grazing him on Christmas Day.

Christmas Day

As the year 2006 gave way to 2007, I had my final visit with Barbaro. Of course, at that time I did not know that would be the case—no one could anticipate the downhill spiral Barbaro would take, given his tremendous, albeit slow, progress to date. Dr. Morrison made a second visit and conducted more work on Barbaro's left hind foot to try to improve the alignment of the foot with the coffin bone. A cast was placed on that foot and reports from New Bolton Center remained upbeat.

....

"Barbaro survived longer because of who he was. There is no doubt some horses tolerate their situation better than others. Barbaro ate very well throughout. His appetite and attitude were remarkable."

—DR. DEAN RICHARDSON

....

Five days after Dr. Morrison's visit, improved alignment of Barbaro's coffin bone and foot was evident in radiographs. Unfortunately, on Tuesday (the sixth day), Barbaro became acutely uncomfortable and the foot cast was removed. New separation of the hoof wall was discovered and additional tissue was removed. Barbaro was now no longer allowed outside to graze and was back using the sling to help keep excessive weight off his other legs. Once the foot cast was removed and replaced with soft bandages, Barbaro seemed more comfortable and appeared to rally, again. Dr. Morrison was quoted in a Kentucky newspaper as saying that the progress of Barbaro's left hind foot had been poor.

A second procedure for the foot took place that weekend, in which a cast was placed on his right hind leg for additional support. His deep digital flexor tendon was cut on his left hind leg for a second time to help with alignment, and the more problematic hoof wall was removed. To this point Barbaro had rallied and overcome many obstacles. This was noted in an article in which Barbaro was described as a "freak." Normal horses would have simply given up long ago. They would have stopped eating and drinking and their kidneys would have failed. Not Barbaro.

Within a week's time, he was taken off his pain medicine and no longer needed his sling. It was another rally, or so we thought.

On Monday, January 22, 2007, Team Barbaro was in California attending the Eclipse Awards. Barbaro was a candidate for two awards: Best Three-Year-Old Colt and Horse of the Year. He won neither. Bernardini won Three-Year-Old Colt (Barbaro was runner-up) and Invasor won Horse of the Year (Barbaro was runner-up again). Team Barbaro did win a special Eclipse Award. All appeared well, even though Barbaro would live for just one more week.

On Wednesday, Barbaro underwent a procedure during which an abscess in his right hind foot was drained. The cast on his right hind leg was changed, and work also occurred on his left hind foot. New shoes were applied to Barbaro's front feet to provide additional support. Clearly the major concern at this point was whether Barbaro would develop laminitis in those front feet. Three days later, Barbaro was less comfortable and underwent further surgery on the right hind leg—by all accounts, this was a last-ditch effort. The right hind foot was unacceptably uncomfortable and Barbaro's medical team needed to design a means to get weight off that foot without overburdening his other legs. An external skeletal fixation was applied, screws were inserted into the cannon bone, and essentially the cannon bone (rather than the foot) was now weight-bearing. Jeannine Edwards spoke to Matz, who was still in Florida, "Michael was subdued and seemed ill at ease," she recalled. "He asked me, 'How many times can you get punched in the nose and keep getting back up?'"

On Sunday evening, Gretchen Jackson spent two hours with Barbaro. For the first time she observed that Barbaro appeared to be in distress. He hunkered in the back of his stall. He did not want to interact. He was sweating. Barbaro appeared to have called it quits after a long fight, and for the first time he appeared to be suffering. The Jacksons had always maintained that they would not continue to keep Barbaro alive if he was suffering.

January 29–30, 2007

My Monday morning started as usual, galloping horses at Fair Hill. This is what I posted on TimWoolleyRacing.com: "It was a chilly morning at Fair Hill, with bright sunshine, but a wind that made the temperatures pretty low. I ended up getting on six, five of which went to the Tapeta track. I was actually first on the Tapeta track this morning on Hawty Creek. The track continues to be very good despite the weather. Hawty Creek did two turns at a jog/light gallop. I rode Chesapeake City Slew for trainer Tim [Woolley], and then three more to the track. One of the keys to keeping warm is wearing plenty of layers (I just counted, nine in my case)...and jogging to and from the racetrack. Anyway, gate day was canceled today due to the weather. I cannot imagine why a gate crew does not want to come out on a lovely day like today and stand around for a few hours."

However, throughout the morning's work I was preoccupied with what might have been going on twenty minutes down the road at New Bolton Center. I knew Barbaro had had a rough few days and I had a foreboding feeling that his fight was nearing the end. I made a couple of phone calls but quite rightly, I was not provided any insight.

Later I learned that Barbaro did endure a painful night on Sunday and was euthanized at 9:30 a.m. Dr. Richardson, the veterinarian who had fought for months to save his life, the Jacksons, his nurse, and Dr. Evita Busschers, were all in attendance. The team had run out of options to keep the ever-aggressive laminitis at bay, and to keep Barbaro out of pain.

Certain events in life become indelibly marked in our memories. Some fade away. No doubt those few that remain do so because of the enormity of the event.

I will always remember where I was and what I was doing when I heard that Elvis Presley had died. I will always remember where I was and what I was doing when I heard that Princess Diana had died. I will always remember where I was and what I was doing when I heard that Barbaro had died.

Kathy Freeborn, at New Bolton Center, called me at about 11 a.m., on January 29. I was driving along Route 213 just outside of Fair Hill, heading toward its back entrance. I pulled over. As she spoke, I knew what she was telling me. Knowing did not reduce the shock and profound sadness of the inevitable. It was overwhelming. Barbaro had lost a battle for the first time, and his life along with it.

A press conference was scheduled at New Bolton Center for later that afternoon. The conference was to announce that Barbaro had been euthanized, but the news had already been broadcast. The press conference was well attended, and critical questions were asked and answered by Dr. Richardson and the Jacksons. Jeannine Edwards recalled, "The Jacksons were gracious, as ever, despite their grief. It was especially difficult to see the anguish in Dr. Richardson's eyes as he choked up. He looked not just drained, but defeated. For the first time ever, Dr. Richardson looked like a broken man."

As the press conference wound down, we were all emotionally exhausted. Jennifer Rench and Kathy Freeborn suggested that we go for a drink. I do not remember where we went, nor do I recall what we discussed. Rich Rosenblatt and Dan Gelston from the AP joined us; it was Rosenblatt's birthday. My enduring memory of that brief evening was seeing Barbaro on each of the television screens as the world learned of his passing.

THREE CHIMNEYS

When Barbaro sustained his injury in the Preakness, it was gut-wrenching. I was very close to the accident and to Michael and D.D. It was a terrible few minutes to see the horse scrambling to stand up, while the recovery team worked feverishly to stabilize him. To see this iconic Derby winner under such duress, while the whole world looked on, gave me an almost nauseous feeling. The public had already adopted him as the next Triple Crown winner.

Case [Clay] and I had visited the Jacksons in February, prior to the Florida Derby, and expressed our interest in the horse. Not only did we love what we had seen physically, but also his precocious two-year-old form, and the way in which he was beating his competition gave us great hope that he could be a Derby contender. Having stood Dynaformer for most of his career, we were obviously interested in standing a stallion that could carry on the Roberto-Dynaformer line.

Several months into his recovery, we went to New Bolton to visit Barbaro, and it appeared that he was going to possibly make a full recovery. We met with Roy and Gretchen and offered to build a special round pen for Barbaro, for further recuperation, in hopes that he could stand at stud the next year (we completed the structure in thirty days). Conference calls with Michael and Dr. Richardson took place to discuss post-New Bolton care. Roy called me on a Tuesday to advise me that the horse was doing so well that he would be ready to ship within a week, and to prepare for his arrival. Two days later, he called me with news of a setback.

Barbaro was another example of a horse that captured America's attention. As we have experienced with Seattle Slew and Smarty Jones, fans of racing need these touchstones in order to remain engaged and enthusiastic about our sport. We take great pride in sharing these icons of racing with the public, and we were looking forward to doing the same with Barbaro. Sadly, we lost this very brave and talented thoroughbred, before the public experienced him fully, and before the breeder could tap his genetic makeup.

We will always be grateful to Roy and Gretchen and the entire Barbaro team, for the confidence they had shown us in their willingness for us to be the next care taker of Barbaro, in his too-short-lived career.

—ROBERT CLAY,
Three Chimneys Farm

Reporting Barbaro's passing

The following day, Dr. Richardson provided an exclusive interview for Debbye Turner Bell of *CBS News*. Turner Bell remembers, "Dr. Richardson was heartbroken. Absolutely heartbroken. More so than almost anyone else, except perhaps the Jacksons. He had bonded with Barbaro. As a surgeon and a horseman, he really wanted to be successful. But there was also a personal bond. So he was heartbroken on many levels. Like all veterinarians, there was the tendency to second guess himself, go round and round, exploring the 'what ifs?' But he could no longer keep Barbaro comfortable. They had to throw in the towel. That had been the plan all along, if they could not keep him comfortable they would not continue. And they stuck to the plan. They did the right thing. Dr. Richardson took comfort in that. That's a blessed place to be, it's not often you can get that solace in such circumstances."

That day, I received the following e-mail from Dr. Richardson:

Dear Alex,

I am sorry I did not get [a] chance to compose myself and speak with you yesterday after the press conference. I wanted to thank you for all of your help with Barbaro. Although I personally didn't have the time to get to your website very often, I know it served a greater purpose. Thanks again for your time and dedication.

All the best,

Dean

Kathy Anderson wrote the following short essay, a day after Barbaro passed:

Dear Fans of Barbaro:

Although I have communicated with you indirectly through Alex and this blog I am writing to you now to share some of my thoughts and emotions at the end of Barbaro's journey through life. First, I would like to thank all who energized and galvanized our will to see this journey through—your frequent messages and notes were very appreciated and a constant reminder of just how many people were touched by Barbaro, the warrior horse.

So, what of Barbaro? Please be reassured that throughout his hospitalization, and indeed his life, Barbaro remained in charge—his eye did not dim nor did his spirit waver until the last. Most of you have come to know him intimately through your research, but for me the best thing about him was he was first and foremost a horse, an equine hero to be sure, but always a horse with all that is so special of our equine friends. He was kind and talented as a two-year-old, he became increasingly confident as his fan base increased, and prior to the Preakness, I believe there could be no happier horse…nor human support team.

Following Barbaro's tragic misstep, we staggered with him, but like him, brushed ourselves off and carried on with the challenging task in front of us— to bring Barbaro back into our lives, healthy and happy. New members joined the team, Dr. Richardson becoming the visible leader: with many behind the scenes caregivers. Despite the odds, Barbaro improved steadily, our hopes rekindled, our fears diminished and Barbaro remained constant—day-by-day inspecting his kingdom and his servants with little patience for the slow or weak of heart. The critical week in July became the fork in the road—he took the path less traveled and still managed to look challenge in the eye and gather momentum toward his future. In early January, I took my children to see him, for I was sure that our next visit would be in a grassy paddock at the farm of his choice. He stood on that sunny afternoon, silhouetted against his large window with a panoramic view of nearby pastures, gazing intently at the lucky equines on the horizon, no doubt plotting what contortions and gyrations he would enjoy when he joined them in the not too distant future—that is the memory I hold in my mind's eye. His inner peace and ever-present confidence that all would be right in his world, his shiny healthy coat, his well-muscled and conformed body, even his wonderfully naked legs with no wraps, casts, or bandages—just his badges of courage—the healed but deformed right hind limb and the lightly padded left hind foot…he was a portrait of health. True, he had lost his perfect body and the innocence of youth but now he stood as a battle-seasoned wise warrior.

This is how I remember him, and although my heart weeps for his loss, I know that he is now cavorting and challenging his cloud mates to those races that he was destined to win. I will see that bright spark in the eye of the racehorses I meet in years to come, and I will wonder if he is mischievously playing with me, challenging me to search for that intangible quality of "champion" amongst future generations. Certainly, I am forever indebted to Barbaro for his gift of courage and grace which he bestowed upon us all from the moment he burst upon the racing scene in 2005. What

a ride it has been "through sickness and health." Barbaro fans hail from around the world with diverse cultural and economic backgrounds but together we have found common ground and realize that heroes come in many shapes, sizes, and species— hail to the hero Barbaro!

UPON REFLECTION

Some do question whether the valiant attempt to try to save Barbaro was worth it.

When the initial decision was made to try to save Barbaro, there was a chance he would live. We should first acknowledge that by trying to save Barbaro, he was afforded the opportunity to survive his tragic breakdown. His chances of survival did fluctuate over the following eight months. Initially his chances were grim, as described by Dr. Scott Palmer at Pimlico. Grim, but he had a chance. A day later, after surgery, Dr. Dean Richardson suggested that his chances were now 50-50. They had increased because of the successful surgery.

Over the remainder of Barbaro's time at New Bolton Center, his chances improved and declined, and improved again before declining to the point at which he was euthanized. Therefore, when analyzing whether the attempt to save Barbaro was worth it, we should first acknowledge that in fact, Barbaro did have a chance to be saved. And at times it appeared he would survive. This was illustrated by the fact that just a month before his death, there had been discussions to move Barbaro out of New Bolton Center to Three Chimneys in Kentucky.

But we now know that Barbaro did not survive. So, in hindsight, can we still make the case, that given the ultimate outcome, that the attempt to save Barbaro was worthwhile?

The attempt to save Barbaro also illustrated that, with the appropriate resources, veterinary medicine can surpass previous boundaries and expectations. Dr. Laura Richardson, wife of Dean Richardson (and herself a small animal vet), noted that the case provided hope. Hope not only that Barbaro was given a chance to be saved, but hope for surgeons like Richardson and for those owners who are willing to try whatever it takes to save their horse. Without the efforts and support of owners, surgeons are unable to help horses and expand their expertise. And the case itself provided opportunities to learn and continue to push the boundaries of orthopedic surgery.

Dr. Palmer, who helped shape the initial decision to try to save Barbaro, has spent time considering what was actually accomplished from the attempt. Most importantly, Barbaro lived for eight more months. And most of those days were happy and comfortable days. Barbaro had a tremendous amount of support and good care over the course of those eight months. If Barbaro had been euthanized on Preakness Day, we would always have been left with the question regarding whether he could have been saved. We know now that it was not to be, but we know that *now*, in hindsight. We would not know that without witnessing the valiant attempt by all those involved, including Barbaro.

Barbaro's plight brought significant attention to horse welfare issues. This has manifested in a variety of ways, including shining a bright spotlight on the disease of laminitis and racehorse retirement. It is not to say that Barbaro's circumstances were good. Race caller Vic Stauffer addresses that most directly: "The tragedy of losing him, the one thing that causes me to bristle, is that what happened to Barbaro was in some way good for racing and breeding. It was good for nothing. There is nothing good in any way shape or form about Barbaro breaking down and dying. 'Nothing Good!' Everyone agrees, we wanted Barbaro the racehorse. We wanted Barbaro the stallion. We wanted Barbaro the pensioned stallion. Not Barbaro the patient, who ultimately succumbed. But Barbaro's tragedy has served his fellow horses well."

"Greatness walks hand-in-hand with grief, because greatness is by its nature ephemeral. Part of the experience of witnessing it is ultimately watching it come to an end. It is this fleeting nature that makes it so wonderful to find and so hard to lose. All of the elements of character that made Barbaro so incandescent a figure on the racetrack—courage, resolve, daring, unwavering will—were summoned a thousand-fold in his fight for his life. To watch this horse meet every morning of that struggle with buoyancy, with joy, with what Emily Dickinson called a rage to live, was to see his greatness truly and fully blossom.

"I think it was impossible for any feeling person to look upon this horse in those difficult days and not feel wonder and admiration. It was this that made our connection to him so sweet, and when the news came that he was gone, it was the knowledge of what greatness died with him that made our anguish so deep.

Godspeed, Barbaro."

—LAURA HILLENBRAND
Author of this short essay for Scott Simon of NPR's
Weekend Edition shortly after Barbaro was euthanized

PART TWO

8

Was Barbaro Great?

As part of my research for this book, I was fortunate to interview various media representatives who followed the 2006 Kentucky Derby trail. I also spoke with many of Barbaro's human connections and other leading horsemen. I asked them, directly, if they thought Barbaro was a great racehorse. Almost universally, their opinion is that, at the very least, Barbaro could have been a great racehorse. Some go further and suggest he simply *would* have been a great racehorse. The only knock on Barbaro is that his resume was incomplete, as he only completed six races.

Here are their thoughts, in their own words.

Steve Haskin of the *Blood-Horse*: "Barbaro had the potential after six races. He had greatness in him. He *would* have been a great racehorse if he had not broken down."

Race caller Tom Durkin: "You never know, but stack his Kentucky Derby performance versus the greats—Seattle Slew, Affirmed, Secretariat. That Kentucky Derby performance at minimum measures up and in some cases surpasses some of the greats."

Dave Johnson, who called twenty-four Kentucky Derbys for ABC, and continues to call the race for radio, places Barbaro's Derby performance in the top four he has witnessed, alongside Affirmed, Alysheba, and Winning Colors. "There is no question Barbaro was greatness, yes. I saw it on the racetrack, personified in his Derby win."

The Associated Press's Rich Rosenblatt: "Barbaro's Kentucky Derby performance has got to be up there in the top. It was not unexpected that he could win, but the way he did it, demolishing those horses was unexpected. Many were

given a shot; to just be so much the best was impressive. In a historic manner, it was mind-boggling the authority with which he won the race. From the mid-1980s, it was the most impressive Derby performance.

"Barbaro is in a class of greatness with an asterisk because of an incomplete career. He could have been one of the greatest of all time, but you cannot put him in the category of greatness with an incomplete career. The way Barbaro won the Kentucky Derby, you are talking about greatness already, but his career was incomplete. It is not fair to judge him on an incomplete body of work."

Courier-Journal's Jennie Rees: "His Derby performance was the best since I started covering the Derby in 1984. It was not like Giacomo's Derby with the fast pace collapsing. It was not like War Emblem's where no other speed materialized. Barbaro was not far off very fast early fractions and then he exploded through the stretch. The shame of it is, they had aspirations to run him as a four-year-old in Europe. They believed he had it in him."

Philadelphia Daily New's Dick Jerardi: "It was the best Derby performance I have witnessed, and that dates back to 1987. The pace was hot and he was close to it, everyone else backed out. When the field was going around the far turn Edgar was just looking around, I knew then he would win. And then Barbaro re-broke. Past the finish line Barbaro galloped out fifteen to twenty lengths in front of everybody. There was no slowing down, and he had a joy for running. Most horses at that point hit a wall, he just wanted to keep running.

"It is difficult to say whether Barbaro was a great horse because his career was so short. There is no question he is one of the greatest Kentucky Derby winners, but anything beyond that is conjecture. He had a chance to be a great racehorse. Few horses are good on the dirt and on the turf, like John Henry and Secretariat. It's very possible he was going to be a great racehorse, but it is hard to say that he was great after six races. Most people's memories of him will be that one race, no question, his Derby win."

Hall of Fame jockey Gary Stevens: "Barbaro did not have the opportunity to prove either way. In my eyes, he was a great racehorse, but his career was cut short by his accident at Pimlico. Unfortunately for everybody, all the connections and fans, we did not get a chance to see his career through. I think his brilliance would have been verified with the talent he had."

Bill Finley of the *New York Times*: "Barbaro's was as good a Kentucky Derby as I have ever seen. The only ones I can compare it to are two of the Triple Crown winners, Seattle Slew and Secretariat. I don't put Affirmed in that category because he did not dominate. That had a lot to do with the fact that he was running against a terrific opponent in Alydar. I didn't cover the Derbys in the '70s but I did follow them closely as a fan. But in my time covering the Kentucky Derby, from 1986 to 2008, it was easily the best and most dominating performance I have witnessed. It was not only just his winning, but it was the type of things he did in winning the race that were so very rare, while running against the best competition. When you are running against that level of competition and can win so convincingly, you know you have witnessed something special. People might say, 'Whom did he beat?' but that's not a relevant point in the Kentucky Derby. The Derby always includes the very best horses of a crop and it's a race that is very hard to dominate. What he did in that race is show that he was in a class by himself. That was the type of performance that left no doubt, he was a horse that comes around only once in a very long while.

"I think he could have been great, but the brevity of his career is the only reason why I would hesitate to say he was a great racehorse. He only won two Grade 1 races and I have a hard time calling a horse 'great' whose accomplishments were that limited. I hate to say that about Barbaro, because I suspect if he had had the opportunity he would have done more than enough to prove that he was a great horse."

Bill Sanborn, who foaled Barbaro: "Barbaro was truly one of the great racehorses. He truly was."

The *New York Post's* Ed Fountaine: "Barbaro would have been a great racehorse, he was an undefeated Kentucky Derby winner, and won by the largest margin since Assault. But he only completed six races."

Barbaro ran the thirteenth fastest Kentucky Derby and won by the largest winning margin in sixty years, in a hand-ride. He could have run faster.

Race caller Vic Stauffer: "Depends on the criteria for greatness—he was brilliant, a short career like Ruffian's. Yes, I definitely consider him a great racehorse with a grade of incomplete. The six races I saw—they struck me as greatness. Certainly the last two, the Florida Derby and the Kentucky Derby."

Trainer Barclay Tagg: "His Derby win was extraordinary, he devastated the opposition. He laid fourth and ran past them like they were tied to a fence. It was as impressive a Derby performance as I have ever seen. Very impressive, he won by more than six lengths, ran the whole race and blew them away. A great horse, certainly, he was undefeated."

ESPN's Randy Moss: "Barbaro's Kentucky Derby performance; it was spectacular, he stumbled a little at the start, then he had that burst of tactical speed to get a perfect stalking position outside horses. He was traveling nice and fluidly, effortlessly. I was not clued in on Barbaro at the beginning of the race, but when I saw him set sail, it was pretty apparent at that point, the way he ran away from those horses down the lane he was really visually impressive.

"In terms of greatness, it depends how liberally you can apply the term. His Kentucky Derby performance qualifies as great, he deserves the label of a great racehorse. But an all-time great racehorse? Barbaro becomes a victim of his fate. He never got to prove he belongs on the list of all time greats."

Pat Forde, senior writer for ESPN.com: "Barbaro's Derby win was brilliant, it was just awe-inspiring. I have covered every Derby since 1988, and there are not many, if any, that left you with your jaw hanging down. That was the case with Barbaro. He looked great before the race and looked better once the race went

off. You immediately thought, Triple Crown.

"From the evidence we have, yes, I think Barbaro was a great racehorse. He cannot be stamped as immortal I guess, there was no Triple Crown, but he was clearly impressive and undefeated. There was nothing to doubt about him, but he just never got the chance to complete a career."

Vic Zast, author of *The History and Art of 25 Travers,* who wrote several articles for MSNBC and NBCSports.com about Barbaro: "Not all Kentucky Derby winners are great racehorses. When Barbaro won the Kentucky Derby, I thought he was a Triple Crown winner and would be a great racehorse. Yes, he was a great racehorse."

The *News Journal*'s Jack Ireland: "One race does not make greatness, but to me it did. He was great that day [Kentucky Derby]."

A few note that not only did Barbaro illustrate greatness in his shortened career, but he also had so much scope to improve.

Daily Racing Form's Jay Privman: "The nagging thing: what could he have done! Maybe he could have been a Triple Crown winner. He certainly had the potential to do that. He could have had a long and varied career. He would have raced as a four-year-old, knowing his connections. Just not knowing how much better he could have been. One of the great tragedies; he looked like he was getting better as he was getting older."

Bill Nack, author of *Secretariat: The Making of a Champion*: "Sadly, Barbaro left us before his time, before he had reached his full potential, before he had the chance to show what he could really do. I thought, after that smashing win in the Kentucky Derby, that he was destined to win the Triple Crown and join the ranks of Secretariat, Seattle Slew, and Affirmed. He had shown that kind of quality. Alas, this was not to be, and the sport was left the poorer for it."

Barbaro's exercise rider Peter Brette: "I think in ten years' time people will look

at him, and say he was a good horse who won the Kentucky Derby in great fashion, which would be wrong. I think he was a great horse who won the Kentucky Derby in good fashion, because that was just the beginning of him, everything suggested he was going to get better with age. His psyche suggested he was going to improve, everything suggested he was going to improve and that was the most exciting part."

Only four other horses had won the Kentucky Derby by a larger winning margin than Barbaro in the first 132 runnings of the Derby: Old Rosebud (1914), Johnstown (1939), Whirlaway (1941), and Assault (1946). Assault and Whirlaway went on to win the Triple Crown. Barbaro's time was comparable to Whirlaway's time and faster than the rest. Barbaro defeated nineteen other runners, Assault defeated sixteen, Whirlaway defeated eleven, Johnstown defeated seven, and Old Rosebud defeated six other runners.

Daily Racing Form's Glenye Cain-Oakford: "We saw a glimmer of greatness in Barbaro's Kentucky Derby. It was the most commanding Derby performance I have seen in twenty years. His pedigree on both his sire's and dam's side suggest he would have gotten better with age. Pedigree aside, he appeared to be maturing, peaking, and gaining momentum. We know that he still physically had room to mature and he was relatively young compared to most of the horses he beat, because he was a late April foal. Both his pedigree and relative youth make me think we were just beginning to see how good he was."

Barbaro's trainer Michael Matz: "I think he was a great racehorse, and I think that probably there's no telling the end result what he could have been. We never saw a limit where we asked, he just did things all the time."

Barbaro's jockey Edgar Prado: "He could run on any track and any kind of surface. I could put him anywhere I wanted (in a race). He had acceleration that was incredible. He was only a three-year-old and was just developing. He had the right to be one of the best horses to ever run a race."

Barbaro's vet Kathy Anderson: "Destined for greatness, as we said, pretty straightforward as he clearly was. But nobody really knew where his greatness would eventually reveal itself. I think that we always define greatness by his race-track performance. But in his case it was clearly bigger than that. Nobody would have ever guessed. The greatness thing, you'll have to come up with the racing stats, but as far as his personality, his character, what contributed to his greatness was his generous heart, and that was exhibited in many ways. He was good with his groom. He was generous with his training. He was very generous with his racing ability and generous with people around him like me. He was professional about everything."

And while as horsemen we are very discerning in terms of how we determine greatness among horses, the general public will have a different perception.

Philadelphia Inquirer's Mike Jensen would argue that by simply winning the Kentucky Derby a horse is considered great in the eye of the general public: "The Kentucky Derby winner is the only brand in the sport that carries over to the general population. The Breeders' Cup Classic winner is usually a champion, but that does not mean anything. The Eclipse Award winner is a champion. But that does not mean much. There is one brand in this sport. Barbaro had it. There's no counter-argument to that."

Obviously, the one knock against Barbaro is the length of his career. This is highlighted by *USA Today*'s Tom Pedulla, who remarked on the topic of great-ness: "I do not subscribe. I believe in a body of work. The body of work was just too small. New York Yankees' Don Mattingly, he was a brilliant offensive player, a defensive player. But he had all kinds of back problems, so did not play enough seasons. We overuse the word great in our society, a lot of times it's nonsense. I needed to see more from Barbaro.

"He was like a shooting star. A horse who raised a lot of 'what ifs' rather than answer questions. Brilliance was there but we did not get a chance to see it play out. If he ran through his four-year-old career how wonderful would it have been? I think he would have won the Triple Crown. He had wonderful connec-tions, his brilliance would not have been ruined by his owners and trainer. It was a missed opportunity for the sport. It was vast potential unfulfilled for the horse. We all wanted more."

Ray Paulick, who was then editor-in-chief of the *Blood-Horse,* agrees: "His Derby win was very impressive. He won by the widest margin in decades, and was drawing off. I had never seen a horse do that in the Derby and I have been covering the race since 1988.

"In regards to greatness it is impossible to say. The closest example for me would be Lukas's Landaluce. The filly in the 1980s won a six-furlong stake by twenty-one lengths, ran two more races, then died as a two-year-old. You cannot really tell until the best three-year-olds face older horses. Because Barbaro never had the opportunity, I have to reserve judgment on greatness. He could have been, he may have been. He was kind of like a star rookie pitcher in baseball, he did great things in a brief period of time. He had no chance to go outside his division to prove himself against older horses."

Michael Blowen, who runs Old Friends, a home for retired racehorses, also agrees: "He died too young to tell. Was James Dean a great actor? He made three movies. He was a major star, in many ways because he died. He did not have the time to make a bunch of bad movies. Barbaro died too soon to figure that out. He was definitely a star."

Accolades for Barbaro were not limited to North America. Clive Brittain, one of the leading trainers in the U.K., who won a Breeders' Cup race with Pebbles in 1985 and came close to winning a Kentucky Derby with Bold Arrangement, was quoted in the Scottish *Sunday Herald* following Barbaro's death: "It is tragic to lose such a horse. There is no such thing as a bad Derby, so the way he skipped away from the field showed he was something exceptional. He may well have become the horse of the century. He was truly a superstar and the way he coped for so long with his terrible injuries indicated the type of horse he was. It is really very, very sad. Let's hope all the good he generated continues."

So let's explore, in more detail, what it was about Barbaro that determines his greatness.

Barbaro was only the sixth undefeated Kentucky Derby winner in 132 runnings. The previous five were Regret (1915), Morvich (1922), Majestic Prince (1969), Seattle Slew (1977), and Smarty Jones (2004). Seattle Slew went on to win the Triple Crown. Barbaro ran his Derby faster than each of his undefeated peers and won by a wider margin.

Barbaro's win in the Kentucky Derby was phenomenal. Many observers consider his Derby performance the best, or one of the best, they have witnessed. Why was his Derby performance considered so good?

The winning margin was one of the factors. Barbaro won by six-and-a-half lengths, which was the largest winning margin since Assault won the race in 1946 en route to capturing the Triple Crown. But it was not just the winning margin that sets Barbaro's Derby performance apart from other Derby performances.

Barbaro won with ease. Prado never went to his stick, he simply hand-rode Barbaro down the lane. In fact, Barbaro might be the only Kentucky Derby winner, dating back to the 1960s, that won the race without the jockey using the stick to ask for extra effort. One can speculate that with some additional urging from Prado, Barbaro may have won the race in a faster time and by a wider margin.

Barbaro dominated his Derby in a fashion not seen since Spend a Buck's wire-to-wire win in 1985. Tom Law expressed that he knew Barbaro had the race won at the three-quarter pole. The race did not simply set up for Barbaro; Barbaro just dominated the race. Spend a Buck's Derby was very impressive in terms of his wire-to-wire performance, but Spend a Buck was a tired horse coming down the lane. He did not finish with the same flourish and ease that Barbaro did.

Barbaro's last quarter of a mile was completed in a little over 24 seconds. This was the fastest closing quarter of a Kentucky Derby since Secretariat's win in 1973. In fact, it is Secretariat's Derby win that some might consider the benchmark with which Barbaro's performance should be measured. Secretariat completed each quarter of a mile faster than the preceding one, which was unheard of in the Ken-

tucky Derby. He came from mid-pack to take the lead at the head of the stretch to accomplish this. Barbaro, on the other hand, was close to the lead throughout his Derby performance. And the early fractions were fast—22 seconds and change for the first quarter and 46 seconds for the first half mile. Horses that were first and second after half a mile, Keyed Entry and Sinister Minister, finished last and sixteenth, respectively. Tom Durkin asserts that if a horse runs the first half mile in the Derby in 47 seconds or less, he will likely not be around at the finish. Barbaro did just that and according to Tom Durkin's race call, he had something left in reserve for another day.

When you look at all the factors of Barbaro's Kentucky Derby win, experts and fans alike will agree that his performance was one of greatness.

••

"His performance in the Kentucky Derby was more than just numbers. His performance was poetry. It was calculated, exact, powerful, and inspirational. He was undefeated going in and still he was not considered the favorite. He played the field like a violin. He was in control the whole time and waited for just the right moment to hit the high note. Peter told me that morning…'These horses will have to have wings to beat Barbaro today.' Barbaro was the one with the wings, and sadly enough, he never used them to their full potential."
—MICHELLE HYLAND

••

Great racehorses should be able to handle all racing surfaces. Secretariat and John Henry are examples of truly great racehorses that excelled on both dirt and turf.

"If Barbaro gave off indications of greatness in his Derby win, he also demonstrated greatness with his indifference to racing surfaces," said Bill Nack. "For really good horses, the type of racing surface does not matter. Secretariat was a great racehorse. Some have argued, including his jockey Ron Turcotte, that Secretariat was a better grass horse than he was a dirt horse, and that the way he handled the grass in both the Man o' War and the Canadian International demonstrated this. His owner, Penny Chenery, has always said that she thought he was better on grass than he was on dirt. I am inclined to believe it myself. Barbaro was also ambidextrous. Turf or dirt, it did not matter."

Many observers will make the case that Barbaro might have been a better turf horse than dirt horse. His first three races, all on turf, were very impressive. He won those three races by a combined twenty lengths. He completed the last eighth of a mile in each of those races faster than he finished the last eighth of a mile in any of his dirt races. While it may be the norm for turf races to finish faster than dirt races, it is the ease and length of victory of his turf races that is also impressive.

There is no doubt that Barbaro's performance in the Kentucky Derby illustrated that he handled the dirt well, and because of that performance Michael Matz does not concede that Barbaro was necessarily a better turf horse. "Was he a better turf horse than dirt horse, we will never know. No one knows how good he would have been on the dirt. It is a question that will always leave people wondering."

One of Barbaro's dirt races, the Holy Bull Stakes, was actually run over a sloppy racetrack. Barbaro handled that also. Perhaps he did not enjoy it, but according to race caller Vic Stauffer, he won the race on raw talent.

There is no doubt that Barbaro excelled regardless of the track surface. Jack Ireland mentioned to Matz, on more than one occasion, that Barbaro could have won on Interstate 95—the surface just made no difference to him.

Barbaro was undefeated in the races he finished—a perfect six-for-six that included the Kentucky Derby, the one race that all owners aspire to win. Some argue that Barbaro was only going to get better. He clearly flourished during the time between the Florida Derby and the Kentucky Derby. He experienced a growth spurt during that time, and celebrated his third birthday on April 29, only a little over a week before his Kentucky Derby win. Only two horses in the 2006 Kentucky Derby were younger than Barbaro (Seaside Retreat and Bob and John), so he certainly did appear to have room for further development and maturity.

Barbaro was a tremendous physical specimen. Certainly, equine photographer Barbara Livingston has seen her share of excellent conformation.

"He had such quiet pride—a certainty of who he was," she said. "He looked like what an English print of a horse would look like. He just looked exactly correctly put together. I am not used to seeing that. There is always something that keeps a horse from looking perfect. But Barbaro, he had a brilliantly intelligent looking eye. Things that would send an ordinary horse into a fit he took in, in a worldly understanding. Every element fit correctly. There is no doubt in my mind; everything just screamed 'great, immortal, history books.' No doubt one of the best horses we would have seen. His professionalism, his power, just so beautifully built, careful attention to his world the way other horses don't."

Barbaro had all the attributes of greatness; he simply lacked a long career to demonstrate that greatness. In the modern era of horse racing, many of our three-year-old stars are swiftly retired to begin their long and more lucrative stallion careers. For Barbaro that was not to be the plan. As tragic as Barbaro's breakdown was, the irony is that his owners had plans to campaign him far beyond his three-year-old season. They are true sportsmen, and aspired to showcase Barbaro both in the United States and quite possibly on the turf in Europe in the Prix de l'Arc de Triomphe.

No definitive measurement defines a great racehorse. Secretariat was great—that is indisputable. Man o' War also was great. And the list probably includes half a dozen more. Barbaro was perhaps going to be great, and demonstrated in one race true greatness. In the long run, history will be the judge regarding Barbaro's greatness. This will take place long after his fans have passed and new generations of fans are following horse racing. These new fans will be encouraged to learn about Barbaro, more so than most other horses of our generation, because of his very prominent memorial at Churchill Downs.

Why Did Barbaro Inspire?

Why did Barbaro become such an inspirational figure? His saga has inspired many people to appreciate their own circumstances more fully and reach out to help others—both human and equine.

As discussed in the previous chapter, Barbaro was great and destined for greatness, or he ran one great race, depending on your assessment of his short-lived career. He was then struck down in his prime and in front of the nation on TV through no fault of his own. His story became a tragedy at a time when the horse racing world was preparing for a coronation. It left a huge sense of "what might have been?"

While Barbaro's prognosis appeared dire, against the odds he fought back and illustrated characteristics that we aspire for ourselves. It is human nature to want a hero, and in Barbaro we found one—an equine hero to a country with deep-rooted cultural ties to the horse. He was a hero that came along at a time of economic uncertainty, global strife, and human failings. We were also introduced to Barbaro's team: his owners, trainer, jockey, and surgeon, all with the singular goal of saving their beloved horse. This chapter represents my best attempt to explain why Barbaro inspired such a strong following in the months following his Preakness accident, and long after his death.

"Well, I think everybody has pretty much said the same thing for a while now, it's hard not to come up with more or less the same conclusions, he was clearly one of those individuals who looked destined for absolute greatness," said Dean Richardson, in describing his most famous patient. "He really looked the part, he acted the part, and he looked like he was going to be a really truly great horse. And he was cut down in his prime, so it becomes a genuine tragedy. It becomes that much more of a story when an individual, and you know we are equating a horse with a human in a lot of ways, but you know that's the way you have to look at these things. When the athlete is cut down in the prime of his career, it becomes a bigger story. You can see a dozen situations like that. If Elvis Presley dies when he is ninety, it is not the same story if he dies in the middle of his career. People in their prime, athletes in their prime, animals in their prime—it just seems more compelling for obvious reasons."

"But on top of that, people can have a visceral affinity to a horse and not even know why," continued Richardson. "Some are animal lovers in general. I mean I received scores of, hundreds of letters from people who were absolutely fascinated with the story and were 'in love' with Barbaro who did not know anything about horses. They owned cats, dogs, but there is something about the story and human affinity for the horse that elicited this kind of response. So I think the fact that he was a great athlete in his prime and struck down, and I think specifically that he was a horse; it got that level of attention."

"Then, beyond that, people started putting their own virtues on him," he added. "People can put their own virtues on a blank page. And Barbaro was a blank page. He was nothing but a paragon of virtue. He had done everything right, so why not give him every imaginable virtue. That's human nature."

I will now explore the characteristics that many associate with Barbaro. It is important to recognize that it is not the reality of whether Barbaro possessed all these characteristics. Rather, it is the perception of whether he did among those who were so enamored by him.

After Barbaro's Preakness accident, renowned artist Fred Stone decided to no longer paint horses. It was four or five months before he then painted his next horse, Barbaro. It was Barbaro's will and fight to survive (and the letters he received) that inspired Mr. Stone to paint horses again. Fred Stone is the most famous painter of horses in the world, according to the *Los Angeles Times* and *Chicago Tribune.*

Barbaro appeared to demonstrate four types of characteristics that contributed to his popularity and fame. Broadly speaking, they are star power, charisma, innocence, and courage.

Star power, presence. Barbaro illustrated star power throughout his racing career. Even early on, after his first race, his connections knew that he was more than special. Anderson called him "next year's Kentucky Derby winner" after only his first win. He mesmerized people both on the racetrack and while he was training. Rengert noted how she reacted when she first saw Barbaro at Delaware Park. It was the same reaction she experienced when she first saw Seattle Slew and Forego. It should be noted that the latter two horses were already famous when Rengert first saw them, while Barbaro had not yet raced. Similarly, John Asher noted that he was in awe when he first saw Barbaro, and this was before he won the Kentucky Derby. Asher usually reserves such reactions for horses that have already established themselves, such as Zenyatta (then 2008 Breeders' Cup Distaff winner and undefeated), who had a brief stint at Churchill Downs in April 2009, and Rachel Alexandra, who won the 2009 Kentucky Oaks with such ease that many believe she would have won that year's Kentucky Derby if entered. The reactions of Jill Baffert and Rick Bozich when Barbaro entered the Kentucky Derby paddock also illustrate his star power and commanding presence. Even when Barbaro was injured, he still illustrated a certain understanding of what was occurring around him. People rallied around him and did their best to help their stricken star. Barbaro's star power gathered mo-

mentum during his stay at New Bolton Center. This was illustrated by his steady stream of visitors, gifts that were sent, and good wishes he received from people across the country. Sabina Louise Pierce, Barbaro's photographer at New Bolton Center, has photographed four U.S. presidents, as well as numerous sports stars and celebrities. Aside from the Dalai Lama, Barbaro is the only subject with whom Pierce wanted to be photographed.

....

"Barbaro's story was a great horse racing story. On a dime, it turned into something else, not a horse racing story, but a horse story. A stress story, something that literally everybody could identify with in some way. To see this animal, through no fault of his own, fighting for his life, in front of national television—whether they saw it live, or through replays, everybody saw that. And then to see the human side of it, to see all the people trying to save this animal, that struck a chord.

"Does it go a lot deeper than that? Yes, it does go a lot deeper; if he had been a typical horse would people have attached themselves? No. I think a Derby winner, in this country, even though it is no longer a mainstream sport, a Derby winner stands for something. It stands for excellence, right up along the lines of Super Bowl winners, Olympic champions. This horse had that label. I don't think that can be underestimated."

—MIKE JENSEN

....

Charismatic, beautiful, breathtaking. It is virtually impossible to find someone who worked with Barbaro who was not wowed by his charisma. Like people, some horses are charismatic and some horses are not. Barbaro was always alert, always inquisitive, and always aware of his own world. Barbaro was also a gorgeous racehorse with a big, beautiful eye. Barbara Livingston saw this during Derby week. According to her, Barbaro was flawless—like what you would expect from a horse in an English oil painting. Reporter Randy Moss noted the ESPN Director's reaction to seeing Barbaro for the first time when the horse was unloaded from the van after he arrived at Pimlico for the Preakness. Of course, when Barbaro ran, he was absolutely breathtaking. Try watching the stretch run of his Kentucky Derby and not get a lump in your throat as Durkin narrates.

Innocent, humble, and heroic. Barbaro never asked for anything more than good care. He was brilliant, yet unlike human athletes, he never let that success affect his character. There were several articles written on how Barbaro compared to other modern-day athletes who held out for better contracts, got themselves in trouble with the law, or gave up during competition.

....

"Barbaro touched so many people because he was a humble hero. He represented everything that every human aspires to be. His Derby performance was inspirational."

—MICHELLE HYLAND

....

Golfer Tiger Woods was embroiled in a very public personal scandal, so took a few months away from golf. Upon his return, at the 2010 Masters, Bill Payne of Augusta National remarked, "It is simply not the degree of his conduct that is so egregious here. It is the fact that he disappointed all of us, and more importantly, our kids and our grandkids. Our hero did not live up to the expectations of the role model we saw for our children."

As a horse, Barbaro was never going to do any of these things. And even during his time at New Bolton Center, he seemed to remain strong, stoic, and for the most part, content, despite his condition. Essentially, Barbaro became a role model for how we should act. Be the best we can be, yet expect that is how we should be, rather than seek out more rewards for better behavior. If Barbaro could be like that, then surely we could do the same.

"Central factor, back to the beginning of time, his life had all the elements of a classic tragedy. He needs a Shakespeare to tell the story because it had so much depth to it. He gave everything and tried so hard, and in the end, that was the end of it. I think the story was just so compelling. It gathered in people. People respected and appreciated he gave his entire being, after winning the race everyone wanted to win, the Kentucky Derby.

"It's almost like Spartacus; at the end of the movie Spartacus dies, it is such a compelling movie. He can't give anymore. That is the quality that Barbaro gave us."

—MICHAEL BLOWEN,
Founder, Old Friends

....

"Barbaro exemplified the hero," said Anderson. "We all need heroes and he was an easy hero with whom to identify. He was also fighting the battle, fighting the war. Now we are fighting the economy. At that time, we were at war in Iraq and still recovering from 9/11. We needed a hero, and I think he was the hero, because he did not give up. Barbaro fought the odds."

Barbaro performed for our entertainment. Richardson included this in a New Bolton Center update during week four of Barbaro's stay: "Why do heroic animals inspire such intense emotions? Partly, I think, because they perform their acts of heroism for us, and not of their own volition. While we may feel intense admiration and concern for human warriors and athletes who put themselves at risk of injury or death, our sympathy is always tempered by the belief that they were aware of the risks and were willing to face them. With animals we cannot shelter realistically behind this assumption."

Bill Finley added: "Horses are so pure and innocent and they are not doing it for the money. They are performing because it is simply their natural instinct to run. Even the most hardened cynics had to appreciate that. His fight and his death made him a heroic figure. He became more famous and more popular than he would have been if he had won the Triple Crown, which is what we had all hoped for."

Dick Jerardi offered his explanation as to why Barbaro became so inspiring, citing "people's general love of animals" as a major factor.

"People want to do something for animals that cannot help themselves," he said. "People adopted Barbaro as their horse; because it was so public it was almost like he *was* their horse."

Debbye Turner Bell added: "People love animals. They always generate a greater emotion and sentiment than human beings. Take the Gulf story for example [the BP Oil spill in 2010]. Eleven men were killed, and all those jobs that have been displaced. But it's the images of the oiled birds that have captured people. We love animals and we cannot stand to see them suffer. Many saw Barbaro that day at the Preakness. They saw the injury happen and just couldn't let go of that image."

Tough, courageous, warrior's spirit. During his time at New Bolton Center, Barbaro demonstrated a toughness that could not have been revealed under any other circumstances. He faced significant adversity as he fought many battles and his condition took turns for the better and for the worse. Each time he bounced back with a fight to live that was more than surprising. It essentially became an ongoing saga.

With Messaging

"The concept of loss is much more personal, understandable, relatable, and compelling than the concept of gain. Even Shakespeare knew that. He became the world's most famous playwright writing tragedies. Barbaro's was the ultimate loss.

"Most examples of gain are about the triumph of imperfection. Barbaro's loss was the unraveling of perfection. He was a beautiful horse with a mysterious name, undefeated and triumphant in America's best-known race. Barbaro's record was irrefutable. He was intelligent and trustworthy, dependable, effective. He was what the leaders of our country were not at the time. America was primed to revere him. Things were not going smoothly, nothing was going right, and along came Barbaro—this symbol of perfection.

"And within the context of Barbaro were these people and their charisma. They epitomized the qualities we expect from royalty. One of the owners was a Rockefeller, a true gentleman before it came time to prove it. His wife was a quiet, classy benefactor. Barbaro's trainer was a humble professional, an airplane crash survivor and hero, an Olympic flag carrier. Ultimately, after the tragedy occurred, a vet emerged who was as devoted to his patient in the same manner as you would want from your own heart surgeon. This was not a raggedy bunch of people in the game for the buck and cheap accolades. These were the kind of people you wanted to win the Triple Crown.

"When you added them into the mix, Barbaro was so ideally cast as a hero. When he fell, he became the ultimate martyr. In his struggles, people found faith in themselves. As long as he stayed alive, people were given hope that they could carry on. His long defiance against passing on caused people to hope against hope."

—VIC ZAST

"It was like an epic poem. Beowulf-like, Odysseus, a dramatic re-enactment," said Bill Nack. "Barbaro was down, and then up again, up and down, it was very emotional. He would have a bad night, then a better day. When you got the positive news, it was like 'good, now I can go to work.'"

Many people noted that some horses, in his circumstances, would have given up on their fight for their lives long before Barbaro did. Lesser horses would have stopped eating and drinking and their organs would have failed, whereas Barbaro's appetite was strong through to the very end. He appeared to want to live. He demonstrated courage to fight his battle. If Barbaro could fight for his life with the determination he demonstrated, others could do the same.

"Barbaro was brilliant, as a racehorse and a patient," said Sandy McKee. "His performance during his injury was amazing. He was phenomenal from start to finish. He never gave up, he just kept on going. There are so many positives from that horse. He was just amazing. Sick people looked to Barbaro and somehow tried harder."

Barbaro's warrior spirit was evident on Preakness Day and acknowledged during his time at New Bolton Center. This was demonstrated by the visit he received from two U.S. soldiers who presented Barbaro with an American flag. What was the rationale for their visit and gift? Barbaro's struggles on Preakness Day reminded them of a wounded soldier who, like Barbaro, would keep fighting despite his injuries.

In the fall of 2006, Prado explained why he visited Barbaro during his time at New Bolton Center.

"I like him very much," said Prado. "He gave me the biggest thrill of my life in the Derby. The courage he is currently displaying in his recovery just shows how special this horse is. A horse like this does not come around too often. I am honored to have been part of his story. He is very special."

Barbaro made people realize that their own situations were not so bad. If he could handle his condition with grace and dignity, surely we should feel better about our own circumstances.

"On Friday morning I visited the hospital for a routine screening that although not painful, I knew was going to be very uncomfortable. As I sat and waited, feeling some dread at the prospect, I looked down at my Barbaro bracelet (that Sharon kindly sent me) and thought of all he had gone through, demonstrating his indomitable spirit and unfailing courage. I suddenly felt my fears were utterly pathetic and wondered how many others had faced much worse and drawn comfort from that colt's great spirit."

—SUE McMULLEN,
A U.K. reporter who contributed to TimWoolleyRacing.com

"Why do people want to be better people because of Barbaro? I think they are better people because they identify with Barbaro, his heart," explained Anderson. "They also took a look at their own lives and said, 'This is not that bad. I am a lucky person. I have my health. I have this, I have that.' Barbaro made them feel more grateful. And when you are grateful, you feel good about the person who gave you that gift. In this case this would be Barbaro."

He also then inspired us to do good things for others. This often manifested in the welfare of other animals that themselves are helpless, such as the thousands of horses saved from slaughter by the Fans of Barbaro.

THE TEAM

The four main support characters in the story of Barbaro were essential to the development of the story and the inspiration that the story provided. They are: Barbaro's owners, Roy and Gretchen Jackson; Barbaro's trainer, Michael Matz; and his surgeon, Dr. Dean Richardson. Not only did this team provide access to the Barbaro story without which a public following could not be galvanized, but they also demonstrated many qualities to which we aspire. Dan Gelston, of the Associated Press, offered his explanation of the Jacksons' role in the story: "The Jacksons felt the pain as a fan, they had the knack of talking as if they were also fans. They were very gracious, thanking people for their support and their letters. This drew more people in. They appreciated Barbaro's fans and consequently he got more fans. They were very proactive in saying thank you. It was like they were giving so much back, like a baseball pitcher giving a ball away. He gets a fan for life."

· ·

"If Barbaro had been owned by a different group of people who said 'we want to save this horse but we will tell you how it works out,' it would have been a different story. Most owners would not have said Dean Richardson can talk, we will issue statements. This obviously was done a different way off the bat.

"And I think from covering this sport just a bit, people get drawn in by the humans, and that became an important part of it. If they had been told just in general terms what was going on with this horse, I mean Dean Richardson was giving very detailed synopses of what was happening. I almost correlate it from when Smarty Jones became a sensation. Part of the reason for that, John Servis [Smarty Jones's trainer] was able to articulate what was going on with the horse and what was special about the horse. He articulated his own enthusiasm about the horse. I think that was important.

"We need to be led into these stories, into these sagas. For the people drawn into it, the people who cared, they could actually see Barbaro fighting. There was TV coverage of that. There was wall-to-wall coverage. Not cameras in his stall, but there were times basically the public was led in."

—MIKE JENSEN

· ·

Anderson noted the importance of the purity of the team: "He had a very charismatic cast about him: the Jacksons, Dean, Michael. None of them appeared to have any financial motivation and I think that's important. That's important because it purifies the process. It would have been far simpler to have just pulled the plug and taken the insurance money. It was heroic action on the part of the group, not just the surgery. It was an early decision, made in the barn at Pimlico."

Prado was a fifth member of the team who proved integral at the beginning of the saga and remained connected through his six visits with Barbaro at New Bolton Center. Prado's anguish at the Preakness as he pleaded with vets to try to save Barbaro established a human connection to the story from the very beginning.

ROY AND GRETCHEN JACKSON

As racehorse owners, the Jacksons are a throwback to the time when racing truly was the sport of kings. Because owners had the financial means to compete in the sport, economic return was not the most important outcome of the competition. Competition itself, the racing of horses, was the goal. We now race in a time in which economics is a major driver for many participants. Under this model, a good horse will race a few times to establish its breeding value, and then be retired to the breeding shed. Typically, a colt that wins the Kentucky Derby is now retired at the end of its three-year-old career to begin its more lucrative breeding career. The Jacksons had aspirations to run Barbaro as a four-year-old and were even considering the possibility of entering the Prix de l'Arc de Triomphe in France.

Roy Jackson, who is a member of the Rockefeller dynasty, comes from a fox hunting family. His father, Roy Senior, was a Master of Foxhounds who loved to hunt. While Roy did not pursue this passion, his wife Gretchen loves the sport. Both Roy and Gretchen come from a deep tradition of horsemen and that tradition persists through their children and grandchildren.

While it appeared that the Jacksons were new to the sport of horse racing when they arrived on the scene with two unbeaten horses in the 2006 Kentucky Derby, that was far from the case. What is true is that they had significantly increased their investment in recent years in the sport they love. The Jacksons have raced horses for more than thirty years, mostly in the Mid-Atlantic region, on a much smaller scale.

(Barclay Tagg, who trained Showing Up for them for the 2006 Derby, also trained for them when they first started out as owners.)

Because the Jacksons have the financial means to compete in the sport, economics was never a driver in terms of decisions made with respect to Barbaro. Euthanizing Barbaro at the track would have been the easiest option at the time, but it was not an option they pursued. During Barbaro's stay at New Bolton Center, the principal considerations were whether Barbaro's pain could be managed, if he could remain comfortable, and if there was a chance that he could live a pain-free life. In fact, the Jacksons took the most expensive course of action with Barbaro in terms of trying to save his life. Live or die, Barbaro was covered by insurance, and the insurance company was not involved in decisions for the horse. The Jacksons were committed to doing the right thing by a horse that had provided them with their most treasured moment in horse racing; it was the least they could do for him. But they have done the same for lesser-known horses.

While the Jacksons were determined to do the right thing by their horse, they endured constant rumors pertaining to the reasons for their actions and the consequences thereof. They were accused of trying to benefit from Barbaro's breeding career as the reason for putting Barbaro through "unnecessary pain and torture." Yet they continued to do what they felt was in the horse's best interests without worrying about responding to rumors. Why fuel the fire, when they knew exactly why they were trying to save their horse's life? And they knew it was the right thing to do, rather than the easy thing to do. Throughout Barbaro's time at New Bolton Center, the Jacksons illustrated a certain dignity that is truly endearing to the public, while demonstrating a simple loyalty to their horse. Interestingly, the term "Lael"—the name of their farm and racing stable—is Gaelic for "loyalty."

The Jacksons' class manifested in many instances throughout Barbaro's life. It was a thank-you note to a Fan of Barbaro who had sent a letter wishing Barbaro well. It was a handwritten note of thanks to outrider Sharon Greenberg who was one of the first on the scene at Barbaro's accident at Pimlico. It was a simple nod of thanks to Dr. Dan Dreyfuss after Barbaro was loaded onto the horse ambulance for his journey to New Bolton Center. It was a signed photograph of Barbaro, as an acknowledgment of thanks, for ICU nursing assistant Lindsey March.

The Jacksons also realized, very early on, that while Barbaro was their horse, he had taken on a public persona. Barbaro had become larger than life, and the Jacksons graciously allowed the public access to his condition in a manner that had not been done before. Allowing this access was essential for the development of the following that Barbaro nurtured through the group Fans of Barbaro. Allowing such access also thrust the Jacksons, who are very private and unassuming people, into the public eye along with their horse.

MICHAEL MATZ

There could not have been a better match for the development of Barbaro, and the inspiration that Barbaro provided, than Matz. He is a "horseman's horseman," a man whose career began in the show-jumping arena. Matz is a six-time U.S. National Champion and won the World Cup in 1981 on Jet Run. He won four gold medals at the Pan American Games and represented the U.S. in three Olympic Games, winning a team silver medal at the Atlanta Games in 1996 on Rhum IV. When Matz retired from show jumping, he was the leading money-winning rider in the sport, with $1.7 million in earnings. In April 2006, one month prior to Barbaro's victory in the Kentucky Derby, Matz was inducted into the Show Jumping Hall of Fame.

It was not just that Matz was a brilliant show-jumping rider, but he also was very good with his horses. His quiet style inspired a following among young riders. He was a hero to many young riders who grew up wanting to emulate his quiet way with his horses—an impeccable horseman whose horses are always well turned out.

Matz is also a hero in another sense. Involved in a plane crash in 1989 where 111 people were killed, Matz not only survived but also helped rescue four young children who were seated near him on the plane. He was named "Person of the Week" by *ABC News* for his actions. It was this act of courage that inspired his teammates at the Atlanta Olympic Games to vote for Matz to carry the U.S. flag at the closing ceremonies. Media stories leading up to Barbaro's Kentucky Derby focused much attention on Matz's airplane heroics, which helped make the developing Barbaro story more human and engaging. Yet if you ask Matz, he will say that his actions after the plane crash were not something extraordinary. Matz would argue that anyone in the same circumstances would do what he had done. But you never really know how you would react to a situation until you are placed in such a situation. What we do know is how Matz reacted.

Matz's composure was evident during the Barbaro saga. After winning the Derby and returning to Fair Hill, he held daily media briefings. While many of the questions were appropriate, some certainly would have stretched the patience of most people. "How many hours does Barbaro sleep at night?" was one question that tested that patience. Matz also displayed professionalism when he gave a media briefing at New Bolton Center on the Saturday evening of Preakness Day. After providing an update, he was asked to identify himself. After the briefing, he mentioned to Dr. Barb Dallap that he was very tempted to say that he was Dean Richardson.

Matz does not let his past life events and accomplishments define who he is, and thus limit his aspirations. He looks forward, not backward. Matz was an airplane crash survivor who helped rescue others from the crash. He did not dwell on this experience nor let this experience define who he is. He moved forward. In another sense, Matz is ambitious. He had achieved all that could be accomplished in one equestrian sport, so he decided to move to another for a new set of challenges. Matz became a racehorse trainer and started training in 1996. He retired from show jumping in 2000 after he did not qualify for the upcoming Olympic Games on a horse named Judgment that he had helped develop. This switch to training racehorses was met with disdain from some of those in the show-jumping community. Regardless, Matz made the switch and in less than seven years, he won the Kentucky Derby with Barbaro and a Breeders' Cup race with the filly Round Pond.

Matz does not let conventional wisdom dictate how he does things. He follows his own rules and remains true to himself. Matz decided not to race Barbaro in the Fountain of Youth Stakes because he wanted a fresher horse leading up to the Triple Crown challenge. This is something that he had learned from his days as a show jumper. He also felt positive about Barbaro having a five-week

gap between his final prep race and the Kentucky Derby despite the onslaught of criticism coming from racing media and traditionalists. This was a cornerstone of the plan Matz and Brette developed for Barbaro's Kentucky Derby trail. The plan was unorthodox, but Matz and Brette never wavered. Not only was the plan successful, but perhaps it inspired other trainers to begin to consider different options in terms of preparing their horses for the Kentucky Derby. Two years after Barbaro won the Derby, Big Brown also won the Kentucky Derby after a five-week break.

Matz is a perfectionist. His philosophy is if you work on the little things and get them right, then greater things will happen. By working hard on all the details, you make your own luck. Plain and simple, Matz is a hard worker and absolutely passionate about what he does. He is one of the first people in the barn every morning at 5 a.m. and works until about 2 p.m., seven days a week. This does not include his time at racetracks with his runners and owners. Matz sets high standards and expects those around him to do the same. His horses are out of their stalls and in training a little longer than is the norm in racing circles. While horse-centric, this approach can prove frustrating for some racetrack employees who are more accustomed to a systematic approach to getting horses trained and back in their stalls. No matter, everything Matz does is with the goal of doing the best for the horse. And he does it with a level of intensity that is rarely matched. That was his style as a rider in the show-jumping ring, which he then carried over to his training career.

DEAN RICHARDSON

Head surgeon for Barbaro and chief caretaker during his time at New Bolton Center, Dean Richardson was the fourth member of this critical team. The choice to send Barbaro to Richardson's care was obvious from the outset; he had prior relationships with both the Jacksons and Matz, dating back to Matz's show-jumping days. Barbaro's breakdown also occurred in close proximity to New Bolton Center, making access to Richardson's care obvious. Beyond those two factors, Richardson is considered one of the world's best large animal orthopedic surgeons.

To be a good surgeon, one must possess a certain self-belief. Some may consider this arrogance, but it is self-confidence that you know you can help your patient, no matter how novel the surgery required. All surgeries present their own unique circumstances. Obviously, Barbaro's surgery was particularly challenging, and Richardson and the team he led needed to be world-class to provide Barbaro a chance of survival. A surgeon needs to be innovative and must have the courage to try new treatments. Richardson had both the confidence and the courage required to undertake the challenge of trying to save Barbaro.

Richardson is also very passionate about what he does. Very similar to Matz in this regard, Richardson would be almost consumed by the Barbaro experience during the eight months Barbaro spent at New Bolton Center. The passion was driven from two fronts: Richardson loves horses and loved Barbaro, so he obviously wanted more than anything for Barbaro to live. The passion is also driven by intellect. Richardson has a remarkable intellect, and Barbaro as a case study presented challenges that would push that intellect to its limit. With all the resources at his disposal, could Richardson lead a team to save the horse he had come to love?

Richardson is also a teacher who has won numerous teaching awards at the University of Pennsylvania. As a teacher, Richardson believes everything is a teachable moment. He can be tough on his students, and there is no doubt some do fear him, especially early in their tenure. But Richardson expects the best from everyone around him, and that will only make those who study with him better.

It was Richardson's passion for horses that nearly led him down a similar path as that of Matz. But then he chose to pursue a career path to become an orthopedic surgeon for large animals, principally horses. His love for horses was clearly illustrated throughout the eight months Barbaro was in Richardson's care. Was Richardson devastated during the period in July when Barbaro first contracted laminitis? Of course. Was Richardson devastated when the realization set in that Barbaro had given up and it was time to euthanize him? Absolutely. Richardson had become attached to a patient that had charisma in bucket loads. Not all surgeons are horsemen, but being a horseman makes you a better caregiver. That's Richardson.

Richardson began his college education as a theater major at Dartmouth College. While he did not complete this path, Richardson is definitely charismatic in front of an audience. Richardson was the interface to the public during Barbaro's stay at New Bolton Center and as such, helped engage his audience with his confidence and easily understandable rhetoric. Richardson was able to balance a level of frankness regarding Barbaro's condition with a level of compassion.

EDGAR PRADO

Edgar Prado was neither core to the team that developed Barbaro, nor the team that attempted to save him; he was a smaller part of both. Prado was also the initial face to the situation on Preakness Day. Many attribute Prado's quick actions on Preakness Day as heroic in terms of how quickly he pulled up Barbaro when it was clear to him that the horse was in trouble. Prado then held Barbaro while others came to their aid. Clearly, Prado was distraught by the sudden change in circumstances and his anguish was displayed, via the media, for all to see. Prado put a human face to the tragic situation and demonstrated very visibly that horsemen really do care. Prado gave the Barbaro story an immediate human angle.

Prado was the face of triumph, after winning the Kentucky Derby, and then tragedy, after pulling up in the Preakness. Prado and Barbaro's relationship developed from moments of their greatest success together to that of a catastrophic event. Those swings of highs and lows bonded a relationship that would play out over the course of eight months at New Bolton Center, as Prado made six scheduled and unscheduled visits to see Barbaro.

Was Prado always bonded with Barbaro, as some would suggest, throughout their relationship? The facts do not necessarily support this. He only rode Barbaro on five occasions. And up until three weeks before the Kentucky Derby, Prado had not committed to riding Barbaro in the big race. Prado had other horses to test. His goal was to be on the horse that would give him the best chance to win the Kentucky Derby. He, and his agent at the time, Bob Frieze, only determined that horse was Barbaro after the Blue Grass Stakes at Keeneland. Some of this "posturing" may have been related to Frieze's strained relationship with Matz, a result of their decision to switch off the Matz-trained Kickin Kris in the Arlington Million in 2004. Kickin Kris won that race, under Kent Desormeaux, on the disqualification of Powerscourt.

Did Prado really bond with Barbaro, or was this a myth developed by the media and supported by those who wanted to see such a bond? Barbaro provided Prado his most prized moment in our sport—a Kentucky Derby win. Then, two weeks later, Prado's Triple Crown dreams were shattered as his champion was now in a new fight for his life. Prado provided the support Barbaro needed to begin that fight, and he then supported Barbaro throughout his eight-month struggle. He visited Barbaro at New Bolton Center on six occasions. Jeannine Edwards described Prado's visible relief when he saw Barbaro for the first time during his first visit to New Bolton Center.

It seems clear that Prado cared deeply about Barbaro.

Prado's own personal story is one of striving and grief. He grew up poor in Peru, the second youngest of eleven children. He began his riding career in Peru, and moved to America in 1986. Prado won a number of riding titles and established himself on the Maryland circuit before breaking into the "big time" in New York. Prado eclipsed five thousand wins in 2004, becoming the nineteenth jockey to do so. He won the Belmont Stakes twice, upsetting two potential Triple Crown efforts, War Emblem in 2002 and Smarty Jones in 2004. Prado won his first Breeders' Cup races aboard Folklore and Silver Train in 2005. In 2006, he won the Breeders' Cup Distaff aboard Round Pond for Matz. Prado's journey to success was punctuated by the loss of his mother to breast cancer, early in 2006. Prado had been trying to get his mother to the United States for treatment; sadly, permission for this to happen was only granted on the day she passed. Prado dedicated his Florida Derby and Kentucky Derby wins aboard Barbaro to his mother.

THE MEDIA'S ROLE

A third critical element that explains why Barbaro inspired was the public's knowledge of the ongoing saga. Traditional media provided much attention to the story, especially at three specific points. Internet media provided persistent coverage of the story.

The Preakness tragedy became a national news event, broadcast on mainstream media and over the Internet. Barbaro's following days at New Bolton Center were closely watched and reported. On Saturday night following the Preakness breakdown, Bloodhorse.com crashed due to heavy traffic. The next evening, Sunday night, TimWoolleyRacing.com did the same. The need for current information about Barbaro's condition seemed insatiable.

As Barbaro's condition stabilized mainstream media's attention began to wane. When Barbaro's left hind foot contracted laminitis in July, however, it re-emerged in a frenzy. Eventually when Barbaro was euthanized he again gained the attention of a national media audience. As far as mainstream media was concerned, the Barbaro story had crossed out of the niche audience of horse racing fans into a much broader audience of animal lovers.

This drove ESPN, the number one sports network in the world, to devote more time to Barbaro than any other equine-related story, *ever*. Barbaro's coverage appeared regularly on *Sports Center*, he was featured on "Outside the Lines," and was covered on ABC's (owner of ESPN) *Good Morning America* several times. ESPN also covered Barbaro updates when they broadcast other horse racing events. For example, when ESPN was covering the 2006 Arlington Million, Jeannine Edwards interviewed the Jacksons, who were in attendance to watch Showing Up run in the Secretariat Stakes on the undercard. During that interview, it was revealed that Barbaro had been outside to graze for the first time during the previous week.

The Associated Press (AP) also made a deliberate decision that this story was important. The main AP reporter for the Barbaro story was Dan Gelston, who published more than fifty stories in the eight months Barbaro was at New Bolton Center. When the AP was not publishing stories on Barbaro's progress, it released daily "charts" on his well-being.

Local media, including the *Philadelphia Inquirer* (Mike Jensen), *Baltimore Sun* (Sandy McKee), and Wilmington's *News Journal* (Jack Ireland) also reported on this story in a fashion that was not typical of a regular horse racing story.

"Everywhere I traveled for work, in the airport or at sporting events, people outside the sport of horse racing, with no connection to it whatsoever, would come up to me and ask about Barbaro," said Edwards. "No one ever asked, 'Why are they putting the horse through that?' It was always genuine empathy and great interest in the horse's condition. I got this from basketball and football players, coaches, other media members, regular John Does on planes. They'd see me and ask, 'How's that horse doing?' There seemed to be an unprecedented amount of interest in his plight; it was incredible how many people were touched by his story."

Of course, there were significant lulls in the story throughout Barbaro's eight months at New Bolton Center. That is where Internet media helped keep the story current and top of mind for those who cared about how Barbaro was faring on a daily basis. New Bolton Center would publish daily updates via the Internet, which sometimes switched to weekly updates. Other sites, including TimWoolleyRacing.com, established a discussion board for fans to share information, comments, and feedback on Barbaro's condition and the pursuit of his legacy.

"You kept people in [referring to TimWoolleyRacing.com and our more-than-daily-updates on Barbaro's condition]; it was another crucial element," explained Jensen. "There was a gathering place and people fed off each other. Twofold: they were getting real-time updates from the principals and they were able to form a community."

"Outside of the community, it was sort of laughed at and mocked," he continued. "It became a source of derision; within the community there were real sentiments, over the top, sure sometimes, absolutely. People were validated. Some people felt that way, some people thought that way. Some went to greater extremes."

Internet media's support of Barbaro's story allowed it to remain current through his time at New Bolton Center, and allowed the story to persist once Barbaro had passed. As one of the Internet media sites, we (TimWoolleyRacing.com) often obtained Barbaro news that was not yet public information. Rather than release the news, work commenced with mainstream media to ensure the news was released appropriately. This occurred during the aforementioned release of the news that Barbaro had been out grazing for the first time. We worked with Edwards so the news would become public in a timely fashion. We did the same with Jensen and the *Philadelphia Inquirer* during the final weekend of Barbaro's life. Our goal was not to break news, but rather to help the public stay informed.

Richardson and the New Bolton Center team received awards for how they worked with media to provide access to the Barbaro story. The entire Barbaro team received a special Eclipse Award. Michael Jensen received an Eclipse Award for a profile story on Dr. Richardson.

The story itself was highlighted as one of the top horse racing and sports stories of 2006 in a variety of media. Steve Haskin considered it horse racing's story of the decade.

Ultimately, everybody seemed to know Barbaro.

WAS IT WRONG TO FOLLOW A HORSE THAT MOST DID NOT KNOW DIRECTLY?

There was some criticism leveled at the notion that Barbaro was simply a horse with whom most people did not have a direct connection. The argument was that there are people starving in this world, and it is more important to focus energies on finding solutions to these bigger problems than to worry about the condition of a horse. All the money spent on trying to save the horse could surely be used more appropriately.

The reality is that, while there are many meaningful issues we need to address, focusing energy on hoping that a horse recovers does not take away from other important efforts. An editorial in the *Japanese Times*, "Sympathy for a Racehorse," noted that compassion is not an either/or proposition. One can have compassion for a horse while also being concerned about broader issues. It is quite likely those who did have compassion for Barbaro are the same people who care about other issues. Barbaro provided inspiration for many good things to occur because of his struggle at New Bolton Center. Those who followed him were inspired to perform good works in his name for other causes, such as supporting laminitis research, and lobbying for anti-horse slaughter legislation. He was a true catalyst for compassion and change.

CULTURAL TIES TO THE HORSE

Barbaro is far from the first horse to prove inspirational and to illustrate humans' strong bond with the horse. Since the beginning of time, man has had a unique connection with the horse. According to an old Arab proverb, "The horse is God's gift to mankind."

Humans have long been enamored with the beauty, grace, and courage of this gallant creature. The horse also represents a sense of freedom, and the fact that horses allow men to "tame" them only contributes to their unique appeal. In ancient Rome and Greece, horses were lauded for their heroics in war; some, such as Alexander the Great's Bucephalus, earned a special place in history. Later, horses such as Robert E. Lee's Traveller and General Custer's Comanche became well-known for their heroic partnerships with man. Horses are praised in various works of art, literature, and poetry. This reverence began with early cave drawings and continues into the present time. Anna Sewell's book, *Black Beauty*, written in 1877, remains one of the best-selling books of all time, with more than 50 million copies sold. Other equine-themed books, such as *The Black Stallion* and *Seabiscuit*, inspired Academy Award–nominated films. Even Shakespeare recognized the glory of the horse when he penned the famous line from *Richard III*: "A horse! A horse! My kingdom for a horse!"

Equines played a crucial role in the shaping of human history. As early colonies developed, horses were utilized to haul plows and other heavy machinery through the fields and to transport crops. With its natural power, a single horse maintained the strength of fifty men, thus originating the term "horsepower." Horses also pulled covered wagons to bring settlers to new frontiers, and saved many people by carrying emergency personnel and equipment when needed. In 1860, with the establishment of the Pony Express in the U.S., mail was delivered ten times faster than it had been in previous years; this allowed people to better communicate via the written word, prior to the creation of the telegraph.

While the advent of the automobile and electric machinery resulted in less work for the horse, equine sports, particularly racing, became popular with folks of varied social classes.

Around the turn of the century, America found a hero in pacer Dan Patch, perhaps the most famous sports star of his time. The colt set various records on the track, and thrilled both the media and the general public with his talent and charm.

Legend has it that Dan Patch would survey the crowds at his performances, which sometimes drew more than sixty thousand spectators. It was said that he would nod his head to the crowds. Dan Patch traveled around the country in a railcar, and people of all ages would wait in line for hours to get a glimpse of the champion horse. Dan Patch became a cultural icon, with more than thirty products (including an automobile) bearing his name, and served as the inspiration for two songs, a feature film, and the book *Crazy Good* by Charles Leerhsen.

In the 1920s, horse racing ranked second to baseball as America's favorite pastime. It was the Golden Age of Sports, in which prosperity reigned and outstanding athletes became bona fide heroes. In baseball, the hero of the era was George Herman "Babe" Ruth; in horse racing, it was Man o' War. The great chestnut, known fittingly as "Big Red," shattered the record books and rewrote history with a series of outstanding victories. While he never raced in Kentucky, the valiant colt handily won the Preakness and the Belmont and is still regarded by many as the greatest racehorse of all time. Man o' War subsequently enjoyed a successful career at stud, siring, among others, 1937 Triple Crown champion War Admiral. (He also was the grandsire, through Hard Tack, of another much-loved champion, Seabiscuit.) After retiring from racing, Man o' War's fan base remained huge; it is estimated that more than a million people visited him at Faraway Farm in Kentucky. In fact, Man o' War was so revered that an elaborate funeral service was held when he passed away in 1947 at the age of thirty. Thousands viewed his body as it lay in state, and his funeral was broadcast via radio. An archived version of the radio broadcast is still available on the Internet. Man o' War's burial site at Faraway Farm was moved to the Kentucky Horse Park in the 1970s, when the Horse Park was built. This move placed Man o' War's Memorial in a much more public location, and as such, helps preserve his legacy for future generations. The memorial at the Kentucky Horse Park is considered by many as the most significant memorial to any horse in North America. Man o' War has also become the subject of various popular books; his legend continues to this day.

While Man o' War was making a name for himself in America, another great chestnut, Phar Lap, took Australia by storm. Born in 1926, Phar Lap gave

Australians a sense of hope as the Great Depression began to take hold. Like the equine heroes before him, Phar Lap represented strength and courage in the face of adversity. His sudden death in 1932 devastated millions, as he had become a cultural icon in both Australia and in his birthplace of New Zealand. Cards and letters of condolence poured in from all areas of the world. Phar Lap would later become the subject of a song, several books, and a film. His body was preserved and has been displayed at the Melbourne Museum, which still celebrates his birthday to this day; his skeleton is on display in the Te Papa Museum in Wellington, New Zealand, which I have visited, and a life-sized bronze statue of Phar Lap in full gallop may be viewed at Timaru Racecourse in New Zealand.

Another of history's most popular equine heroes was a plucky bay colt by the name of Seabiscuit. An unlikely hero—being small and knock-kneed with questionable conformation—Seabiscuit entered the scene at the height of the Depression. Folks were able to identify with the feeling of being an underdog, and pinned their hopes for victory on him. When Seabiscuit defeated Triple Crown champion War Admiral in a match race in 1938, Americans felt that they too could overcome adversity. Seabiscuit became a hero for the common person. His story would reach greater heights several decades after his death, when author Laura Hillenbrand penned the bestseller, *Seabiscuit: An American Legend*.

While several horses made history in 1940s, '50s, and '60s, the great Secretariat eclipsed them all in 1973. The early 1970s was a time of unrest, as political tensions mounted and the U.S. was faced with various crises such as the Vietnam War and the Nixon Watergate scandal. Secretariat, a magnificent chestnut colt, became a horse for the ages as he won the Kentucky Derby in a track record that has stood the test of time, and won the Belmont by thirty-one lengths to become the first Triple Crown winner in twenty-five years. Nicknamed "Big Red" (a moniker shared by both Man o' War and Phar Lap), Secretariat helped bring the nation back to its feet, introducing a whole new generation to the meaning of greatness in sport. He became a true celebrity. In a single week, Secretariat's photo appeared on the cover of *Time*, *Sports Illustrated*, and *Newsweek*. As his owner Penny Chenery once stated, "This red horse with blue and white blinkers and silks seemed to epitomize an American hero."

The 1970s would also witness the brilliance of Ruffian, a stunningly beautiful filly whose life was cut short by tragedy. Tall, strong, and undefeated, Ruffian became a symbol of courage for anyone who dared to challenge adversity. She became a hero to women who admired her strength in taking on the male establishment. Ruffian's heroic spirit became even more evident when she continued running on three legs after sustaining what would ultimately become a fatal injury. It was a match race against the reigning Derby champion, Foolish Pleasure, a colt—and Ruffian's great heart was not about to give up. As she underwent surgery to repair the injury, fans prayed for the great filly to survive. The nation mourned when she was euthanized later that night. Like the various equine heroes before her, Ruffian was a warrior whose heart would not give out. To this day, she remains a symbol of hope to those who face tremendous challenges.

Equine heroes are aplenty in Great Britain. Horses that have long and highly successful careers are revered there. Oftentimes these are steeplechase horses, but also some campaigners on the flat, like Yeats and Persian Punch, are able to capture the imagination of the public as they race at the highest levels year in and year out.

Of the steeplechase horses, Arkle, Red Rum, and Desert Orchid stand out as exceptional. Arkle, who campaigned in the 1960s, is considered the best steeplechase horse of all times. Among his many victories were three Cheltenham Gold Cups. Arkle was a national legend in Ireland and was often referred to simply as "Himself."

Red Rum developed a large fan base while winning three Grand Nationals and coming second in his two other attempts, from 1973 to 1977. I attended all five races. Upon retirement, Red Rum developed a second career, as a celebrity attending events and opening ceremonies.

"A three-year-old racehorse is like a college athlete, blooming in front of us. The very best ones not only show they can make it in open company—until something proves otherwise, they let us enjoy the idea of unlimited potential.

"Ever since his brilliant three-year-old season in 1920, Man o' War has represented that highest standard. He retired from racing with the impression of something still untapped. Fifty-three years later, Secretariat reached the same heights and left the track with a similar aura of still unknown possibilities. We are still waiting for their heir.

"In the brief time given him, Barbaro could not prove whether he belonged with Man o' War and Secretariat on the racetrack. But until that awful moment at Pimlico, he had taken the right steps toward that highest threshold. Like Secretariat, he excelled on both turf and dirt. Like Man o' War (who suffered one controversial defeat), he remained unbeaten through steeper and steeper challenges. Like both, he relished a classic distance and exalted in his own ability. This quality burst forth in his Derby stretch run, with Barbaro rocketing away from the pack at his rider's signal, then increasing his margin under no urging but his own energy.

"Like Man o' War, like Secretariat, Barbaro left racing before he reached his prime. Like them, he opened hearts and imaginations wide. Although he never can reach the standard set by both 'Big Reds' at the track, his great spirit found an answering spirit: good will and generosity."

—DOROTHY OURS,
Author of *Man O'War: A Legend Like Lightning*

More recently, Desert Orchid created a huge following by winning four King George Steeplechases from 1986 to 1990. It was his win in the Cheltenham Gold Cup in 1989, however, on a racecourse he disliked and in heavy ground that he detested, that illustrated his sheer courage. Upon retirement, Desert Orchid made a number of charitable appearances attended by people throughout the United Kingdom. These examples illustrate that racehorses in the U.K. are bona-fide stars.

Because horse racing is a more popular sport in Great Britain than in the United States, even some of the stars of the flat that are not around for too long are able to generate a passionate following. The Jackson-bred George Washington, "Gorgeous George," who was as well-known for his quirky behavior as his brilliance (he was champion two-year-old and three-year-old in the U.K.), fits this category.

Equine heroes in Great Britain are not limited to racehorses. The show jumper Milton generated a huge fan following and IRA bombing survivor Sefton died a national hero.

Other countries have equine heroes as well. In Japan, a gray colt named Oguri Cap became a household name in the late 1980s with twelve graded race wins in twenty starts. Affectionately regarded as the "Grey Monster," he began his career at the local government tracks and quickly became a fan favorite. In 1990, he capped off a highly successful career with a victory in the Arima Kinen in front of a record crowd of 177,779. Many fans regard this win as the greatest moment in Japanese racing history. According to sources, the horse was so popular in retirement that the stallion farm constructed bleachers near his paddock in order to accommodate his many fans.

In Hungary, Overdose is their modern-day equivalent of Seabiscuit. Purchased almost by accident for 2,100 British pounds at a sale in Newmarket (U.K.) in 2006, Overdose's future did not look bright. Taken to Hungary to train, he reeled off fourteen wins before he was beaten for the first time. He won in Hungary as well as at other prestigious racetracks in Europe. Overdose has helped bring pride back to a nation that was dismantled by the Trianon Treaty of 1920, and the communist regime that followed. Overdose won the Prix de l'Abbaye, a top sprinting race in Europe, only for the victory to be voided by a faulty starting gate. Ironically, this event occurred not far from where the Trianon Treaty was signed. In a culture that is accustomed to failure and doom, Overdose has demonstrated a winning mentality. Known as the "Budapest Bullet," Overdose has also allowed the memories of the great race mare Kincsem to resurface. Kincsem won all of her fifty-four races in the late 1870s, setting an unbeaten record that still stands today. Kincsem was a national treasure and when she succumbed to colic later in her life, Hungarian flags were flown at half mast.

When Barbaro was born in 2003, the world—and America in particular—was at a crossroads. The nation was reeling from the devastating impact of the terrorist attacks of September 11, 2001, and the threat of another assault loomed large. Troops were fighting what appeared to be unending wars in Iraq and Afghanistan. Natural disasters and school shootings made the news, and the economy began to fail. Employment rates plummeted. Even baseball had become tainted, as its athletes were found to have used performance-enhancing steroids and bats made of illegal materials. The message was clear: America was desperately in need of a hero.

Barbaro became that hero. Like Man o' War, Phar Lap, and Secretariat before him, Barbaro showed tremendous speed and power on the track. He had the swagger of an athlete, the bravery of a warrior in battle, and the stunning good looks of a movie star. Like Seabiscuit, Barbaro arrived at a time when fans were in need of inspiration. He brought interest back to the "sport of kings," a sport in decline. And like the beautiful and talented Ruffian, he represented great promise unfulfilled—and the bravery to continue fighting in the face of severe injury. It was a perfect combination of all of these things that made Barbaro a cultural icon.

"In the past fifty-five years, which is about the same length of time that I have been following horse racing, only three events come to mind which were of a transcendent nature—in other words, events that moved people who were outside of our sport," explained Vic Zast. "Only two of those three events included horses racing during this period. The other was Laura Hillenbrand's Seabiscuit

book and the Oscar-nominated movie that followed about a horse that captivated the public's attention in the 1930s. The two events that involved horses racing during the period were the triumph of Secretariat in the mid-1970s and the tragedy of Barbaro at the beginning of this century."

"Other great events may seem monumental to people in our sport, like the rivalry between Affirmed and Alydar, the string of victories by Cigar, the deaths of Ruffian and Eight Belles," he continued. "But they weren't transcendental in effect when compared to Secretariat and Barbaro. Secretariat and Barbaro were events that moved the needle; they caused a stir. They enabled people to tap into a phenomenon."

Overdose

"The stories of Seabiscuit and Barbaro hit a core myth of humanity, the Hero's Journey—every religion that exists today has this myth in some form or another. To context how this myth plays out in both horses you can look at the times they lived in—Seabiscuit raised a broken nation off its knees, became the horse of the common man—made possible by the collective team of Howard, Pollard, Smith, and Seabiscuit himself.

"I believe Barbaro struck a different chord in us, because we had to see (via TV) the horrific nature of his injury, the footage of him trying to move away from that pain, triggers that in all of us. Barbaro showed us that something so powerful could be so vulnerable and the Jacksons showed us that racing may not be dispensable after all. Barbaro became the wounded king (fracture was on the right, side of the masculine), and perhaps, Dr. Richardson became Parsifal, looking for a way (the Holy Grail) to heal the wounded king.

"Finally, I think the larger theme here is what horses teach humans every day, because they solely exist in the present moment—we saw that in Barbaro's relationship to his injury, taking everything in stride, but being pretty real about when he wasn't feeling well. We could take a lesson from that."

—FOB JULIE BRIDGE

HOW DID THE INSPIRATION MANIFEST?

While Part Three of this book will explore the effect of Barbaro's legacy, here I will highlight the means with which that legacy has worked by examining two ideas; "little things add up and make a difference," and "many people, working together, can make a difference."

In 1969, anthropologist and poet Loren Eiseley wrote an essay called "The Star Thrower." As part of this essay, Eiseley told a tale that illustrated how even the smallest acts of kindness can make a difference in the world. The story began with an older man walking along the beach where thousands of starfish had been washed upon the shore. His attention was quickly drawn to a figure that appeared to be dancing on the sand. Upon closer inspection, he realized that the figure was, in fact, a child. He was not dancing, as it had initially appeared, but rather was gently picking up the starfish and throwing them, one by one, back into the ocean. The man was puzzled by the child's actions and asked what he was doing. The boy replied that he was trying to save the starfish. When the cynical old man replied that the boy could not clearly save all of the starfish, the boy picked one up, tossed it softly into the sea, and smiled, "It will make a difference to this one!"

Eiseley's story has appeared in several incarnations since its original publication. It has been used by motivational speakers and translated into several languages. Sometimes the child is a boy, sometimes a girl, but the message remains the same. Acts of kindness, no matter how small or seemingly insignificant, can have a greater impact on the world. The affect that Barbaro had on people mirrors Eiseley's message. In fact, a significant part of the Barbaro story is the work done in his name by those who followed his condition and were inspired by his courage.

"After his surgery at New Bolton Center, when things started arriving from all parts of the U.S. and around the world, we realized he had touched a lot of people's hearts," said Gretchen Jackson. "People were standing on the overpasses of I-95 when he was in transit from Pimlico, and then they followed up with notes and gifts at New Bolton Center. It was amazing. The unidentified donor who began the Barbaro Fund in Barbaro's honor started a momentum all of its own. The momentum has continued; it is just amazing how wide reaching it has become. We are honored."

Often when a crisis occurs, people react quickly and work together to help out; however, once the crisis is over, attention begins to fade. People move on with their lives, and new events generate media attention. Yet Barbaro's situation was far from typical. The courage he displayed during his eight-month struggle inspired and unified people from all walks of life. Some were lifelong horsemen, while others had never even seen a horse up close. Their common denominator was that each had been touched by Barbaro's courage and grace, and were committed to do whatever they could to contribute to a larger cause—horse welfare. If they could not help Barbaro, they could help another horse in his memory.

"Barbaro's coverage was inspiring and those who supported the story were also inspiring," said ESPN's Edwards. "Regular people, contributing $50 here, $100 there all in Barbaro's name. Generosity feeds upon itself and it was truly amazing. The devotion they showed was what made the whole story so remarkable."

Like the child who made a difference by saving the starfish that had washed up on the shore, small contributions by so many people have made a major difference in the equine world. While one person cannot be expected to tackle the larger issue of horse welfare, many people working together can make a difference. In saving a horse, for example, many people work together. One person notes that the horse is in need; another person agrees to save the horse from slaughter; yet another provides transportation; and others contribute to the horse's expenses. Like the starfish, the rescue of even a single horse makes a difference for that horse, and thus contributes to the larger issue of horse welfare.

"Greatness was the beginning; the goodness is what is going to go on forever," summarized Kathy Anderson. "The legacy of that is tremendous. His followers can impact an outcome. With this you can make a difference. It will have a name on it. It will be Real Lace. It will be so and so. But it will be a horse you can identify. That's huge."

A Photographic Essay

▲ **1** KATHEE RENGERT initiated the discussions that led to the purchase of La Ville Rouge, Barbaro's dam, by the Jacksons. Kathee is a friend of the Jacksons and is a lifelong horsewoman. She was a steeplechase rider for Hall of Fame trainer Mikey Smithwick. Kathee is now a bloodstock agent, photographer, and works at Fair Hill Training Center.

Kathee attended Barbaro's first race at Delaware Park. Her reaction to seeing Barbaro for the first time was similar to the reactions she experienced when she first saw Seattle Slew and Forego. Kathee was very helpful during my writing of this book. *Kathee Rengert*

▼ **2** LA VILLE ROUGE, Barbaro's dam, was purchased by the Jacksons early in her racing career. She ran for three years and earned more than $250,000. She was graded stakes placed. As of 2010, La Ville Rouge has produced six foals: Holy Ground (by Saint Ballado), Man in Havana (by Quiet American), and three full brothers to Barbaro—Nicanor, Lentenor, and Margano. Holy Ground is a stakes winner and now a stallion. Man in Havana did not race, but is now a show jumper and fox hunter.

Both Nicanor and Lentenor have shown promise early in their careers. Margano was just a yearling at the time of this writing. In 2010, La Ville Rouge was bred back to Dynaformer and confirmed in foal. The Jacksons are hoping for a full sister to Barbaro. *Courtesy Mill Ridge Farm/Joy Gilbert*

▲**3** DYNAFORMER (1), Barbaro's sire, earned $671,207 in a career spanning three years. He won two Grade 2 races: the 1988 Jersey Derby (photograph) and the 1988 Discovery Handicap. He won 7 of 30 starts and equalled two track records. D. Wayne Lukas referred to Dynaformer as "the most difficult horse" he has trained. *Courtesy Three Chimneys Farm*

▲**4** DYNAFORMER ENTERED stud for a $5,000 fee at Wafare Farm, Midway, Kentucky, in 1990. He moved to Three Chimneys Farm in 1995. When La Ville Rouge was first bred to Dynaformer, his stud fee had increased to $50,000. By 2010, his stud fee was $150,000, and he was considered one of the leading sires in North America. Dynaformer's stud fee had increased at a time when the majority of stallions' fees were being reduced due to the poor economy and a downturn in the business of horse racing. While Barbaro is his most famous son, Dynaformer has sired a number of good runners that have had long careers. These include Perfect Drift ($4,714,213), Dynever ($2,640,444), and Film Maker ($2,203,730). *Courtesy Three Chimneys Farm/Tony Leonard*

▼ **5** BILL AND SANDY SANBORN ran Sanborn Chase, a breeding operation, at Springmint Farm, in Nicholasville, Kentucky, until 2005. Bill has worked in the breeding business for more than thirty years, and had boarded horses for the Jacksons since 1994. Barbaro spent seventeen months in the care of Bill Sanborn before heading to Florida and the care of John and Jill Stephens. This photograph was taken in July 2006. *Anne Eberhardt*

▲ **6** BARN FOUR, Sanborn Chase, at Springmint Farm, is the birthplace of Barbaro who was born on April 29, 2003. Barbaro spent the majority of his first seventeen months in Barn Four when he was not turned out in one of the paddocks. Here I am, visiting the site, in October 2010. *Matt Wooley/Equisport Photos*

▲ **7** THIS IS ONE of the very few foal pictures of Barbaro. It is a snapshot of a photograph from the Jacksons' collection. Barbaro was about six weeks old when this picture was taken. He is standing outside his barn. Barbaro is being held by groom Jimmy Preston, who worked for Bill Sanborn for eleven years. Barbaro was foaled by Bill Sanborn and night watchman Irvin White. *Courtesy Roy and Gretchen Jackson, and Rai Phelan*

▼**8** HEADLEY BELL is the bloodstock advisor for the Jacksons, and in that capacity would visit the Jacksons' foals and yearlings, take notes, and fax those reports to the Jacksons. Here are three of Headley's notes on Barbaro. The first note describes Barbaro as a two-month-old foal. The second was from a visit on January 7, 2004, and the third was from the beginning of April that year. In all three reports, it is clear that Barbaro was impressive from a very early age. *Matt Wooley/Equisport Photos*

'03 Colt by Dynaformer/La Ville Rouge – A very big colt who is quite strong and has very good use. Considering he is a Dynaformer, he has good quality and hopefully won't be too big.

'03 Colt by Dynaformer/La Ville Rouge – Also a very nice individual especially for being by Dynaformer. He has good scope and balance with the scope. He is also a natural mover and has a very good presence.

'03 Colt by Dynaformer/La Ville Rouge – I am very pleased with this colt as well. When you breed to Dynaformer you never quite know what you are going to get. But he is an excellent stallion as demonstrated by his ever-increasing stud fee. This is a strong colt that is quite athletic and a racehorse.

▲**9** JILL AND JOHN STEPHENS at Saratoga in 2008. Barbaro was sent to the Stephenses' farm in Florida in September 2004 to receive his early education. He spent seven months at Stephens Thoroughbreds, where he progressed from being a yearling that had never been ridden to a two-year-old that was "two-minute-licking" three-eighths of a mile. Jill was the first person to sit on Barbaro. *Courtesy Jill and John Stephens*

▲ **10** THIS VICTORIAN era lithograph of six foxhounds, belonging to a French nobleman, Comte de Barral, was the inspiration for naming Barbaro and his three full brothers, Nicanor, Lentenor, and Margano. The lithograph hung in the kitchen of Roy Jackson's family home during his childhood. Years later, the Jacksons discovered the lithograph in an attic. It now hangs in their living room at Lael Farm. Mrs. Jackson confessed that it is becoming more and more difficult to name horses. This lithograph simply provided her a new source of names. *Rai Phelan*

▼ **11** BARBARO ARRIVED at Fair Hill Training Center, into the care of trainer Michael Matz, on April 29, 2005. Michael can be seen each day out on his pony Messaging. Messaging is a thoroughbred, born in 2000, by Jade Hunter. Michael trained Messaging as a young horse; he had four official workouts, but never raced. He was Barbaro's constant companion throughout the time Michael trained Barbaro.

Michael was a world-class show jumper and Olympian before switching his attention to training racehorses. He also survived a plane crash where he helped save the lives of four young children.

Michael adopted an unorthodox training schedule for Barbaro that was heavily criticized in the media leading up to the Derby, but then lauded for its genius after the Derby. Michael would be a constant visitor to Barbaro during the colt's stay at New Bolton Center before heading south to Florida in November 2006 with the rest of his horses in training. *Rai Phelan*

▲ **12** PETER BRETTE rode Barbaro in most of his gallops and his breezes. In fact, Michael Matz asked Peter if he wanted to ride Barbaro in his first race; Peter declined the offer.

A native of England, Peter was a jockey in the U.K. before moving to Dubai (United Arab Emirates) for ten years; there he became a champion jockey and then a trainer. In 2005, Peter, along with his wife Kim and young son Nicholas, moved to the United States and soon joined Michael Matz. Peter and Michael worked closely together to plan out Barbaro's career. Peter also visited Barbaro regularly during his time at New Bolton Center before leaving for Florida in November 2006. *Rai Phelan*

13 – 14 ADAM DAVISON and TERESA THOMAS also had the pleasure of riding Barbaro from time to time. In fact, including his jockeys, twelve people rode Barbaro. Teresa rode him a bit when he first arrived at Fair Hill. She also rode many of his work partners when Peter worked Barbaro. Adam rode Barbaro a few times in Florida, when Peter had a day off. *Rai Phelan*

15 DR. KATHY ANDERSON, a partner in Equine Veterinary Care, based at Fair Hill Training Center, is Michael Matz's main veterinarian and, as such, was Barbaro's vet. Kathy is originally from western Canada. Kathy called Barbaro "next year's Kentucky Derby winner" after his first start. Kathy hosted parties for the horsemen at Fair Hill to watch both Barbaro's Derby win and the Preakness. Kathy would be a constant visitor to Barbaro during his time at New Bolton Center, and was very helpful during my writing of this book. *Rai Phelan*

16 JOSE CARABALLO was Barbaro's jockey for his first two starts—the two races that yielded Barbaro's largest winning margins. Jose is based in the Mid-Atlantic region, riding at tracks such as Delaware Park (where this photograph was taken in 2010) and Philadelphia Park.

In his career, Jose has ridden more than two thousand winners. Originally from Puerto Rico, Jose began his U.S. career at Thistledown Racetrack in Ohio. After a stint at Suffolk Downs in Boston, he relocated to the Mid-Atlantic region. Jose attended both parties hosted by Kathy Anderson to watch Barbaro's Triple Crown races. *Andie Bicho*

17 JOHN CURRAN is Delaware Park's race caller, and, as such, called Barbaro's first race. "This could be a good one" was his remark as Barbaro was heading to the wire many lengths in front. John had not picked Barbaro from a handicapping standpoint for the race, but when he saw him leave the paddock, he changed his mind quickly. That December, John was in Las Vegas and placed a wager on Barbaro to win the Kentucky Derby; he got odds of 85-1! *Author*

18 MAIDEN WIN at Delaware Park October 4, 2005: This is the only publicly available photograph of Barbaro's first win in his first race, which was on the turf. Jose Caraballo is just perched on top, guiding Barbaro to this emphatic win by a little over eight lengths. It was enough to convince Michael Matz to put Barbaro in a stakes race for his very next start. *Hoofprints.com*

19 SECOND WIN in the Laurel Futurity, November 19, 2005: Barbaro displayed his high knee-action on his way to winning his second start, just as easily as he won his first start, again on the turf. He also appeared to be "flying," with all four feet off the ground. This was very typical of Barbaro and is seen in all the subsequent racing photographs in this book. *Lydia Williams*

▶ **20** THIRD WIN in the Tropical Park Derby, January 1, 2006: After his Laurel Futurity win, Barbaro moved to Florida along with the rest of Michael Matz's horses. From his new base at Palm Meadows, Barbaro won the first Derby of 2006, the Tropical Park Derby at Calder Race Course. This was his third straight win on the turf, and his first win under his new jockey Edgar Prado. It was another very easy win. Questions were now being asked as to when Michael Matz would try Barbaro on the dirt and whether he would be pointed toward the Triple Crown.

The 2006 Tropical Park Derby was a Grade 3 event. Graded stakes races are more prestigious than non-graded stakes. Grade 1 is the most prestigious graded stake and thus, the most prestigious type of race. Money earned in the Tropical Park Derby would help Barbaro gain a place in the Kentucky Derby if he was pointed toward that race, as graded stakes earnings are used to prioritize which horses earn a berth in the Kentucky Derby. *Jim Lisa*

◀ **21** EDGAR PRADO became Barbaro's jockey for the Tropical Park Derby and the remainder of the horse's career. Jose Caraballo's job was well done, but Barbaro had now moved to a different racing circuit. Because he was looking like one of the better three-year-olds in America, many of the nation's top jockeys' agents had been contacting Michael Matz to try to secure the mount on Barbaro. Prado was a favorite of Michael Matz, although Michael was not as keen on his agent at the time, Bob Frieze.

From Lima, Peru, Edgar Prado is the second youngest of eleven children. He came to the United States in 1986 and started out riding in Florida, then at Suffolk Downs in Boston, before making his mark on the Maryland circuit. He then moved permanently to the New York and Florida circuits after a successful Saratoga meet. Prado capped off his 2006 season with a win at the Breeders' Cup on the Michael Matz-trained Round Pond, and won his first Eclipse Award as the leading jockey for 2006. Edgar attributes his Eclipse Award to the love everyone had for Barbaro. Prado has ridden more than five thousand winners, and is considered one of the leading jockeys in North America. His services are sought for most major races. *Chad Harmon*

▼ **22** FOURTH WIN in the Holy Bull Stakes, February 4, 2006: Barbaro's first try on the dirt was in the Holy Bull Stakes, another Grade 3 event at Gulfstream Park. Unfortunately, it was not a true dirt test, as the track became sloppy due to the rain. Despite the conditions, Barbaro did win, but it was not as spectacular a win as we were used to seeing. The win was, however, his first win on the dirt, so he did answer some questions regarding whether he could handle a surface other than the turf. *Photos by Z*

23 – 24 FIFTH WIN in the Florida Derby, April 1, 2006: Barbaro did not return in the Fountain of Youth, as is more typical for horses on the Triple Crown trail in Florida. This was a first clue that Michael Matz and Peter Brette were doing things differently with their horse. After an eight-week break, Barbaro ran in his first Grade 1 event, the Florida Derby. Held five weeks before the main prize, the Kentucky Derby, the Florida Derby had a weakened field because of its timing. Most horsemen did not want to go into the Kentucky Derby after such a long break. Michael Matz and Peter Brette were not like most horsemen.

Barbaro drew the 10 post for the Florida Derby. No horse had won a mile-and-an-eighth event from that wide a post position since the racetrack at Gulfstream Park had been reconfigured in 2005.

After the break, Edgar Prado moved Barbaro to the front, alongside Sharp Humor. The first photograph shows them both at the top of the stretch, while the second photograph is closer to the wire. Barbaro eventually got the better of Sharp Humor, but it was the first time Barbaro had been pushed and challenged in his career. This was an event that, some have suggested, toughened him up a little in preparation for the Kentucky Derby. *James Clark*

▶ **25 SHORTLY AFTER BARBARO** won the Florida Derby, he flew to Kentucky, via Tex Sutton Horse Transportation, and trained at Keeneland for three and a half weeks. Keeneland was chosen due to the access to the Polytrack on the training track, which would allow for uninterrupted training. Barbaro worked twice at Keeneland before moving to Churchill Downs ten days before the Kentucky Derby. This photograph illustrates how well Barbaro was doing. Peter Brette was concentrating very hard in order to keep Barbaro under control. In Brette's words, Barbaro was a "monster" in training. *Anne Eberhardt*

◀ **26 ONCE AT CHURCHILL DOWNS,** Barbaro continued to thrive. Peter Brette again had his hands full galloping Barbaro. He had one workout at Churchill Downs, the Saturday before the Kentucky Derby. Barbaro's workout was exceptional, and he continued to train very well throughout the following week leading up to the Derby. Those who saw him training at Churchill Downs were becoming more impressed. *Barbara Livingston*

▶ **27 BARBARO MADE** such an impression during Kentucky Derby week, not only with the energy he displayed galloping, but also with his presence. Here he is gazing at the iconic Twin Spires of Churchill Downs, as if he knew he owned his surroundings. Barbara Livingston, who took this photograph, was one of many onlookers who were effusive in their admiration of Barbaro during Derby week. *Barbara Livingston*

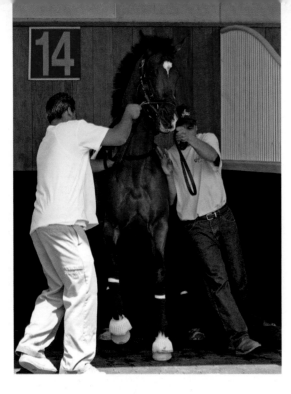

▲**28** PRIOR TO THE Kentucky Derby, many of the horses school in the paddock to become accustomed to the surroundings. Barbaro was no exception. Here he displayed some of his more quirky behavior; he was a handful to saddle. In fact, saddling for the Florida Derby was not without incident. Michael Matz was wiping Barbaro down when the colt kicked out and sent Matz to the back of the saddling stall. Matz's shirt was torn and he hurt his wrist! *Barbara Livingston*

▼**29** WHEN BARBARO ENTERED the paddock for the Kentucky Derby, he caught the attention of many people who were seeing him for the first time. Bob Baffert's wife, Jill, was one of those who was impressed and said so to her husband, who had three horses to saddle for the race. Rick Bozich from the *Courier-Journal* was similarly impressed, and noted that it was the first time, in thirty years of covering horse racing, that he had ever seen a horse who had impressed him in such a way. *Shawn Foley*

▲**30** BARBARO BEGAN to draw clear of his pursuers as he came around the final turn in the Kentucky Derby, flying! *Chad Harmon*

▶ **31** BARBARO WAS ALL ALONE as he galloped down the lane at Churchill Downs to win the Kentucky Derby and remain undefeated, one of only six undefeated Kentucky Derby winners at that time. Barbaro won by the largest winning margin since Assault in 1946. He ran the fastest final quarter of a mile since Secretariat in 1973. Barbaro had sat close to the pace for the entire race and just drew away from the field at the quarter pole. Beyond the finish line, he galloped out further ahead of the field. It was simply an overwhelming victory that convinced many people that he would become the first Triple Crown winner since Affirmed in 1978. *Kris Johnson*

◀ **32** THIS IS A VIEW of Barbaro's lead down the stretch, from a fan in the grandstand. While it appears that Edgar Prado has his stick up, he only showed Barbaro the stick, he did not actually use it. Showing a horse the stick helps keep him focused. Barbaro was running in rhythm, and Prado decided that he did not need any extra urging from the stick. This was the first time in many years that a horse has won the Kentucky Derby in a hand-ride. While it is only speculation, one can assume that if Prado had used his stick, Barbaro would have run faster and won by a wider margin. *Patricia Schroeder*

33 EDGAR PRADO celebrated with the crowd as he and Barbaro were brought back to the winner's circle by head outrider Greg Blasi. Prado dedicated this win, and his Florida Derby victory, to his mother, who had succumbed to cancer early in 2006. *Barbara Livingston*

34 EDUARDO HERNANDEZ met his star, as Edgar Prado cooled off Barbaro with some water. Eduardo was also the groom for Barbaro's brothers Nicanor and Lentenor and has worked for Michael Matz since his show jumping days. *Barbara Livingston*

▼ **35** TO BE IN THE WINNER'S CIRCLE for the Kentucky Derby is the dream of all racehorse owners in North America. Barbaro provided that moment for the Jacksons, something for which they will always be grateful.

There are three unusual things about this winner's circle celebration. Barbaro is not wearing the garland of roses, something he did not want to do after his Florida Derby win. For a quick photo opportunity, the roses were placed on him, but were swiftly removed as Edgar Prado jumped off! There was also an interloper, who is crouched down in front of Mrs. Jackson, in the winner's circle. The number 8 saddle cloth also disappeared.

Also in the photo are Roy Jackson (behind Gretchen Jackson); Michael Matz; Ritchie Orozco, Barbaro's hot walker (on Matz's left); and Rafael Orozco, another Matz groom (in front of Matz). Eduardo Hernandez is hidden by Barbaro. Michael Matz's brother, Douglas, and mother are also in the photograph, as are two of the Jacksons' grandchildren, Hardie and Grace. *Anne Eberhardt*

▶ **36** THE KENTUCKY DERBY trophies for the winning Owner and the Breeder are displayed on the Jacksons' mantelpiece at their Lael Farm residence. *Rai Phelan*

▲ **37** ON DISPLAY in Michael Matz's office at Fair Hill is half of the garland of roses that Barbaro did not want to wear. The other half of the garland of roses is at the Brettes' house. Kim Brette took the garland of roses that were, at the time, hanging on the Vanity Farms sign outside Matz's bottom barn at Fair Hill, and had them preserved. *Author*

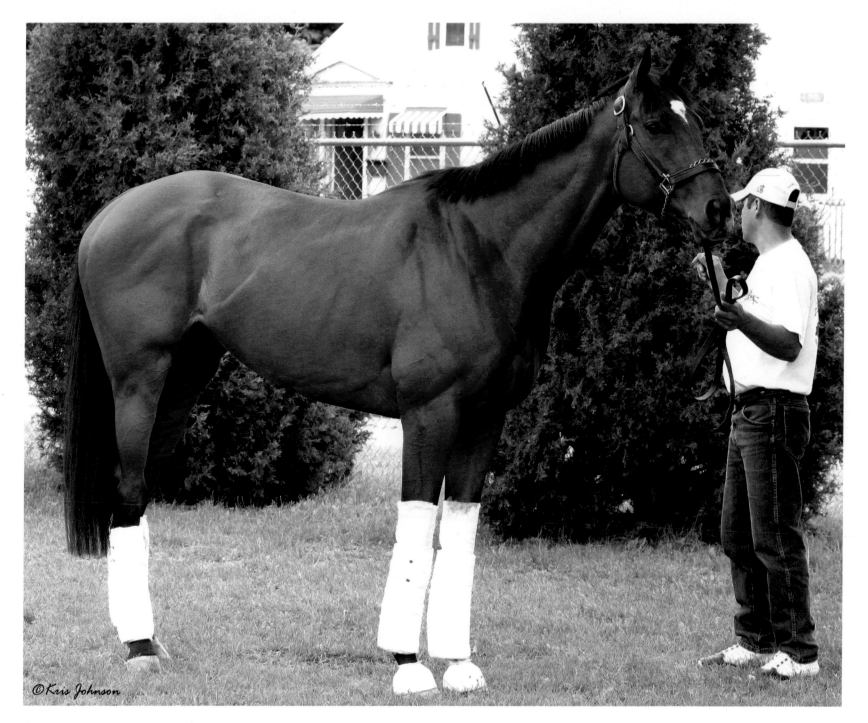

©Kris Johnson

▲**38** BARBARO LOOKED RESPLENDENT the day after his Kentucky Derby win. Tom Pedulla, of the *USA Today*, took note of this as he was one of the media in attendance. Tom remarked that horses do not usually look that good the next day after running in such a grueling race. This was further evidence that Barbaro's Kentucky Derby win had been accomplished with ease. *Kris Johnson*

©Kris Johnson

▲ **40** A DAY AFTER his Kentucky Derby win, Barbaro received a visit from Peter Brette's wife Kim and their young son Nicholas. Because Nicholas was not able to pronounce "Barbaro," Peter nicknamed the colt "Bobby." Bobby was also Phar Lap's barn name. *Kris Johnson*

▲ **39** A LOVELY HEADSHOT of Barbaro, just one day after his Kentucky Derby win. He had a big, beautiful eye and the "look of eagles." He appeared to know he was just that good. *Kris Johnson*

▶ **41** TWO DAYS AFTER the Derby, Barbaro returned to Fair Hill Training Center to prepare for the Preakness Stakes. One distinguishing characteristic of Fair Hill Training Center, versus racetracks, is the abundance of paddocks available for horses to graze. Barbaro was able to take full advantage of this. Here he is four days after winning the Kentucky Derby, on Wednesday, May 10 at 10 a.m. without a care in the world, just enjoying being a horse. He had returned to the track to train for the first time that morning after his Kentucky Derby win. *Lydia Williams*

42 – 50 BARBARO AND PETER BRETTE were accompanied to and from the racetrack by Messaging and Michael Matz. These photographs were taken on the first Friday, May 12, between the Derby and the Preakness (Brette in red sleeves), and on the following Tuesday, May 16, (Brette in blue jacket), five days before the Preakness. Barbaro trained at Fair Hill through to the Friday before the Preakness. He worked an easy quarter mile two days before the Preakness. *Jennifer Duffy*

▲ **51 – 53** BARBARO WAS ALSO turned out in a smaller round pen. Like any horse, Barbaro enjoyed a good roll. Typically, when he was turned out, he would dance around a little, buck, and then get down and roll. He would then get up, buck and squeal a little, and get back down again and roll. He would then finally settle down. These photographs were taken on Friday, May 12.
Jennifer Duffy

▲**54** BARBARO ARRIVED at the Preakness with the swagger of a rock star. His preparations at Fair Hill had gone flawlessly. Barbaro looked terrific, and those in attendance at the arrival were duly impressed. *Cindy Dulay/Horse-Races.net*

▼**55** BARBARO WAS READY, as his groom, Eduardo Hernandez (partially hidden), led him over from the Stakes barn to the paddock. Preakness Day was also Eduardo's birthday. *Dr. Rachel Beard*

▼**56** BARBARO WAS TAKEN to the Preakness starting gate by Gladys McHargue and her pony, Paco. Gladys remembered that nothing bothered Barbaro during the warm-up; the only thing he was intent on doing was nibbling the flowers braided into Paco's mane. Some observers noted that Barbaro took a couple of funny steps behind during the warm-up, which triggered a reaction from Edgar Prado. Dr. David Zipf, the state vet who was close enough to observe this said that an insect, a yellow jacket, had landed on Barbaro and the colt reacted accordingly. Once the insect left, Barbaro was fine. *Lydia Williams*

▶**57** BARBARO BROKE EARLY from the gate—a false start. It is apparent that Barbaro heard a noise and mistook that sound for his cue to leave the starting gate. At the time, the crowd noise was very intense, and the majority of the crowd was focused on one horse, Barbaro. Because the gates are held closed by magnets, a horse is able to push them open with significant forward momentum. This is designed to limit the chances of injury. Once Barbaro had broken early from the gate, he was quickly caught by outrider Sharon Greenberg and her thoroughbred pony, DJ. Many horsemen, including jockey Javier Castellano (who was aboard Bernardini), assumed that Barbaro was now a vulnerable favorite. There is just something about breaking early from the gate that seems to affect how a horse subsequently races. *Brandon Benson*

▼**58** BRUCE WAGNER was the official starter for Barbaro's Preakness. He explained how Barbaro broke early from the gate. Wagner noted that Barbaro was not anxious, he was just very focused. It was just one of those very unfortunate events. Barbaro was ready, and he left the gate when he thought he needed to run. *Author*

◀ **59** DR. DAVID ZIPF was the head state veterinarian, one of three state vets who were present at the Preakness to observe the runners. Dr. Zipf observed Barbaro breaking from the gate and watched him closely as he jogged back to the gate. He also made sure there were no visible injuries. Barbaro appeared to be okay, and Zipf conferred with Edgar Prado, who agreed. For Dr. Zipf to scratch Barbaro, something had to be visibly wrong. He could not scratch Barbaro "just because." Nothing appeared to be wrong with Barbaro and he was reloaded into the starting gate. *Author*

▶ **60** DAVID RODMAN called the Preakness for the record crowd at Pimlico. Once Barbaro was pulled up after breaking down, he was out of Rodman's sight but not out of his thoughts. Rodman struggled to call the race as the front runners seemed to be standing still. It was not until Bernardini made his move around the far turn that Rodman was able to regain his focus. *Author*

61 EDGAR PRADO quickly pulled Barbaro up when he realized there was a problem. Edgar then held Barbaro until help arrived. Many people credit Prado's quick actions on Preakness Day for giving Barbaro a chance at recovering from his terrible injuries. *Chad Harmon*

▶ **62** RAFAEL OROZCO, a Michael Matz groom (but not Barbaro's groom), was the first on the scene to help Barbaro and Edgar Prado. Rafael is also the father of Ritchie Orozco, who was Barbaro's hot walker. Sharon Greenberg, on her pony DJ, arrived next. *Terence Dulay/Horse-Races.net*

▲ **63** THE PREAKNESS CROWD anxiously looked on as Barbaro was being attended to. The race was still ongoing, but for many a much more important situation was now unfolding. The Derby hero, whom they had come to witness firsthand, was now in a very different battle—one for his life. Shouts could be heard from those offering good wishes or to implore the caregivers not to put Barbaro down. These shouts could be heard amidst a strange vacuum of noise that resulted from the stunning turn of events. *Chad Harmon*

64 JAVIER CASTELLANO won his first Triple Crown race aboard Bernardini in very impressive fashion. It was not until after he crossed the wire, as he gazed to his right, that Javier realized all was wrong with Barbaro. Javier had assumed that he had beaten Barbaro, whom he had seen momentarily early in the race before what he thought was a tactical adjustment by Edgar Prado. Javier had been celebrating his win before seeing the drama unfold to his side; his emotions just dropped. He no longer knew what to think. He could not celebrate his horse's victory in such dire circumstances. After the winner's circle ceremonies, Javier returned to the jockeys' room to apologize and offer his condolences to Edgar Prado.

With Barbaro (as Bernardini galloped by) were his groom Eduardo Hernandez, Rafael Orozco, Pimlico track worker Glen Kozak, and Peter Brette (hidden). Soon others would be on hand. Sharon Greenberg, on her pony DJ, was directing traffic. *Barbara Livingston*

65 AS THE AMBULANCE brought Barbaro to the Stakes barn, the Pimlico crowd could see Barbaro's head. This sight provided many with a little hope that Barbaro might be saved. The Associated Press's Rich Rosenblatt remarked that when he saw Barbaro being vanned off, it demonstrated to him how gutsy the horse really was. *Cindy Dulay / Horse-Race.net*

66 DR. DAN DREYFUSS was one of four veterinarians who helped with Barbaro from the time he was injured to the time he was vanned to New Bolton Center. The other three vets were Dreyfuss's practicing partner Dr. Nick Meittinis; Dr. Scott Palmer, who is a lifelong friend of Michael Matz and was a guest of Matz for the Preakness; and Dr. Rachel Beard, who was an intern of Dr. Palmer's and attending the Preakness as a guest. Matt Hartmann, a vet tech assistant for Drs. Meittinis and Dreyfuss, was also in attendance. They helped get Barbaro back to the Stakes barn, and took X-rays of the injured right hind leg in order to perform early diagnostics. They also assisted with the decision to send Barbaro to New Bolton Center and communicated with Dr. Richardson, who would undertake Barbaro's surgery the following day. Richardson was in Florida at the time, helping his friend Dr. Byron Reid perform surgeries. *Author*

67 A CROWD GATHERED outside the Stakes barn at the Preakness as many awaited the fate of the horse that they had been rooting for moments earlier. The horse ambulance to the side of the Stakes barn was visible, as well as a canopy that covered the stage that was being used as a briefing area. *Lydia Williams*

68 BALTIMORE CITY POLICE astride their motorcycles awaited the horse ambulance in order to help escort Barbaro out of Pimlico and on his way to New Bolton Center in Pennsylvania, about ninety minutes away. *Lydia Williams*

▲ **69** DR. LARRY BRAMLAGE was the "on call vet." His job, in a crisis, was to relay ongoing events to the media. Here he is updating the media regarding Barbaro's situation. To his right is Dr. Nick Meittinis and behind them is Dr. Dan Dreyfuss. Dr. Scott Palmer was with Dr. Bramlage when Michael Matz contacted Bramlage to ask him if he knew where Palmer was, shortly after Barbaro was pulled up. When Palmer heard the message, he sprinted to the Stakes barn to help out as the consulting vet. He advised Matz and the Jacksons of the best course of action going forward. *Lydia Williams*

▶ **70** ME with outrider Sharon Greenberg and her thoroughbred pony DJ at the 2010 Preakness. *Wendy Wooley/Equisport Photos*

▲**71** AT 8:08 P.M. Sunday night, Barbaro had successfully completed surgery, had recovered in the swimming pool, and was now being transported back to a recovery stall under the watchful eye of Dr. Dean Richardson. He was then lowered so he would stand on his legs. Once stood up, Barbaro was led back to his own stall. This photograph appeared in every national newspaper the following morning and was shown on all of the national news stations. The photograph was chosen by *Time* magazine as one of the best for 2006. *Sabina Louise Pierce*

▼ **73** DR. DEAN RICHARDSON was the head surgeon for Barbaro, and led his care throughout the time Barbaro was at New Bolton Center. Dean knew Matz and the Jacksons well, and had worked on their horses on a number of occasions. Dean is considered one of the best large animal orthopedic surgeons in the world. Throughout the Barbaro saga, Dean communicated effectively with the public, and made the Barbaro story more engaging. This photograph shows Richardson addressing the media at the press conference at New Bolton Center, following Barbaro's initial surgery. *Sabina Louise Pierce*

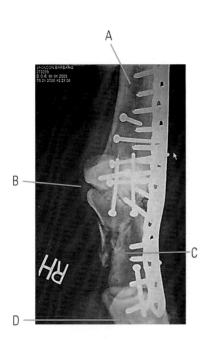

▲ **72** BARBARO'S right hind leg suffered a condylar fracture of the cannon bone (A), a fractured sesamoid (B), and a shattered long pastern bone (C). Three significant injuries that together created a very complex case. Twenty three screws and a locking compression plate were inserted into Barbaro's leg. The distal screw was inserted into the intact short pastern bone (D), which helped anchor the plate. *Unknown*

▲ **74** WHILE DR. RICHARDSON LED the surgical team that performed on Barbaro, there were many other people involved in the surgeries and aftercare. Dr. Liberty Getman (photograph) was part of the initial surgery team, along with Dr. David Levine and Dr. Steve Zedler. The anesthesia team for that surgery consisted of veterinary anesthesiologist Dr. Bern Driessen, anesthesia nurse Shannon Harper, and surgery resident Dr. Sarah Dukti. There were also two operating room nurses, Kate Cole and Erin Ortell. *Author*

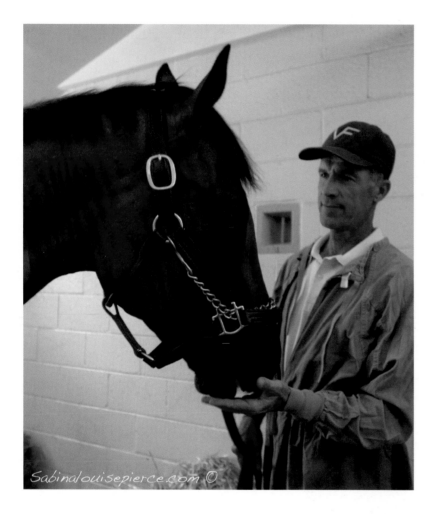

76 MRS. JACKSON was Barbaro's most frequent visitor. She would often visit twice a day. Mrs. Jackson would bring grass from the Jacksons' Lael Farm for Barbaro to munch on, which also helped pass the time during the visits.

Barbaro is wearing a cooler that was signed by the racing office at Churchill Downs. *Sabina Louise Pierce*

75 MICHAEL MATZ was a constant visitor of Barbaro's before Michael moved his horses to Florida, in early November, for the winter. There was rarely a day that would go by that Matz would not visit. It was fortunate that New Bolton Center was not only close to Pimlico, but also close to both Fair Hill Training Center and Matz's home. Visits to Barbaro were not only beneficial for the horse, but likely also for the horsemen who visited. As Barbaro had given them their greatest moment in our sport, supporting their star in his time of need was an easy decision for all involved. *Sabina Louise Pierce*

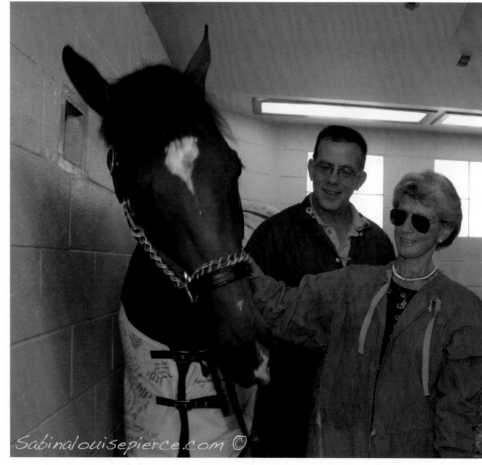

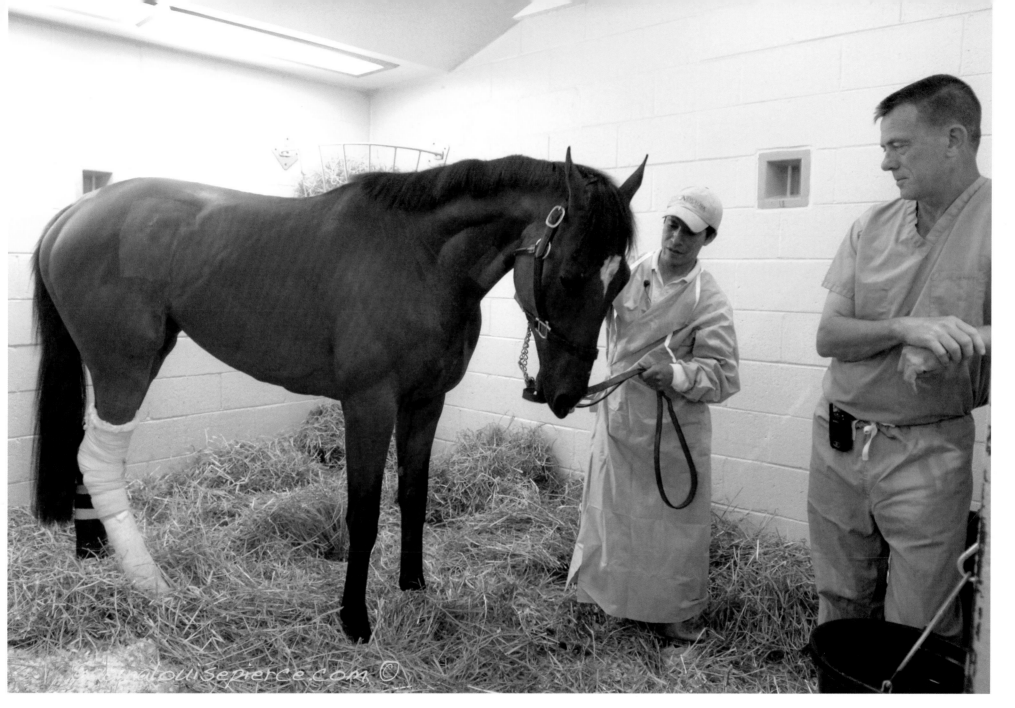

▲ **77** THIS PICTURE was taken during jockey Edgar Prado's first visit to Barbaro at New Bolton Center, on May 30, 2006. ESPN's Jeannine Edwards was along for the visit and noted Prado's visible reaction to seeing Barbaro for the first time—relief. Prado would visit five more times during Barbaro's stay at New Bolton Center. *Sabina Louise Pierce*

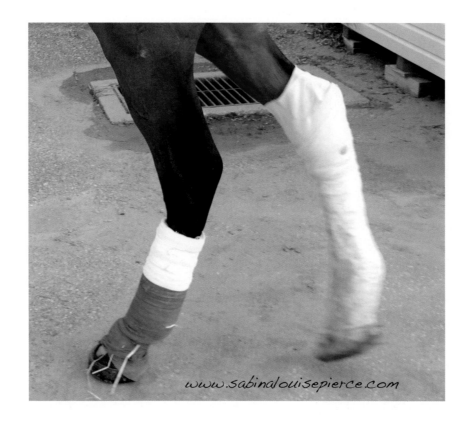

www.sabinalouisepierce.com

▲ **78** AFTER SEVEN WEEKS of recovery, which appeared to be going very well, Barbaro contracted laminitis in his left hind foot. There was rotation and sinking of the coffin bone, and nearly the entire hoof wall had become detached from the coffin bone. The laminitis was most likely the result of Barbaro shifting his weight off his injured right hind leg after he experienced some soreness from a bent screw, the distal screw referred to previously in caption 72.

The Jacksons, Richardson, Matz, and his wife D.D., met to discuss whether it was time to euthanize Barbaro. The meeting was held in full view of Barbaro, who appeared to be expressing that he could handle this setback. The team decided to give him a chance. A hoof wall resection was undertaken, in which 90 percent of Barbaro's hoof wall was removed.

A press conference, to announce the laminitis, was held a couple of days later, on Thursday, July 13. During the press conference, the laminitis was described as "as bad as it can get." Barbaro's prognosis had now become dire. *Sabina Louise Pierce*

Sabinalouisepierce.com ©

◀79 IN AUGUST, a little less than a month after the announcement of laminitis, Barbaro was allowed out of the ICU for the first time to take a little walking exercise and to graze. This was considered a major step forward in his recovery. Here he is with Dr. Richardson on August 11. He had only started to graze the week prior to the taking of this picture. *Sabina Louise Pierce*

▶80 I WAS FORTUNATE to visit Barbaro on eight occasions during his stay at New Bolton Center. The first time I visited was also the first time I met the Jacksons. My fondest memory was the thirty minutes I spent with Barbaro, on Christmas Day, outside the ICU while Barbaro happily grazed. This photograph was taken on Thursday, December 28. I was at New Bolton Center that day adding more posters from Fans of Barbaro to the outside fence line. *Sabina Louise Pierce*

▲ **81** SABINA LOUISE PIERCE was Barbaro's photographer during his time at New Bolton Center. Like many of those who were privileged to interact with Barbaro, Sabina fell in love with the champion. Sabina has photographed U.S. presidents, movie stars, and sports stars, but Barbaro and the Dalai Lama were the only two subjects with whom she wanted to be photographed. Sabina also suffered a nasty riding accident during the time Barbaro was at New Bolton Center. Barbaro was Sabina's inspiration during her own recovery. *Jennifer Rench*

82 – 83 NEW BOLTON CENTER received many posters in support of Barbaro from Fans of Barbaro, school children, and many others who were inspired by the horse's courage. These three posters were among the many hanging on the fence line at the entrance of New Bolton Center on July 15. *Author*

▲ **84** TAYLOR BARNES was at Delaware Park with her family and brought this poster for the Delaware Handicap weekend, July 16. Taylor had Michael Matz sign the poster before she placed it on the fence line outside New Bolton Center when she and her family journeyed home from the races. *Author*

85 THIS WAS THE ONLY TRIBUTE on display at Fair Hill Training Center, outside Parlo 3, Michael Matz's second barn. This photo was taken on July 20. *Author*

86 AFTER BARBARO'S LEFT HIND HOOF succumbed to laminitis in July, FOBs understood the need for that hoof to grow back. FOBs adopted the "Grow Hoof Grow" mantra as a way to support Barbaro. This poster was placed on the fence line in early September by FOB Jean Mansavage. It became one of the most widely recognized posters, and was so popular that Jean made a second one in December to replace the original when it became faded by the weather. ESPN interviewed Jean who represented the Fans of Barbaro in a segment that aired on one of its programs. *Jean Mansavage*

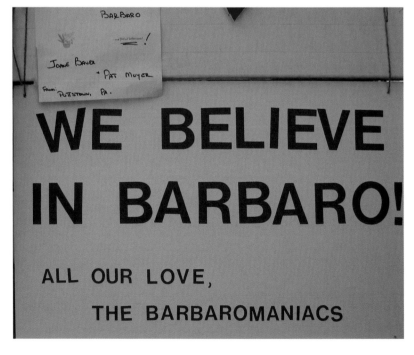

▲ **87** ON AUGUST 5, a family arrived at New Bolton Center to hang a poster to show their support for Barbaro. *Author*

▶ **88** THIS POSTER is from the "Barbaromaniacs," the name that preceded Fans of Barbaro. The name change was determined to be appropriate as the group started to become active in terms of lobbying for the horse slaughter issue. Fans of Barbaro is a group that developed following Barbaro's time at New Bolton Center, using the TimWoolleyRacing.com website. *Author*

▲ **89** PETER BRETTE in the lobby of New Bolton Center, on August 5. One of the cards from Churchill Downs is displayed behind him. The card noted, "Once a Derby winner, always a Derby winner." Churchill Downs sent six of these cards, all signed by fans. Other racetracks, including Belmont Park, Delaware Park, and Pimlico, also had fans sign cards in support of Barbaro.

Peter was also a frequent visitor to Barbaro. If Michael Matz was away, Peter would definitely visit; he would also visit three to four times a week while Michael Matz was in town. Peter also left for Florida, with Michael Matz, in early November. *Author*

▶ **90** A LOCAL FLORIST in Kennett Square, Pennsylvania, Kennett Florist became a conduit between Fans of Barbaro, and New Bolton Center and Barbaro. At times, they would deliver flowers and gifts from Fans of Barbaro on a daily basis. They would then report back, via TimWoolleyRacing.com, the mood at New Bolton Center. Kennett Florists would also help organize fundraising celebrations, such as Dr. Richardson's birthday.
Courtesy Kennett Florist

▲ **91** MARTINE PALERMO was an exercise rider for Michael Matz during the summer of 2006. Like many other horsemen, Barbaro was never far from his thoughts. Martine showed his support by displaying a bumper sticker on the back of his safety vest that read: "Go Barbaro." *Jennifer Duffy*

▲92 FOLLOWING A COUPLE OF TOUGH WEEKS for Barbaro after the laminitis diagnosis, things started to settle down a bit. To help decompress and relax a little, a few horsemen from Fair Hill and New Bolton Center got together at the Whip Tavern, July 20. Fans of Barbaro contributed to the evening. Included in this photograph are Peter and Kim Brette, Dr. Kathy Anderson, Sabina Louise Pierce, Tim and Penny Woolley, Adam and Lisa Davison, Grae Kennedy and Jill Barnes, Jennifer Rench, Catlyn Spivey, Emily Daignault, Amanda Spence, and me. *Jennifer Duffy*

▶93 BARBARO APPEARED to be recovering well from his bout of laminitis, and discussions were underway in December regarding where Barbaro would go after New Bolton Center. Three Chimneys Farm, in Midway, Kentucky, was selected as his next destination. Whether he could become a breeding stallion, or simply live out his life comfortably, Three Chimneys prepped for his arrival. In this photograph is an Equicizer, specifically built to help Barbaro with his rehabilitation. It has a walking machine around its perimeter; inside the walking machine is a round pen. Jen Roytz, marketing and communications director at Three Chimneys, and Catherine King, intern, are also photographed. *Author*

◀ **94** THINGS BEGAN TO UNRAVEL in early January. The laminitic left hind foot's hoof wall was not growing adequately. Work was undertaken to try to improve the situation, but Barbaro's right hind foot soon became uncomfortable. On Saturday, January 27, a last-ditch effort was attempted to improve the comfort of the right hind foot by placing an external fixation device on that leg, which was designed to take the weight off that foot. On Sunday night, Barbaro was very uncomfortable, as laminitis had now affected his two front feet. He was euthanized on Monday morning.

A press conference was held that Monday afternoon and the world became aware of Barbaro's passing. *Author*

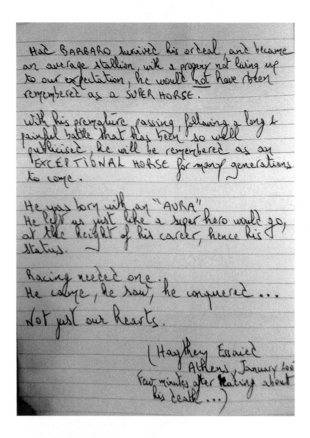

> **95** PEOPLE REACTED to the news of Barbaro's death in many different ways. Exercise rider Haythem Essaied wrote this note, which he intended to send to the Jacksons, a few minutes after he had read the news on the *Daily Racing Form*'s website. Haythem was in Greece at the time.

I met and befriended Haythem at Woodbine during my travels, two years later. He had kept this note, and gave it to me when he heard I was writing this book. It was in his Woodbine dorm room. *Author*

> **97** THE JACKSONS displayed class and grace throughout Barbaro's ordeal. They often would personally thank those who contacted them with well wishes for Barbaro. This type of behavior would help nurture the support that Barbaro received during his time at New Bolton Center. This photograph is of a letter the Jacksons wrote to Pimlico outrider Sharon Greenberg, thanking her for all the help she provided during Barbaro's early break from the gate, and for helping with Barbaro after his accident. *Rai Phelan*

> **96** FRED STONE is considered one of the leading equine artists in the world. When Barbaro broke down in the Preakness, Stone decided that he could no longer paint horses. It was not until months later, as Stone followed the progress of Barbaro, that he was inspired to begin painting horses again. This painting of Barbaro was the first that Stone completed since the Preakness accident. This photograph is of the painting displayed at the Jacksons' Lael Farm. *Rai Phelan*

LAEL STABLE

West Grove, PA 19390

June 11, 2006

Dear Sharon,

We would like to thank you personally for all you did as the outrider at the time of Barbaro's injury. Things are a bit of a fog to us as to everything that happened so quickly, but I do remember your protecting him from the horses in the race in a very calm and professional way.

So far he is doing well and still has many days to go in his recovery.

Again thanks for all you did in making it possible to get him off the track and on his way to New Bolton Center.

Sincerely,

Roy Jackson

Gretchen Jackson

▲ **98** ANOTHER EXAMPLE OF THE GRATITUDE the Jacksons displayed. This is a Barbaro print, signed by the Jacksons and given to ICU nurse Lindsey March. *Lindsey March*

▼**99** MICHAEL MATZ'S career as a show jumper helped garner support for Barbaro during his time at New Bolton Center. Michael was not only an outstanding show jumper in terms of an overall career, but he was considered a very quiet horseman whose style was revered by young children who aspired to follow in his footsteps. *Victoria DeMore*

▲**100** BARBARO is not the only horse that has proven inspirational. Horses have inspired humankind for millennia and have helped advance human civilizations. Man o' War, Secretariat, Ruffian, Seabiscuit, Phar Lap, and Dan Patch are a few of our racing stars that have been inspirational during the twentieth century. This is the Breyer model of the British show jumper Milton, whose long and successful career, as well as his patented buck after the last fence of a course, endeared him to many followers in the U.K. and worldwide.

Breyer's Barbaro model has been the fastest-selling Breyer product in the company's sixty-year history. Proceeds from the model raised $240,000 for the Laminitis Fund and Barbaro Fund at New Bolton Center. This is the largest single gift from Breyer products. *Rai Phelan*

▶**101** OVERDOSE IS ANOTHER EXAMPLE of an inspirational horse. Nicknamed the "Budapest Bullet," Overdose captured the imagination of Hungarians during a time of economic woe. Purchased inexpensively from a sale in England (about $3,000), in November 2006, Overdose won his first fourteen races, including prestigious races in Europe. He was unlucky in the Prix de L'Abbaye, which he won, for the race to be voided because of a faulty starting gate. Ironically, the race is run not far from where the Trianon Treaty of 1920 was signed. This treaty essentially dismantled the Hungarian empire.

Overdose reminded Hungarians of better times, and brought back memories of the great race mare Kincsem, who won 54 straight races in the late 1870s, a record that stands to this day. *Mirus Luna*

11.06.2010 17:07

102: ZENYATTA STIRRED THE EMOTIONS at the 2010 Breeders' Cup when her attempt to remain an unbeaten 20-for-20 just fell short. Zenyatta's undefeated record, up to the 2010 Breeders' Cup, had inspired a large following that admired her strength, beauty, gentleness, and charisma. She allowed people to believe that, no matter the circumstances and competition, anything is possible.

Like Barbaro, Zenyatta had owners who understood she had fans who wanted access to the great mare. John Shirreffs, her trainer, provided that access by posting online videos of her in training, as well as letting her fans interact with her while she grazed outside her barn. Like Dan Patch, Zenyatta appeared to interact with the crowds at the races. Dan Patch would nod to the crowd; Zenyatta would dance. Zenyatta's running style was also endearing to her fans. She would start slowly, and then try to overtake all the horses in her races to win. It created drama, and it almost gave her an "underdog" status, when in fact she mostly overmatched her rivals easily. When she got to the lead, she would prick her ears, as if to signal that she required little effort despite the visual drama.

In this photo, from left to right, are Linda Fewox Stringer, Madison Crawford, Laura Crawford, Shannon Thomason, and Taylor Thomason (front). They are from Georgia and drove eleven hours to attend the 2010 Breeders' Cup to cheer on Zenyatta.

Laura started following Barbaro at his Florida Derby. She was a fan of Michael Matz and saw him ride in the Atlanta 1996 Olympics. She admired Matz as a horseman, and liked the fact that Barbaro was undefeated. She was elated when he won the Derby, and could not wait for the Preakness. At last, she thought, we would see a Triple Crown winner. At the Preakness, she could not believe what she was seeing; it felt like she had been kicked in the gut. A few days of frantically searching for information about Barbaro's status, she came across TimWoolleyRacing.com. She checked the site four to five times a day, prayed for Barbaro, and became more drawn into the sport. She started following Lava Man, Fleet Indian, and Better Talk Now. The more she learned about the sport, the more she came to love it, because of the horse. She recognized the sport had some problems, but also saw that there were many good horsemen, like Matz, doing the right things.

Laura decided to attend the Breeders' Cup in 2006, because of Lava Man, Fleet Indian, and others. It was only the second time she had been to the races. While Invasor was brilliant, she left with a broken heart because of the breakdowns of Pine Island and Fleet Indian. A year later, the loss of George Washington nearly drove her away from the sport for good. When asked by her friend, Shannon, why she kept following a sport that she almost gave up on, she referred to a book she had about Seabiscuit, and said simply, "Because one day we will see another horse like him, and I don't want to miss it."

Zenyatta is now here, and Laura has watched all twenty of her races; at the Breeders' Cup 2010, she watched her run in person for the first time. *Author*

103: ZENYATTA IS GRAZING, after training at Churchill Downs, the Thursday before the 2010 Breeders' Cup Classic. Fans line the fence line on Longfield Avenue, to get a look at the star. Foreman Frank Leal is holding Zenyatta. Despite Zenyatta's narrow loss in the Classic, she was voted Horse of the Year for 2010. *Author*

104: RACHEL ALEXANDRA was another mare that created a large fan following. She was voted Horse of the Year in 2009, over Zenyatta, after winning the Preakness Stakes, the Haskell Stakes, and the Woodward Stakes, defeating the boys. This photograph was taken in the Spring of 2009 at Oaklawn Park, while Rachel was still in the care of trainer Hal Wiggins. She was purchased by owner Jesse Jackson after her Kentucky Oaks win and transferred to trainer Steve Asmussen. *Author*

▶ **105** THIS IMAGE HAS BEEN ON DISPLAY on **TimWoolleyRacing.com** and **AlexBrownRacing.com** since FOBs started gathering online. As such, it serves as the symbol for everything that is meaningful to Fans of Barbaro. *Lydia Williams*

▼ **106** TIMWOOLLEYRACING.COM served as the means to connect Fans of Barbaro with each other and with the latest Barbaro news while he was at New Bolton Center. I worked for Tim Woolley as a freelance exercise rider at the time, and set up his website in 2004. Until we started following Barbaro, the site received about three visits per day. Site traffic grew exponentially once we started following Barbaro before the Preakness, and then grew to its peak of 15,000 visits per day during July 2006. When I left Fair Hill, and Tim's employ, in the summer of 2007, we created AlexBrownRacing.com to host Fans of Barbaro.

In this picture, taken in the summer of 2010, Tim is on one of the horses he trains, while his wife Penny is on their stable pony, Strike. *Rai Phelan*

▲ **107** SHARON CLARK designed these wristbands as a means to raise funds to support the Barbaro Fund at New Bolton Center. She raised $10,000 for the Barbaro Fund by selling the wristbands to Fans of Barbaro and others. Kellogg, the company where Sharon worked, matched the gift, allowing Sharon to donate $20,000 in honor of Barbaro.

The Barbaro Fund was established by Mrs. J Maxwell "Betty" Moran, who contributed $500,000 as an anonymous donor, at the time. As of June 30, 2010, the fund had accrued $1.4 million. Two other funds have also been established in Barbaro's name. The Laminitis Research Fund at New Bolton Center, which had accrued $1.9 million as of June 30, 2010, and the NTRA's Barbaro Memorial Fund, which had dispersed nearly $400,000 as of June 30, 2010, via the Grayson-Jockey Club Research Foundation. *Sharon Clark*

▼ **108** BIRTHDAYS became a time for Fans of Barbaro to celebrate and raise money for various related causes. As shown in this photo, Dr. Richardson received a check for $3,851 for the Barbaro Fund at New Bolton Center on August 25, 2006. More than $30,000 has been raised in total for either the Laminitis Fund or the Barbaro Fund, for Dr. Richardson's birthday and Barbaro's birthday, through 2010. Dr. Corinne Sweeney is pictured with Richardson holding the check. *Jennifer Rench*

▲ **109** THE NIGHT BEFORE the Delaware Park Celebration on April 29, 2007, an auction was held that raised a little more than $20,000 for the Thoroughbred Charities of America. Here I am, the auctioneer, taking a break with the traveling Beanie Barbaro. Beanie Barbaro is a Barbaro ambassador who seems to simply get around and do a lot of visiting. A goodwill ambassador of sorts! *Julia Brown*

▶ **111** FOB JULIA BROWN listens to Edgar Prado's words, read by Jeannine Edwards. *Wendy Wooley/Equisport Photos*

◀**110** THE JACKSONS were the keynote speakers at the Delaware Park Celebration. This added credibility to the entire event. Other speakers included ESPN's Jeannine Edwards, who read a message from jockey Edgar Prado; Dr. Corrine Sweeney, who represented New Bolton Center; and Dr. Kathy Anderson. Even Eduardo Hernandez, normally quite reserved, came up to speak a few words of gratitude. *Wendy Wooley/Equisport Photos*

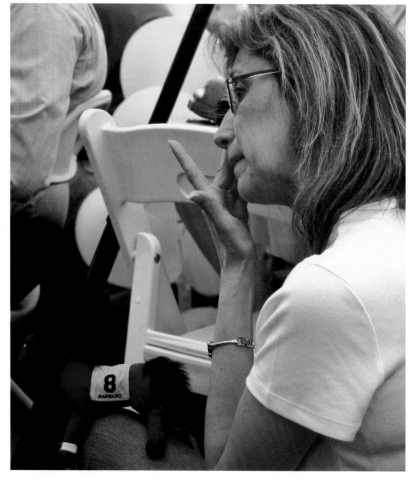

▲**112** ON THE MORNING of the Delaware Park event, Fans of Barbaro visited Fair Hill to observe training. It was likely the largest crowd that has gathered at Fair Hill, or at least the largest crowd since the Fair Hill Dash events of the 1980s (yes, I have been at Fair Hill that long). The morning's events almost went without a hitch (there was one loose horse on the track), and we were entertained by trainers Michael Matz, Michael Dickinson, and Tim Woolley, among others. *Wendy Wooley/Equisport Photos*

◄**113** FANS OF BARBARO listening to the speakers at the Delaware Park Celebration. *Wendy Wooley/Equisport Photos*

114 FANS OF BARBARO raised money for a memorial bench at New Bolton Center. The bench was dedicated in May 2007, and a $3,000 check was presented for the Laminitis Fund. *Susan Hopkins*

115 ABOUT 120 FANS OF BARBARO attended the unveiling of the Barbaro Memorial at Churchill Downs in April 2009. An entire weekend of events was planned for the group, including a dinner across the river in Jeffersonville, Indiana, the night before the unveiling. *Shoot-it*

▼ **116** FANS OF BARBARO have supported many people and horses. Lost in the Fog, a spectacular sprinter that succumbed to cancer, was one recipient. Not only did the FOBs follow the Fog's saga closely once he was diagnosed with cancer, but they also sent this wreath to Golden Gate Fields for the memorial to the Fog, held September 30, 2006. The banner reads: "For a Warrior and a Champion We Love You 'Lost In The Fog' – From the Fans of Barbaro." *Bill Vassar*

◀ **117** MIKE REA, a trainer at Fair Hill who was involved in a horrific accident shortly after Barbaro's Preakness tragedy, was another recipient of FOBs' support. Here is Mike, taking a riding lesson at Carousel Farm, near Newark, Delaware, in January 2010. *Author*

▶ **118** FANS OF BARBARO enjoy getting together to go to the local races. Here we have some of the Midwest FOBs representing Wisconsin, Illinois, and Indiana. They have gathered for the fourth consecutive summer just outside Chicago for a day of racing at Arlington Park in August 2010. Pictured (from left) are Patti Hammell, Sally Bonneau, Colleen Morrison, Deb Taw, Chris Taw, Walt Remondini, Gloria Nussbaum, and Mary Remondini. *Terry Bonneau*

▲**119** ONE ASPECT OF BARBARO'S LEGACY is a heightened scrutiny on thoroughbred retirement issues and horse slaughter. It was on this aspect that I chose to focus subsequent to Barbaro's death. After working at Fair Hill Training Center on and off for twenty years, I left in 2007 to travel via North American racetracks. I decided it was a better way to really understand horse welfare and horse racing issues, as well as develop a stronger network throughout North America. While I did not make it out to California, I worked at Penn National (PA), Presque Isle Downs (PA), Keeneland (KY), Churchill Downs (KY), Sam Houston Race Park (TX), Woodbine (Toronto, Canada) and Oaklawn Park (AR). I worked for Murray Rojas, Tim Kreiser, Clovis Crane, Chuck Lawrence, Liz Hendricks, Eddie Kenneally, and Steve Asmussen. In this photograph, I am on Jimmy Simms for Steve Asmussen, at Woodbine in 2009. *Wendy Wooley/Equisport Photos*

▲**120** PART OF THE RACETRACK culture that I was interested in exploring is what happened to the racehorses at the end of the race meets. Woodbine has a long meet (April through December), and many horses are given the winter off, while some head south for the winter to either train or race. In this photograph, taken in December 2009, is a stock trailer, parked outside a barn at Woodbine. The driver was looking for horses to buy. This type of transaction can lead to the slaughter pipeline. As soon as the racing office was alerted of this truck's presence on its backside, the driver was paged. The driver then left the backside, empty-handed.

Many racetracks are now trying to be more vigilant in terms of not allowing their horses to go to slaughter. Woodbine is one of those racetracks. Woodbine also supports a racehorse retirement program, the Long Run Thoroughbred Society. It is the longest running such program in North America. Other racetracks have similar programs. I have also visited the program at Finger Lakes, the Finger Lakes Thoroughbred Adoption Program. *Author*

▶ **121 FERDINAND** won the 1986 Kentucky Derby (photo) and the 1987 Breeders' Cup Classic. In the latter, Ferdinand defeated Alysheba, winner of that year's Kentucky Derby. Ferdinand was selected as Horse of the Year for 1987. After a much less successful stud career in the United States and Japan, Ferdinand was disposed of in Japan. It is assumed that he was slaughtered for his meat. When the news of Ferdinand's demise reached the United States, there was an outpouring of concern. Along with Exceller, who defeated two Triple Crown winners in one race and was slaughtered for his meat, Ferdinand became an inspiration for the anti-slaughter movement in the United States. This led Mrs. Jackson to become more outspoken on the issue, and hence generated support for the issue among Fans of Barbaro. *Bill Straus*

◀ **122 I WENT TO WASHINGTON D.C.** two times in order to lobby for horse slaughter legislation. The first time was an event I helped organize, Americans Against Horse Slaughter, in March 2008. The event was conceived while I was in Houston, Texas, galloping horses for Steve Asmussen at Sam Houston Race Park. I met with fellow horse advocate Julie Caramante, from Houston, and we planned the event over a series of meetings.

Approximately a hundred people lobbied during the two-day event; it was the largest horse slaughter lobbying event to occur to date and included many Fans of Barbaro who were lobbying their government for the first time. This group shot includes about half of the participants who attended an evening reception. In this photograph are leading anti-slaughter advocates John Holland and Vicki Tobin (Equine Welfare Alliance), Sonja Meadows (Animals' Angels), Julie Caramante, Nancy Perry (HSUS), Shelly Abrams (Americans Against Horse Slaughter), Shelley Grainger (Canadian Horse Defence Coalition), and former Kauffman Mayor Paula Bacon. Kauffman, Texas, was the site of the last Texas slaughter plant, which closed in 2007. *Jill Fisher*

▼ 123 THE RESCUE OF CLEVER ALLEMONT was a classic case of the effectiveness of the Fans of Barbaro network. Clever Allemont was a very good horse in his early races. In 1985, he won the Southwest Stakes and the Rebel Stakes at Oaklawn Park to remain undefeated. He was on the Triple Crown trail, and was a heavy favorite for the Arkansas Derby but did not win. Clever Allemont ran as an older handicap horse to some success. He then went on to be a breeding stallion of only modest accomplishment at various locations, including Illinois, Washington, and Kansas. His whereabouts then became unknown. In 2009, he re-emerged in a horse broker's lot in Kansas; slaughter was a possible next step. A rescue organization posted his situation on the ABR discussion board and a quick succession of events took place that guaranteed a lifetime home for Clever Allemont at Old Friends in Kentucky (where this photograph was taken). More than a hundred Fans of Barbaro have visited Old Friends to see some of the horses that they have helped to retire. *Wendy Wooley/Equisport Photos*

Wendy 2009

▲ **124** THE SECOND TIME I went to Washington D.C. to lobby was in December 2009, to attend a hearing on the issue and to present at the hearing. Here I am speaking about all the support anti-slaughter has within the horse racing industry, and the steps taken by many racetracks that have adopted a zero tolerance for their horses heading to slaughter. *Michelle Riley/The HSUS*

▶ **125** TO SHOW LOBBYING is not all hard work, here I am with the lovely actress and model Kelly Carlson. Kelly has been an avid rider since childhood, and is a devoted horsewoman. *Michelle Riley/The HSUS*

126 – 128 AS PART OF MY RESEARCH on the horse slaughter issue, I visited low-end horse auctions. While at Fair Hill, I visited the New Holland Auction in Pennsylvania on a number of occasions (third photo) and while at Woodbine in Canada, I visited OLEX, in Kitchener, Ontario, on many occasions. I also visited auctions in Kentucky, Texas, and Arkansas.

The first of the two OLEX photographs is of me riding a horse before it enters the ring. I only performed as a catch rider on this one occasion, and the horse was not sold for slaughter. The second photo is of a horse in the ring, being sold by the pound. Its weight is displayed above. Typically, two or three kill buyers would be there bidding, along with a couple of rescue people, a few dealers, and perhaps one or two private parties. Many times, more than half of the horses sold at OLEX go to slaughter. *Author*

129 I PURCHASED KISS MY HOOF in 2008 from a kill buyer at OLEX. I paid a $50 premium to the kill buyer after he had already bought the horse. Kiss My Hoof might well have been one of the slowest horses in Canada. He was beaten forty-nine lengths in a $5,000 maiden claiming event in his last start at Fort Erie. His very quiet temperament allowed him to become an excellent trail horse.

This type of transaction is actually very controversial within the horse slaughter movement, as many believe that rewarding kill buyers with a premium simply makes their business more lucrative. However, this transaction fits the mission of ABR, where we do not "forsake a single horse for the horse slaughter movement." Like the starfish parable, rescuing Kiss My Hoof will not change the world, but it does change Kiss My Hoof's world. *Ellie Ross*

Phenylbutazone	Butazone 400 Butazone 1000 Butazone Concentrate Butequine Buzone Concentrate Phenylbutazone Phenylbutazone Injection Phenylbutazone Powder Phenylbutazone Tablets Phenylbutazone Tabs	**Note: All of the products listed carry an indication for use in equine (but not equine intended to be slaughtered for food)**
Resorcylic acid lactones including zeranol	**Zeranol** Ralgro	Beef **Note that this product carries only a cattle indication**
Stanozolol	No active products for veterinary use in Canada.	N/A
Steroidal hormonal implants used for growth promotion purposes	Equine animals treated with steroid containing hormone implants used to promote growth are not eligible for slaughter in Canada.	**Note that these products carry only a cattle indication.** Hormonal implants containing oestradiol or melengestrol acetate singly, or the combinations of oestradiol and progesterone; oestradiol and testosterone; oestradiol and trenbolone acetate etc. sold under different brand names for use in cattle.
Stilbenes, stilbene derivatives, and their salts and esters including diethylstilbestrol	Banned by regulations₁ for sale in food producing animals in Canada. **Diethylstilbestrol** Stilbestrol	Dog, Cat
Stilbenes, stilbene derivatives, and their salts and esters including diethylstilbestrol	Stilbestrol Tablets	Dog, Cat
Thyrostats, antithyroid agents administered under any circumstances for the purpose of growth promotion	Approved for use in humans. Use in animals would be under veterinary control, but animals treated with these substances would not be eligible for slaughter.	N/A

▶ **130** THIS IS A DOCUMENT from the Canadian Food Inspection Agency (CFIA), which lists drugs banned from the food chain entirely, regardless of when the drugs were ingested. Bute is on that list; any horse that has ingested bute at any time is not eligible for slaughter. This should eliminate most domestic horses from the food chain. More specifically, it would be difficult to find a racehorse in North America that has not had bute at one time or another. In a study of all horses that ran in California in 2009, 99 percent pre-raced on bute (7,391 out of 7,443) source: *Daily Racing Form*

▶ **132** THE RICHELIEU PLANT in Masseuville, Quebec, is one of five federally licensed horse slaughter plants in Canada that are approved to export to the European Union. Many of the slaughter-bound horses purchased at OLEX, and some of those purchased at New Holland, are ultimately shipped to this slaughter house.

The last remaining slaughter houses in the United States were closed in 2007. U.S. slaughter-bound horses are now shipped to either Canada or Mexico. *Author*

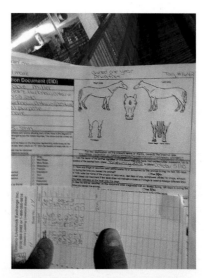

◀ **131** IN JULY 2010, new rules were introduced by the CFIA that required a six month quarantine period for horses that have been administered specific drugs (for example, acepromozine, a common tranquilizer), before a horse is viable for slaughter. These rules were put in place as a directive from the European Union, a major market for Canadian horse meat. This Equine Information Document (EID) needs to be completed for horses that are being sold for slaughter, in order to document whether the horse satisfies the six-month threshold. I attended two auctions in September and October of 2010, at New Holland and at OLEX. For both auctions, the loose horses were advertised as to whether they had the required documentation. Only a very few were sold without the documentation. This is a photograph of the EID for a horse sold at OLEX, "owned one year, drug free."

It is clear that kill buyers are concerned about this six-month issue, and pay more per pound for horses that have this documentation. Otherwise, they need to hold the horses for the additional months that they need to prove that they are drug free. What does not seem to be addressed by this document are the drugs that are permanently banned, like bute. *Author*

133 TOP BUNK WON twenty-one races and made more than $500,000 in his career, but was descending down the claiming ranks. I met Top Bunk at Presque Isle, where he was running for a $10,000 claiming price. He won that race. About four months later he was running for $4,000. Fans of Barbaro attempted to claim him to retire him. The claim was voided; however, we purchased him shortly after the race. The experience inspired the Top Bunk List, where we identify horses that have made more than $500,000 and are running for $5,000 or less. The list usually includes about a dozen horses at any given time. About twenty horses from the list have now been retired, including Dashboard Drummer, Lights on Broadway, Rudirudy, Frazee's Folly, Easy Grades, Pay Attention, and Lord of the Game. Some of the horses were retired with the help of FOBs, some with the help of their original breeders, and some by their current connections. Sadly, three did not make it. *Wendy Wooley/Equisport Photos*

134 ANOTHER RESIDENT of Old Friends, Tour of the Cat was a $1 million earner on the race track and had also raced at the Dubai World Cup event. Sadly for the Cat, his career spiraled downhill and he was running in low claiming races in the northeast, far away from the successes he had enjoyed in Florida. He had also been a vet scratch on a couple of occasions. When he was entered for a $5,000 claiming price at Presque Isle Downs, he became part of the Top Bunk List. Tour of the Cat was claimed and retired to Old Friends. *Rick Capone*

▲ **135** MANY RETIRED RACEHORSES can have very productive second careers, if given the right opportunities. Transitioning from the racetrack can take a little time, but, if done correctly, an off-track thoroughbred (OTTB) can compete in many disciplines. Here Grade 1 Stakes winner Ashkal Way is performing some of his dressage moves at an event in Saratoga during the summer of 2010.

Owner Jeannine Edwards, riding Ashkal Way in this picture, was one of the key reporters of the Barbaro saga. Jeannine also wrote the foreword to this book. Jeannine is a lifelong horsewoman. She has been a jockey, trainer, and exercise rider. *Adam Coglianese*

◀**136** SHOW JUMPING is another discipline in which OTTBs can excel. To prove that the OTTB does not have to have been a successful racehorse in order to excel in another career, here is Judge Beautiful, who was slow. JB ran thirty-nine times. She only won three races, and in her last five starts, she was beaten a combined 150 lengths. JB simply was not cut out to be a racehorse, but put in the right hands, and given a new direction, she has excelled in the show jumping arena. Here she is, with her partner Priscilla Godsoe, jumping a five-foot Puissance wall, bareback! *Janine Rapone*

▶ **137** THE MAJORITY of my racetrack travel experience was spent at Woodbine in Canada. I worked there during the 2008 and 2009 meets for Steve Asmussen. 2008 was the first year in which Steve had set up a stable at the Woodbine meet. A part of my daily routine, after finishing galloping, was stopping by the Horsemen's Benevolent and Protective Association (HBPA) office and reading the *Daily Racing Form.* Corinne Phillips (pictured) manages the backstretch HBPA office. The HBPA helps take care of many issues for the horsemen on the backside at Woodbine, and also hosts a yearly event on Lake Ontario. I attended the event both of the years I was there. I also met many other horsemen from the backside of Woodbine during my daily visits to the HBPA office. *Author*

◀ **138** MEGGY WATSON works in the Backstretch Cafeteria at Woodbine, which serves the culinary needs of the backside workers. I would usually visit during the track renovation break to get my morning coffee. If we had runners in the afternoon, I would oftentimes grab my lunch in the kitchen too; shepherd's pie and fish cakes were among my favorite dishes.

My fondest memory from the kitchen was watching the 2009 Kentucky Derby, and cheering on 2008 Canadian Champion two-year-old Mine That Bird. *Margaret Lopez*

◀ **139** KENNY ROMINE is a groom at Woodbine and lives in the dorm rooms. Here is Kenny, in December 2009, photographed in the dorm room that he shared with retired Canadian Champion jockey Lloyd Duffy.

The Woodbine dorm rooms cater to about 300 of the approximately 1,500 workers at Woodbine. Some live at Woodbine year-round, while others leave Woodbine during the months when there are no horses at Woodbine (about eight weeks during the winter). Some of the workers at Woodbine have worked there for 25 years and more; this is their life. They have become accustomed to a backstretch lifestyle that could not be replicated in any other environment.

Kenny has been at Woodbine since 1991, at the suggestion of his brother, who had moved to Woodbine, from Nova Scotia, two years prior. Kenny began as a hot walker, and then worked as a groom for a number of trainers including Conrad Belaire, Jimmy Day, Sandy McPherson, and Earl Barnett. I met and befriended Kenny when he came to work for Steve Asmussen in 2009. Kenny and I would also often attend "Soul Survivors," a weekly program offered by the racetrack chaplaincy. *Author*

▼ **140 – 141** THE RACETRACK CHAPLAINCY is another important aspect of the backside of a racetrack. It provides both spiritual and practical guidance for backstretch workers, and general support. The Racetrack Chaplaincy of Ontario is run by Chaplain Shawn Kennedy (first photograph), who also gallops a few horses in the mornings at Woodbine. The chaplain's office is housed in the Jake Howard Center, a facility available to all backstretch employees, which includes a library, a computer learning center, and a used clothing depot. Having made good use of the center myself, I designed and taught a class for backstretch workers who wanted to access the Internet, but did not know how to use a computer. "Internet for First-Time Starters" was a great teaching experience for me and allowed me to meet more backstretch workers on a one-on-one basis. In the second photo, I am with three students who completed the three-session course.

The Jake Howard Center, the HBPA office, the Woodbine Backstretch Cafeteria and Recreation Room, and the dorm rooms serve as the facilities that are available for the backstretch workers at Woodbine.

The Jacksons have supported backstretch workers through their support of Backstretch Employee Service Team (BEST), which provides a full range of health and human services to support workers on the backstretches of the racetracks at Belmont Park, Aqueduct, and Saratoga. They also support the Belmont Child Care Association (ANNA House). *Author, Shawn Kennedy*

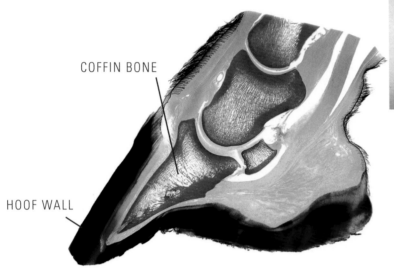

COFFIN BONE

HOOF WALL

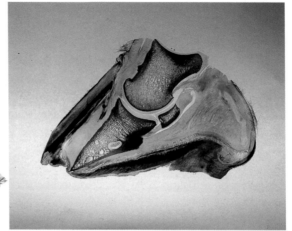

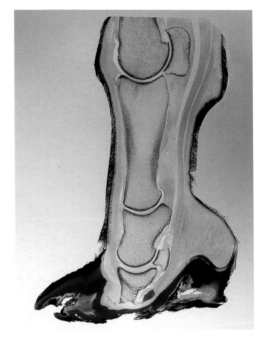

▲**142 – 144** LAMINAE are the thin intricately folded, interlocking sheets of tissue that connect the coffin bone (the last bone of the foot) to the hoof wall (outside of the foot). A major purpose of the laminae is to transfer weight from the skeleton to the hoof wall. The laminae also help reduce the compressive forces, preventing the hoof wall from crushing blood vessels, nerves, and other vital tissues, against the coffin bone. They act somewhat like the shock absorbers of a car, keeping the car from sinking too low or bouncing too high.

Laminitis is the inflammation of the laminae. Severe cases of laminitis, known as "founder," result in the rotation of the coffin bone away from the hoof wall, or the "sinking" of the coffin bone, or both, as was the case with Barbaro's initial bout of laminitis. Mild cases of laminitis do not involve any movement of the coffin bone, and are more manageable.

While horses do not die directly from laminitis, they are often euthanized as a result of the excrutiating pain they experience. Laminitis is the second largest killer of horses, behind colic, and it has claimed many of our racing stars.

These three illustrations indicate a normal foot, where the coffin bone is perfectly aligned with the hoof wall; a foot with a case of laminitis that includes some rotation of the coffin bone (note the increased distance between the tip of the coffin bone and the hoof wall); and a severe case of laminitis where the coffin bone has rotated and sunk. It is also evident in the third case that the horse suffered from laminitis for a long period of time, and did not receive any treatment.

C. V. Horst DVM / Plastinate.com

▲ **145** SECRETARIAT is considered one of the truly great horses to race in North America. He won the Eclipse Award for Horse of the Year as a two-year-old and a three-year-old, his only two seasons of racing. His Kentucky Derby winning time, 1:59.4, remains the track record and the fastest time for the Kentucky Derby. He ran each quarter of a mile faster than the preceding quarter of a mile in his Derby win. Secretariat's thirty-one length winning margin in the Belmont is considered by many as the greatest victory of all time; he ran that mile and a half race in 2:24. Some believe that Secretariat was a better turf horse than a dirt horse. Known as "Big Red," the same nickname given to Man o' War and Phar Lap, Secretariat captured the hearts of a nation. ESPN ranked Secretariat 35th of the top 100 athletes of the twentieth century.

After a stud career where he was more notable as a sire of broodmares, and the sire of 1986 Horse of the Year Lady's Secret, Secretariat succumbed to laminitis at the age of nineteen. The cause of Secretariat's laminitis was never revealed, as his medical records were never made public. Oftentimes older horses suffer from insulin resistance, which is one of the conditions that precipitates the onset of laminitis. In this photograph Secretariat is being led from the Preakness winner's circle by his groom, Eddie Sweat. *Cappy Jackson*

▼ **146** KIP DEVILLE won the 2007 Breeders' Cup Mile. After a bout of colic in October 2009, Kip contracted laminitis. In March 2010, it looked as if he was going to recover from laminitis and live out his life. Sadly, that was not the case and he was euthanized in the summer of 2010. This photograph was taken in 2008; Cornelio Velasquez, who rode Kip Deville to his Breeders' Cup victory, is aboard the colt. *Sherackatthetrack*

▲ **148** DR. JAMES ORSINI heads the Laminitis Institute at Penn Vet (New Bolton Center). I interviewed Dr. Orsini for this book in order to gain a better understanding of the progress in laminitis research in recent years. Dr. Orsini noted that there is now hope of discovering the root cause of laminitis, and is working on a strategic plan that would outline when that goal is achievable and how much, in terms of funding, will be required. He noted that advances in research techniques over the last ten to twenty years, and better means of collaboration, are reasons for optimism. As horsemen, we have been dealing with laminitis for two millennia. *Author*

▲ **147** BLACK TIE AFFAIR won the Breeders' Cup Classic in 1991 and was voted Horse of the Year for that season. Black Tie Affair went to stud initially in Kentucky (1992), and then to Japan (1997). He returned to the United States, to stand at stud first in Virginia and then in West Virginia, before retiring to Old Friends. Black Tie Affair suffered from laminitis and was euthanized in the summer of 2010. Old Friends also lost Academy Award to laminitis in the summer of 2010. *Matt Wooley/Equisport Photos*

▼**149** LENTENOR, a 2007 full brother to Barbaro, made his debut at Keeneland on October 31, 2009. Lentenor finished third in his debut. This photograph is of Lentenor's second race, and his first turf start, at Aqueduct. In this race, he finished second. In his next start, he won his maiden race in Florida. Lentenor went on to show enough promise to be entered in the Florida Derby, a race won by Barbaro on the way to his Kentucky Derby win. Lentenor finished fourth in the Florida Derby. Fans of Barbaro love the Barbaro brothers, and come out to the races wherever they run.

Sarah Andrew, who took this photograph, has also helped rescue horses by going to a low-end auction in New Jersey and photographing all the horses to ensure wider exposure among the horse community and Fans of Barbaro. *Sarah Andrew*

◀**150** A 2006 FULL BROTHER to Barbaro, Nicanor started out racing on dirt in Florida. In his second race, he ran a very creditable second behind Custom for Carlos, who soon became a graded stakes winner. Nicanor was switched to the turf at Delaware Park and ran two explosive races. Those performances earned him the role of favorite for the Virginia Derby, from which he was unfortunately scratched due to an injury. After significant time off to recover, Nicanor returned to the turf in early 2010. *Elaine Deutsch*

▶**151** THE BARBARO MEMORIAL at Churchill Downs was unveiled in April 2009. Principals in attendance at the unveiling were Dr. Dean Richardson, Gretchen and Roy Jackson, Michael Matz, and sculptor Alexa King.

In meetings with the Jacksons, Alexa King was charged with designing a statue that showed Barbaro's joy for running, to illustrate his power and beauty. This required Alexa to show Barbaro with all four feet off the ground, a significant design challenge.

Four Kentucky Derby winners—Broker's Tip (1933), Swaps (1955), Carry Back (1961), and Sunny's Halo (1983), and Eight Belles (who finished second to Big Brown in the 2008 Kentucky Derby before tragically breaking down)—are buried on the grounds of the Kentucky Derby Museum. Barbaro is the *only* horse buried on the grounds of Churchill Downs. Two other statues are also on the grounds of Churchill Downs (jockey Pat Day and the 1875 Kentucky Derby winner Aristides), but neither are as publicly accessible as the Barbaro statue. *Shoot-it*

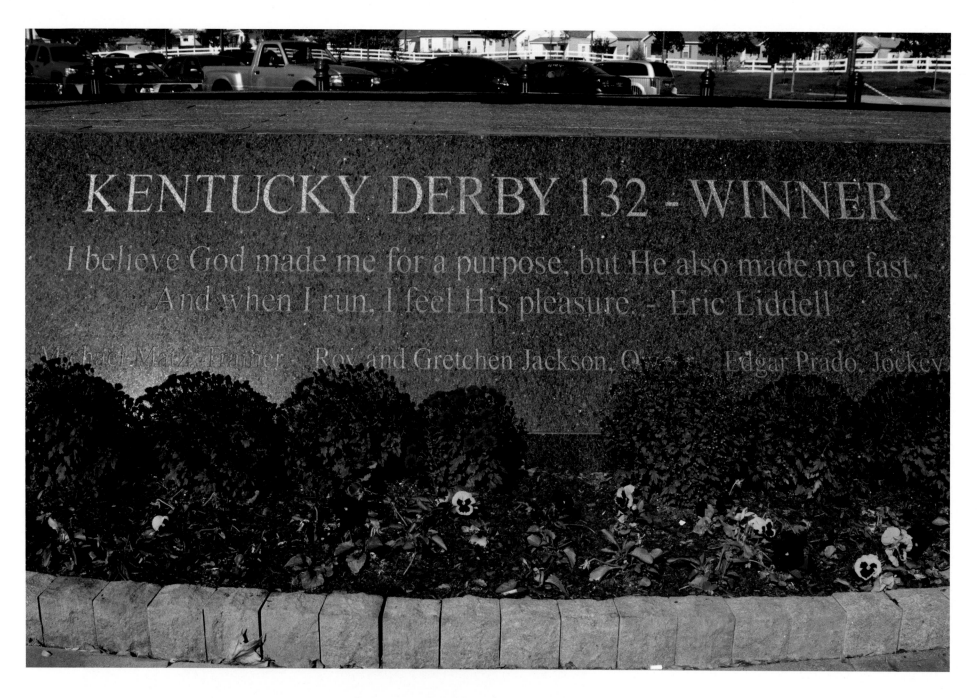

KENTUCKY DERBY 132 - WINNER

I believe God made me for a purpose, but He also made me fast.
And when I run, I feel His pleasure. - Eric Liddell

Michael Matz, Trainer   Roy and Gretchen Jackson, Owners   Edgar Prado, Jockey

▲**152** THE QUOTE USED IN THIS INSCRIPTION on the Barbaro Memorial is by Scottish athlete and missionary Eric Liddell, as portrayed in the award-winning movie *Chariots of Fire*. Born in China, the son of Scottish missionaries, Liddell became the first Scotsman to win an Olympic Gold Medal, before he pursued his missionary work in China. Liddell was always deeply religious, but chose to pursue his athletic career before embarking on his religious mission. When the Jacksons heard the Liddell quote, they thought it could have been written with Barbaro in mind. *Wendy Wooley/Equisports*

▲ **153** THE DAY AFTER the 2009 Kentucky Derby, the winning connections of Mine That Bird paid tribute to Barbaro by placing the garland of roses worn by Mine That Bird in the winner's circle on the Barbaro Memorial Statue. They then handed out the 400 roses to fans visiting the Barbaro Memorial. Co-owner Mark Allen and trainer Chip Woolley (with crutches) are in the picture. *Amanda Brown and the Kentucky Derby Museum*

154 THERE ARE AT LEAST twenty-five memorials to thoroughbred horses throughout North America, at racetracks, breeding farms, and private farms. If you include simple gravestones, there are several hundred.

The Man o' War Memorial at the Kentucky Horse Park is considered by many as the most impressive memorial to any horse. This is appropriate, as many will argue that Man o' War was the definition of true greatness in a near perfect career. He was beaten once and the circumstances of that defeat were considered questionable. Many times Man o' War won so easily his jockey would ease him down toward the finish line.

The Man o' War Memorial was moved from its original location, Faraway Farm, in the 1970s when the Kentucky Horse Park was built. The move placed the Memorial in a much more visible location, which in turn helps preserve his memory for future generations.

Statues and memorials are symbolic tributes that help preserve our history. The Barbaro Memorial at Churchill Downs, given its location and design, may well become as influential as the Man o' War Memorial, in terms of preserving a horse's legacy. *Cindy Dulay/Horse-Races.net*

Photographic Essay Addendum

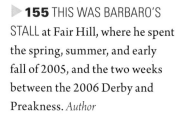

155 THIS WAS BARBARO'S STALL at Fair Hill, where he spent the spring, summer, and early fall of 2005, and the two weeks between the 2006 Derby and Preakness. *Author*

156 BARCLAY TAGG has trained for the Jacksons on and off since the Jacksons first entered the sport about thirty years ago. Barclay was a childhood friend of Gretchen Jackson. Barclay trained the Jacksons' Showing Up, who was also undefeated as he entered the 2006 Kentucky Derby. In fact, this was the first time in the history of the Kentucky Derby that an owner had two undefeated horses running in the race. Barclay was on hand at the Preakness, after Barbaro broke down, to console his close friends. Barclay also trained Funny Cide, who won the 2003 Kentucky Derby. *Rai Phelan*

157 MIKE LAPOTA was Barbaro's blacksmith during the time Barbaro was with Michael Matz. He worked with Barbaro at Fair Hill, as well as in Florida and Kentucky. The only time another farrier worked on Barbaro was the morning of the Kentucky Derby, when his back shoes were replaced by Todd Barton. *Kathee Rengert*

158 THE JACKSONS presented me with this gift during the Barbaro Celebration in April 2007. The shoes in this design are modeled after the shoes Barbaro wore in the Florida Derby. *Author*

159 GEORGE WASHINGTON was bred by the Jacksons and foaled the same year as Barbaro, in Ireland. He was sold as a yearling for about $2 million. George Washington was a champion as a two-year-old and three-year-old in Europe. He won the English 2,000 Guineas, the first leg of the English Triple Crown, on the same day Barbaro won the Kentucky Derby. Thus, the Jacksons bred the winner of the first leg of both the English and American Triple Crowns in the same year. This is likely a unique feat.

Known as "Gorgeous George" for his stunning good looks, George Washington ended his three-year-old career placing a disappointing sixth in the Breeders' Cup Classic. He was then retired. Unfortunately, he was only able to get one mare in foal as a stallion (the foal's name is Date with Destiny), so he was returned to the races. After a less remarkable campaign in Europe as a four-year-old, George Washington returned to the United States for another run in the Breeders' Cup Classic. Unfortunately, he broke down in the Classic and was euthanized on the track. *Wendy Wooley/ Equisport Photos*

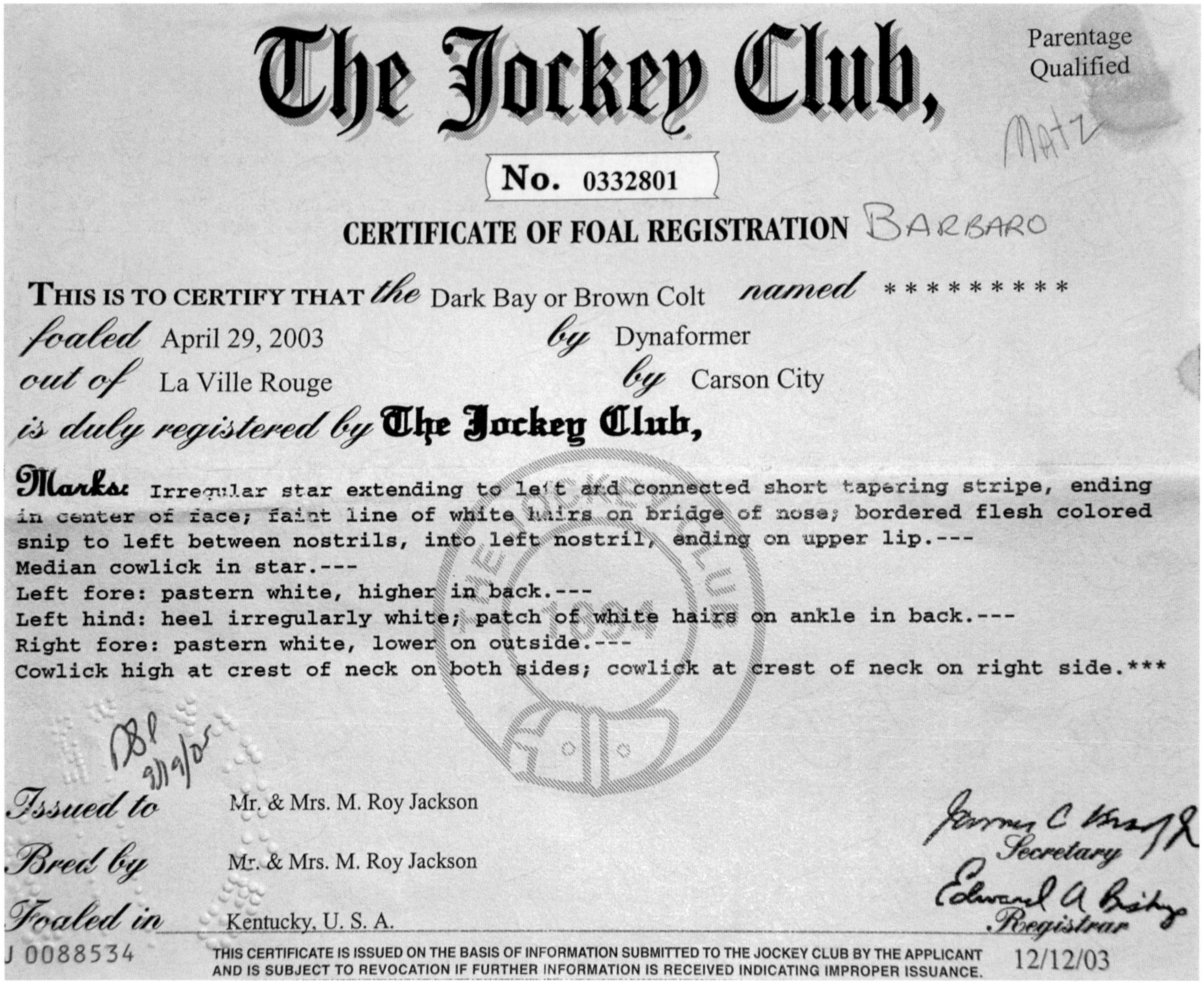

The Jockey Club,

Parentage Qualified

Matz

No. 0332801

CERTIFICATE OF FOAL REGISTRATION BARBARO

THIS IS TO CERTIFY THAT *the* Dark Bay or Brown Colt *named* * * * * * * * *

foaled April 29, 2003 *by* Dynaformer

out of La Ville Rouge *by* Carson City

is duly registered by **The Jockey Club,**

Marks: Irregular star extending to left and connected short tapering stripe, ending in center of face; faint line of white hairs on bridge of nose; bordered flesh colored snip to left between nostrils, into left nostril, ending on upper lip.---
Median cowlick in star.---
Left fore: pastern white, higher in back.---
Left hind: heel irregularly white; patch of white hairs on ankle in back.---
Right fore: pastern white, lower on outside.---
Cowlick high at crest of neck on both sides; cowlick at crest of neck on right side.***

Issued to Mr. & Mrs. M. Roy Jackson

Bred by Mr. & Mrs. M. Roy Jackson

Foaled in Kentucky, U.S.A.

J 0088534

Secretary

Edward A. Bishop
Registrar

THIS CERTIFICATE IS ISSUED ON THE BASIS OF INFORMATION SUBMITTED TO THE JOCKEY CLUB BY THE APPLICANT AND IS SUBJECT TO REVOCATION IF FURTHER INFORMATION IS RECEIVED INDICATING IMPROPER ISSUANCE.

12/12/03

▲ **160** BARBARO'S JOCKEY CLUB Foal Papers. Every racehorse is registered with the Jockey Club, and the papers prove the horse's identity. On the front of the papers you can read his markings, which help describe Barbaro as unique. You can also determine his "lip tattoo," from the registration number, which would be G32801. The "G" replaces the first two digits, the year Barbaro was born. The lip tattoo number is checked against the Jockey Club papers to confirm the identity of a horse when it races. Barbaro's lip tattoo was checked when he entered the paddock for each of his races. *Rai Phelan*

0 3 3 2 8 0 1

OFFICIAL RECORD

OF RACES WON IN THE UNITED STATES, CANADA AND PUERTO RICO

HORSE: Barbaro   SEX: C   FOAL OF: '03 SIRE: _____ DAM: _____

	DATE WON	NET VALUE TO WINNER	TYPE OF RACE	DISTANCE	NAME OF STAKE OR HANDICAP	NAME OF TRACK	RACING SECRETARY OR/BY
1	10/4/05	24,000	MDN	1m Ⓣ		Del	Sam Abbey
2	11/19/05	$60,000	STAKE	1 1/16 Ⓣ	"The Laurel Futurity"	Laurel	Denver Beckner
3	1/1/06	60,000	STK	1 1/8 Ⓣ	Tropical Park Derby III	Trpl/Crc	R. Umphrey
4	2/4/06	90,000	STK	1 1/8	Holy Bull III	GP	D Bailey
5	1/06	600,000	STK	1 1/8	GRADE I The Florida Derby	Gulfstream	D. Bailey
6	5-6-06	1,453,200	STAKE	1 1/4 mi	GRADE I "The Kentucky Derby"	Churchill	Doug Bredar
7							
8							
9							
10							

△ **161** ON THE BACK of the papers is listed each race a horse wins. This is important as a horse can only run in races in which it is eligible. Of course, it's just a cool piece of history to see the handwritten entries, from the racing secretaries, of Barbaro's wins! *Rai Phelan*

◀ **162** PRIZZIO'S, a deli close to the intersection of 273 and 213 by Fair Hill Training Center, serves as a breakfast and lunch place for many of the horsemen at Fair Hill. Michael Matz is a customer, as are many of his team. Prizzio's serves as a gathering place for news, and hosts many news clippings of the Barbaro saga.

Ron, who was the proprietor, asked Michael Matz (before he left for Florida in 2005) if he had any Derby hopefuls. Michael replied that he had a two-year-old named Barbaro that looked good. Ron is posing in front of some of the news clippings on display. *Rai Phelan*

▶ **163** FROM TIME TO TIME, a few of us who were covering the Barbaro saga would meet at the Whip Tavern to catch up with a few of the people we had met from New Bolton Center. This gathering took place in December 2009, shortly after I returned to the area from Woodbine, in Toronto, Canada. In this photograph are Dan Gelston (Associated Press) and his wife Keri and their young son Cooper; Michael Jensen (*Philadelphia Inquirer*) and his wife Lisa; Jennifer Rench, who was at New Bolton Center during the Barbaro saga, working in public relations; Dr. Dean Richardson; Sabina Louise Pierce; and Rob Menzies. *Unknown*

▲**164** AND BELIEVE ME, it was not all work. I got to hang out with some cute people. Here is Canadian jockey Chantal Sutherland with me, after riding one of Maggie Moss's horses, trained by Steve Asmussen at Woodbine. Chantal was selected as one of *People* magazine's 100 Most Beautiful People in 2008. Like many people who work in horse racing, Chantal wants to help end horse slaughter. *Wendy Wooley/Equisport Photos*

PART THREE

Fans of Barbaro

*"Like the Fans of Barbaro, I decided to turn my emotion
into positive action for others."*

—EDGAR PRADO,
My Guy Barbaro

Barbaro has proven truly inspirational to people from all walks of life. One such group of people is Fans of Barbaro (FOBs), a self-organized horse advocacy group that evolved from the devotion exhibited by those following Barbaro's progress at New Bolton Center. Fans of Barbaro has existed as a group for four years as of this writing. In that time, the group has raised more than $1.4 million to rescue more than 3,600 horses from slaughter. FOBs have also done much more for horses in honor of Barbaro, including supporting the Laminitis Fund at New Bolton Center, the Barbaro Fund, which helps support ongoing care and expansion initiatives at New Bolton Center, and the Barbaro Memorial Fund created by the National Thoroughbred Racing Association (NTRA) to assist with equine health and safety initiatives. Here I explore the Fans of Barbaro phenomenon.

In the early part of Barbaro's three-year-old year, I was managing a website for a Fair Hill-based trainer and friend, Tim Woolley. We had set up a blog in 2004 and called it TimWoolleyRacing.com. It was designed to provide updates on Tim's horses, Fair Hill events and happenings, and horse racing in general. Very few people took notice of the website at the time.

When Barbaro returned to Fair Hill after his Derby win, I suggested to Tim that we provide Barbaro updates as he prepared for the second leg of the Triple Crown. Tim agreed and wrote the daily updates. At the time, I was teaching an Internet marketing class at the University of Delaware. As a project for the class, we began to study the traffic patterns of the site. We also started a Google advertising campaign, promoting Barbaro's training regimen, to draw additional traffic to the site. The experiment worked. In the two weeks leading up to the Preakness, we increased the audience of the site from approximately three visitors to 120 visitors a day.

On the Sunday following the Preakness, as Barbaro was undergoing surgery, an insatiable demand for information about his condition was very evident on the Internet, illustrated by the number of Google searches conducted for the term "Barbaro." Fans wanted to know his prognosis, and recognizing the precarious nature of the situation, they wanted real-time updates. Because I had connections to Barbaro's caregivers, I decided to try to get updates and post them on TimWoolleyRacing.com. I contacted Dr. Chuck Arensberg, a colleague of Dr. Kathy Anderson, who was on duty that Sunday at Fair Hill. Arensberg updated me and let me know the plan that was in place for when Barbaro would come out of surgery. This is what I put on the site:

A SOCIAL EXPERIMENT

The website TimWoolleyRacing.com became the original host of Fans of Barbaro. It started out as a blog in 2004. With very little traffic, we began providing updates as Barbaro prepared for the Preakness. Traffic moved from three visits to 120 visits per day. During Barbaro's time at New Bolton Center the traffic increased to close to 15,000 visits a day at its highest levels (July 2006). During that time, the blog was receiving 500 comments a day. It soon became clear that the medium was limiting the conversations.

A discussion board was needed to host the conversations more effectively. On August 8, 2006, the discussion board was added, and the conversations soon turned into action. The discussion board was and still is the heart of Fans of Barbaro activity. As of July 2010, 1.65 million messages have been posted, and more than 1,000 new messages are posted each day. FOBs Wendy Uzelac Wooley (Michigan), Mary Locarumo (Illinois), Katarina Villanueva (Colorado), and Amy Spear (Wisconsin) have been instrumental in managing the success of the discussion board.

To help manage the information at TimWoolleyRacing.com, a wiki was added on May 13, 2007. The wiki allows rescue organizations to tell FOBs more about themselves, as well as document their history with FOBs. The wiki allows content development for horse slaughter issues and much more. As of July 2010, there have been more than 5 million page views of the wiki.

In August 2007, the home of FOBs moved from TimWoolleyRacing.com to AlexBrownRacing.com, as I stopped working for Tim Woolley and began a more than two year trip around North American racetracks. Essentially, all the content from TimWoolleyRacing.com was copied to AlexBrownRacing.com; the move was relatively seamless.

In November 2008, we added the Alex Brown Racing Facebook group to the media mix. This group eclipsed 5,000 members in June 2010. The Facebook group allows Alex Brown Racing to reach out to the non-FOBs who are interested in horse welfare and horse racing issues. Many FOBs are also active on Facebook.

Toward the end of 2008, we also began to tweet. Twitter includes a higher proportion of media people. It is useful to push out content from the discussion board and other relevant horse racing and horse welfare news. As of December 2010, Alex Brown Racing on Twitter had 1,600 followers.

Update 4: Barbaro's surgeon, Dr. Richardson, was flown up from Florida this morning. The procedure after the surgery is designed to have Barbaro "wake up" in a swimming pool. He will be placed on a sling and transported to the pool. This is to help ensure that when he does wake up he does not cause himself further damage. When a horse comes out of anesthesia, there is a chance he will start thrashing around; this environment limits the chances of causing further trauma from the thrashing. As he is already "stood up" by the sling in the pool, he won't need to get up, which could obviously cause further harm to the leg. It is anticipated that this procedure will occur sometime early this evening.

I restarted the Google advertising campaign to allow people who were searching for Barbaro news to see an advertisement for TimWoolleyRacing.com that highlighted Barbaro's latest status.

Dr. Arensberg called me as soon as Barbaro came out of surgery; this update followed shortly thereafter:

Update 5: Barbaro is now in the recovery pool (7:40 p.m.). He has a bone plate fusing his ankle and pastern, and a cast has been placed over this. Dr. Richardson described the surgery as one of the toughest he has performed. Barbaro is awakening from anesthesia in the pool, and once he completely comes around, he will be transported via a sling back to his stall later this evening (it usually takes an hour from when they are placed in the pool to when they are able to return to their stall).

We received three thousand visits to the site in the hour after we published the above update. The site crashed. That was the beginning of a new role both for TimWoolleyRacing.com and for me.

On Monday, with the site back up and running, I committed to providing updates on Barbaro's condition on a frequent and regular basis, as long as Barbaro's team provided me with access to that information. A process soon developed. Dr. Richardson would provide Michael Matz with a morning report on Barbaro's condition. Matz would then provide me with that information when I saw him on the training track, or horse path, at Fair Hill. I would then update the site with that most recent news, often by calling a friend, Jennifer Duffy, as I was jogging a filly named

Chappy around the dirt track for trainer Judge Jackson. If someone I knew had visited Barbaro (Peter Brette or Kathy Anderson, for example), that person would also provide me with updates on his condition. Additionally, we would post New Bolton Center's Barbaro updates to the site. Thus, updates were sometimes provided two or three times a day. This type of rapid updating fed the insatiable appetite of those following Barbaro's progress and nurtured the devotional behavior that Barbaro inspired among "Barbaromaniacs," a label soon applied to the group.

Word of mouth across the Internet and the Google advertising campaign were all it took to inform those interested in Barbaro's condition that TimWoolleyRacing.com was the place to find the latest updates. We also had a means to form a community of people—one that could discuss Barbaro's status as well as grieve. Members of the community provided mutual support in their shared grief, and bonded with each other in their concern for Barbaro, their hero. Barbaromaniacs would not only discuss Barbaro's condition, but would also write poetry, produce online videos, seek out meaningful quotations, hold vigils, and light candles in support of Barbaro.

As Barbaro's condition began to stabilize, discussions of other themes started to emerge. These conversations were specific to the broader issues of horse racing and horse welfare. They were occurring on the discussion board, which was added to the initial blog site to manage the community more effectively. Soon, there were postings regarding specific horses that needed to be rescued. Conversations turned to action, and the site allowed many people to work together in rescue efforts. Each rescue or contribution provided further inspiration for additional action. It fed on itself. People felt they could make a difference, no matter how large or small their individual contribution. Many projects ran simultaneously, and those that were successful received support from the community while also attracting new members. This pattern continued through 2010.

Mission Statement

ABR, a horse racing site and home to the Fans of Barbaro, is a community dedicated to honoring the legacy of Barbaro by improving the welfare of horses and the humans involved with them.

How: ABR is dedicated to the fight of ending horse slaughter; to finding a cure for laminitis; to sharing horse welfare and horse racing knowledge within the community; and to promoting action to accomplish these purposes.

ABR is committed to helping rescue and support horses at all stages of the slaughter "pipeline" and not forsaking a single horse for the horse-slaughter movement. ABR supports other animal welfare and spiritual interests of FOBs as they evolve.

Note: ABR (AlexBrownRacing.com) is the successor of TWR (TimWoolleyRacing. com). This mission statement was developed in the summer of 2007, the result of a collaborative effort of FOBs.

One of the major initiatives to develop from the site pertained to horse slaughter. Because the group was evolving into an activist group, a more appropriate name for the group was sought. While "Barbaromaniacs" was very descriptive for the passion shown by many people following the progress of Barbaro at New Bolton Center, it was not a name that would evoke respect when communicating with legislators in Washington. Mrs. Jackson suggested, via Kennett Florist, that the group should call itself "Fans of Barbaro." Essentially a "Fan of Barbaro" is someone who is inspired by Barbaro and is associated with the website TimWoolleyRacing.com (which became AlexBrownRacing. com in 2007).

A Fan of Barbaro may have forgone his or her association with the website, but to be a Fan of Barbaro the person must have had some association to build that bond—not only with Barbaro but with other Fans of Barbaro.

Fans of Barbaro began as an online group, and remains as such through 2010. However, many have now met personally at local events and at larger national events. The first such meeting was the Delaware Park Racetrack Celebration on April 29, 2007, a date that would have marked Barbaro's fourth birthday.

More than 700 FOBs gathered for the weekend at Delaware Park, and a number of other FOBs gathered at other venues across the country. An auction held the previous evening raised more than $20,000 for the Thoroughbred Charities of America. Donations were gathered that day to support laminitis research, and essentially, the event served as a time to celebrate Barbaro's life.

While an event of this magnitude has not been repeated, other gatherings have been organized and the connections among FOBs continue to strengthen. Approximately a hundred FOBs traveled to Kentucky to participate in activities related to the unveiling of the Barbaro Memorial Statue at Churchill Downs in April 2009. Many returned a year later to watch Super Saver win the Kentucky Derby.

One of the more fun and enduring projects undertaken by Fans of Barbaro has been the "Adventures of Beanie Barbaro." This project was the concept of FOB Lisa Morin. Explained Morin:

"'I'm so sorry, Madison, Barbaro died this morning.'

"I couldn't believe that I had to tell my little girl that Barbaro was gone. All the nightly prayers, wishes, hopes, and dreams that she had—that we all had for Barbaro—were not enough for him to stay. Just a month or so before, we had daydreamed about meeting him someday, and now that would never be. We would often take our Beanie Barbaros (an anniversary gift from my husband) and groom them, run them in the 'Kentucky Derby,' then put them to bed, projecting our real life wishes onto these miniature plush toys. These tiny stuffed animals soon became a sorrowful reminder though, and, even as an adult, it was difficult to look at them and not feel sadness."

"But there was some measure of comfort in knowing that we all shared in this loss," she continued. "The FOBs were leaning on each other, looking for a spark of light, a distraction perhaps, a reason to laugh and smile, but to never forget our collective heartbreak. Maybe a visit from Barbaro would do the trick—Beanie Barbaro that is! I proposed the idea of a journey in which Beanie Barbaro would become sort of a goodwill ambassador for horses. He could visit a horse rescue, a landmark, an event—anywhere his FOB host would desire. I saw it as a win-win: a visit from 'Barbaro' and the opportunity to convey the message of horse-related issues such as slaughter and laminitis to the general public and to provide the opportunity to raise funds for shelters, rescues, and other equine charities. The only requirement was that the FOB document their visit through writings and photos, then send Beanie Barbaro on to his next host. The concept was gleefully accepted by the FOBs and 'hosts' and 'hostesses' began to line up for a visit from 'Barbaro'!

"Beanie Barbaro's initial excursion was perhaps his grandest—a visit to meet an entourage of FOBs at the Kentucky Derby on the one-year anniversary of Barbaro's dramatic win. News of the journey traveled through the stands at

The Jacksons

Churchill Downs, and FOBs clamored to have their pictures taken with our tiny ambassador. As the joy of his whimsical journey spread, so did the opportunity to open a dialogue about the issues most important to FOBs.

"Beanie Barbaro's journey continued with visits from the coast of California to the steps of the U.S. Capitol and just about everywhere in between. His travels have taken him to each race of the Triple Crown, to countless horse rescues, and national monuments, and to meet Barbaro's connections, including Roy and Gretchen Jackson, Edgar Prado, Dr. Dean Richardson and the New Bolton staff, and even Barbaro's sire, Dynaformer. Beanie Barbaro's travels continue to this day, weaving a tapestry that continues to bond the FOBs in an imaginative, poignant, and unique celebration of the life and legacy of Barbaro."

As a group, Fans of Barbaro have sometimes been mocked by those outside the group who view some of the behaviors of its members as extreme. Maintaining vigils for a horse may be perfectly normal to some, and downright bizarre to others. Adding online candles to a website is an acceptable way to show support for some, but seems rather odd to others. The fact that some FOBs chose to display some of this behavior does not detract from the valuable work that the group, as a whole, has accomplished—and continues to accomplish to this day. But it has provided fodder for the naysayers to ridicule the group.

Deadspin was one website that took aim at Barbaro and Fans of Barbaro. Articles included: "Not to Beat a Dead Horse But…," "ESPN Trots Out Barbaro Crazies Again," "He Has Risen, and Is Demanding Oats," and "Think You Can Avoid the Legend of Barbaro, Go Ahead and Try."

FOB INSPIRATION FROM DISCUSSION BOARD

I posed a two-part question on the AlexBrownRacing.com discussion board, asking FOBs why Barbaro inspired them, and how that inspiration played out. Following are a few of those responses. They cluster around the themes of Barbaro's

EDGAR PRADO ADDRESSES FANS OF BARBARO

Barbaro, what a beautiful name to pronounce. He gave me the biggest thrill of my life, second only to my kids being born.

He changed the lives of so many people, not only because he won the Derby, but because of the heart, courage, and will to live he showed, even against the odds. He never gave up. He fought so hard every step of the way. He taught us that to give up is not an option. He began the flame of hope that nearly anything is possible, but we must put our hearts into it; it is up to us now to ensure that the flame is not extinguished.

We have to remember him as a true champion and a fighter. Those who saw him saw greatness; he left his mark on horse racing. To all the fans, thank you so much for all the support through the rough times. Your calls, e-mails, and letters helped me to stay on my feet. Barbaro brought a lot of people together, people who really love our sport, and more importantly, really care about animals. Barbaro stole those hearts forever.

Thank you for being loving, caring people. We have found out that there are still great fans all around the world. We must continue to raise our voices together, especially in the name of a horse that we loved so much and brought so much joy into our lives.

Barbaro is gone, but still lives in our hearts, and will forever. Thank you, Barbaro, for making me a better person. Thank you for giving me the ride of my life. Thank you for making my dreams come true. Thank you for letting me love you.

I miss you, my friend, and always will. Hope to see you down the road and we can be reunited for one more ride.

—EDGAR PRADO'S WORDS,
Delivered by ESPN's Jeannine Edwards, to FOBs during the
inaugural Barbaro Celebration at Delaware Park, April 29, 2007

characteristics, demeanor, and strength; horse rescue and legislative efforts to end horse slaughter; and personal development and introspection inspired by Barbaro's courage.

FOR THE LOVE OF A HORSE, AND BARBARO

"When Barbaro broke down, I was at my sister's home, dog sitting, with intermittent access to the Internet. Two days later, I found TWR and a new home. You kept us updated daily and sometimes thrice daily with quotes from Dr. Richardson. What I found at TWR and ABR were people who were as crazy about horses as I was. A lot knew tons more than I did. But the love I had for this horse, and the hopes I had for his recovery—everyone else had those same feelings. It was magical.

"It was magical watching Barbaro on Belmont Stakes Day. Via TV I could sit and watch Barbaro all day long. Whether it was eating, sleeping, or just standing in contemplation, I could watch to my heart's desire and not have to worry about bothering him as he was trying to heal." —*Margaret*

Kennett Florist, located in Kennett Square near New Bolton Center, became a conduit between FOBs and New Bolton Center and Barbaro. FOBs would contact Kennett Florist to contribute toward gifts or send their own gifts to New Bolton Center and Barbaro. Kennett Florist would prepare those gifts and deliver them to New Bolton Center. They would then report back to FOBs, via TimWoolleyRacing.com, regarding the mood at New Bolton Center.

"Barbaro inspired me because he was such an athlete and fighter. But his supporters also inspired me with their love, care, and devotion to him and all horses. Barbaro inspired me to gain knowledge about the plight of our horses and do what I can to not only help, but spread the word. I continue to do both. I am honored to be part of the FOB family!"—*kathyb5783*

"It was my granddaughter who introduced me to Barbaro. It was just after the Preakness that my heart belonged to Barbaro forever. I had never seen a horse with so much courage and strength. He has inspired me to fight and not give up in the face of all the trials I face in my life. He became an inspiration for me to help with donating to the Barbaro Laminitis Fund on his birthday and the date of his death. I have also donated to several rescue organizations for thoroughbreds, mares, and foals. I have also supported the FOBs by buying items that they sell in support of fighting laminitis and anti-horse slaughter. Barbaro will always live in my heart. I follow his brothers, Nicanor, Lentenor, and Margano, for I see Barbaro in each of them. They will carry on his legacy and the fight against laminitis."—*Lou*

"Barbaro inspired me because of his beauty, charisma, and perseverance. I was inspired to volunteer my time and professional services to produce two DVDs about the FOB celebrations at Delaware Park, with all of the proceeds of the DVDs donated to the Laminitis Research Fund at UPenn. Because of Barbaro, I've become a horse lover, and appreciate all animals as never before." —*Amy A in NJ*

"More than 100 FOBs have visited Old Friends to see how much their impassioned generosity has meant to these great racehorses. They've helped these amazing athletes by spreading the word and donating money to ensure more and more deserving thoroughbreds receive the retirement they so richly deserve."

—MICHAEL BLOWEN,
Founder and President of Old Friends
(FOBs have helped retire a number of horses to Old Friends, including Clever Allemont, Cappucino Kid, and Tour of the Cat)

The Inspiration

"As a racing fan for many years, I sensed Barbaro possessed a unique, intangible quality—'a presence,' as Mrs. Jackson once described. His presence may have caught our attention, but his indomitable spirit bonded us to him. Barbaro inspired people by his breathtaking speed, strength, natural athleticism, intelligence, courage, beauty, and heart. His spirit was indomitable on the track, as well as in the hospital stall. His will to live inspired millions around the world. Barbaro was a true champion!" —*Gina*

"Barbaro inspired me because he was the first horse since Secretariat that took my breath away when he raced…and then after he was injured, he awed me with his will to live. Barbaro, and this community of FOBs inspired me to finally be my authentic, horse-crazy self. That led me to become political for all kinds of causes involving the benefit of horses, raise money for laminitis research and horse rescue, and meet wonderful people from all over the country. My life is far richer because of a beautiful bay horse named Barbaro." —*Kathy*

"Barbaro inspired me because he showed the world what pure courage is and for many months, without faltering! He touched so many of us, and encouraged us to be better people and help the animals, especially the horses! Barbaro inspired me to learn about laminitis, and donate regularly to his fund to find a cure! When I broke my wrist in 2009, I knew it was nothing compared to what Barbaro had to endure, and that made my recovery easy!" —*IL FOB Linda*

"Barbaro inspired me because of his grit—an amazing racehorse and an amazing patient. Barbaro inspired me to move to Nevada and get a horse of my own—Barbaro taught me patience."—*NV Sally*

INSPIRED TO ACT: HORSE RESCUE TO ANTI-SLAUGHTER LEGISLATION

"Barbaro inspired me to implement a grassroots organization that included FOBs from each state. The movement was called 'Campaigning for Barbaro.' We campaigned to end horse slaughter, to raise funds for laminitis, to campaign for safer racetracks. Campaigning for Barbaro ultimately inspired me to launch my own non-profit Animal Fairy Charities, which has spawned Animal Advocate Television. Of course, Americans Against Horse Slaughter was inspired by Barbaro as well."—*Debra, WI*

"I moved to Washington State thirty years ago, horse racing in the far distant past. I started watching the Triple Crown races again, watched Barbaro win—and break down tragically in the Preakness. With the advent of the Internet, I started tracking his treatment on TWR from the beginning, never realizing how attached my present would be to my past. I grieved inconsolably over his demise and continued reading ABR where my past and present converged and became educated regarding the situation with equine health, welfare, and outcomes. All my memories merged, reading all the books as a child by Marguerite Henry and Walter Farley, movies watched, horses ridden, and realized I wanted to once again experience being around those I had loved so long ago. It led to contributions to rescue operations, writing my Congressmen and Senators about various bills, and signing many petitions. I had never been an overt activist before, but now know that had I not followed the path which Barbaro opened I would have never found my childhood once again." —*Pam Stiefel Gerla, Everett, WA*

"Barbaro's story, and the local people I came to know through interacting on this board, did inspire me to try to make a difference locally. Several other Minnesota FOBs and I have rescued two off-track thoroughbreds (OTTBs) from our local track. I've also been inspired to try to help as many retired—or needing to be retired—racehorses through this board that I can, by helping to donate to get them off the track, and then help support them as they transition to their new lives or homes." —*Linda J., Minneapolis*

"Because of Barbaro, I learned about horse slaughter and I work to help our American horses be spared from that end. I work by contacting Congressmen and women and Senators in Washington D.C. and our President on a regular basis, asking them to help us help our American horses who helped us settle this land."—*murphsmo3*

IN THEORY: A TRIBE

Fans of Barbaro (FOBs) would be described as a "Tribe" by author Seth Godin in the book *Tribes.* A tribe is a group of people who are joined together with a shared interest. In the case of Fans of Barbaro, that shared interest was the progress of Barbaro's condition at New Bolton Center, and remains the welfare of all horses.

Fans of Barbaro are able to communicate among each other via the medium of the website, which was TimWoolleyRacing.com and is now AlexBrownRacing.com. Now, it is essentially a horse welfare advocacy group, which has a number of leaders fronting different welfare initiatives. Those horse welfare initiatives include: lobbying government for legislative change, raising funds for laminitis research, raising funds for horse rescues, retiring "war horses" from racing, celebrating birthdays, and much more.

It is Barbaro who brought the Tribe together, and it is the memory and inspiration of Barbaro that remains the glue that unifies the group. As a Tribe, Fans of Barbaro have accomplished many things in the name of Barbaro. As of July 2010, more than three years after Barbaro was euthanized, FOBs have rescued more than 3,600 horses from slaughter, raising more than $1.4 million in doing so. They have contributed money toward laminitis research, have reached out to their local horse rescue organizations, and have lobbied the government regarding horse slaughter legislation.

As a tribe, Fans of Barbaro have disrupted the status quo with respect to horse welfare, while also raising the bar in terms of the level of scrutiny of horse sports.

"I still find it amazing what we have been able to accomplish these last four years. Part of the reason, I think, is that we have resisted the urge to become too organized, or to become a legitimate organization; instead we have remained an informal community. This loose structure is probably the reason why we can accomplish so much, so quickly."

—MARYGRAN

"I was married on a horse farm on Preakness Day in 2004, so in 2006 while celebrating our anniversary, we went to watch Barbaro hopefully win. Seeing him break down before my eyes reminded me of when I saw Ruffian do the same as a little girl. It was only then that it dawned on me, 'what happens to thoroughbreds once they are not able to race or are no longer valuable on the racetrack anymore?' My quest began…I couldn't get enough information about Barbaro, his recovery and his future, and for the hundreds of thousands of other horses that aren't as fortunate as Barbaro was, to have the Jacksons—owners who truly loved and cared for their horse. Two months later (7/21/06), and at the age of forty (it's never too late to fulfill your dream!), I *finally* was a first time owner/adopter of a thoroughbred rescue through Bright Futures Farm. I vowed to Foreveramber—whom I adopted in honor (at the time) of Barbaro—to never give up on her and that she would have all of the love and care that she and every horse deserved until her last days. In 2008, my husband and I bought a twelve-acre farm, turned it into a horse farm for Amber and our other two rescues, Cody (a blind wild mustang adopted in 2007) and Passion (an abused and starved Haflinger that we rescued with the help of ABR last April 10, 2009). We take the ones that many others won't even think about looking at. If we can ride them, great—that's a bonus, but that's not what it's all about with us…it's about helping them in the

name of Barbaro—no matter what their illness or deformity! Barbaro's photo was the first one to hang on our wall of photos in our barn." —*Michele*

"Barbaro has inspired me with his incredible will to survive. He has shown me to never ever give up and keep fighting to the end. His spirit lives on in the many horses that have been saved because of him. Barbaro has inspired me to fight for the end of horse slaughter. Normally I am a shy person but because of Barbaro, I make daily phone calls to my Representatives and Senators. I help to fundraise for horse rescues and am an Angel to many of the horses of Forgotten Treasures Equine Rescue. I also help to coordinate the many adventures of Beanie Barbaro." —*melody1963*

"What Barbaro inspired me to do—get involved with rescues. Because of Barbaro, I learned about rescues, which I never knew existed. I now volunteer many hours a week at a local cat rescue at Pet Smart called 'Animals Can't Talk.' It was through this rescue that I adopted two of my cats, Remington and Bashful. And I volunteer on occasion at Ponytales Rescue." —*Grandma Bea Gobèe*

"Barbaro inspired me because of the sense of hope that permeated his story—from the hope that he would win the Derby to the hope that he would win the Triple Crown to the hope that he would survive. That hope inspired me to join the effort to end horse slaughter and move outside my comfort zone to contact legislators in person. That hope also inspired me to follow racing closely year-round instead of just in the spring for the Triple Crown and in the fall for the Breeders' Cup." —*Peggi*

"Barbaro inspired me to learn more about horses in general. Horses that race, horses who need help at rescues, and horses who have been heroes as a family member or on the race track. He inspired me to meet a great group of people here, who share their love for Barbaro and admire the way he fought daily to live, love, and to be loved." —*Carleen in CA*

ORGANIZING FANS OF BARBARO

I think the FOBs have been able to help a lot of horses and raise money quickly because this website serves as a clearinghouse for rescue groups and has allowed groups to highlight individual animals in need of immediate help. More formal charities often have a lot of bureaucracy, which often prevents them from reacting quickly to a desperate situation. Because of the ad hoc nature of the FOBs and the fact that the site reaches people all over the country, individual animals can often be helped in a matter of days or hours.

On the downside, there is a lot of infighting among rescue groups, although that happens within and among more formal organizations too. There also is the possibility of scam artists as well but my sense has been that the good results have greatly outweighed the bad. The lack of a formal structure has also allowed creative solutions to problems that might take months to implement within the confines of a structured organization.

In addition, while there are some conflicts between rescues and individuals, the site has tended to encourage a lot of cooperation between various groups to help horses in bad situations that might not have happened without the contacts made on the website.

—PETEHORSE24

I would love to see what a so-called "management" or "organization" expert would say about how this remarkable forum works. I don't think they have a model for the FOBs that they could rely upon. I think we have created a new and different organizational structure to accomplish those unfinished tasks Barbaro left for us. So often in this world, people prefer to be put into and to stay in their little comfort zone boxes. At least speaking for myself, this place has helped me to get out of my "box" and has rekindled that idealistic spark I once had to agitate for change and to make things better for those who have no political voice, specifically horses and other creatures.

What is stunning to me is how folks here pick up the mantle on an issue and become leaders. Whether it is rallying others to make those calls to Congress, helping to fundraise for laminitis, organizing an event at a track, working with OTTB rescues to get a claimer out of a bad situation, tracking down a lost horse, people here always *step up* to the task at just the right time. No president, no board of directors, no management structure, no orders from headquarters, just caring and committed people who see a need and sometimes move heaven and earth to fill the need.

The best one word term I can think of is "collaborative." However, nothing captures precisely the magic that happens here daily. All I know is that I am deeply proud of my association with everyone here.

—TERRIC324

"One important facet of the impact of the FOBs has been to track old 'war horses' that are running at the bottom level at cheap tracks and get them retired. An early example was Tour of the Cat, a horse that earned $1.1 million but was running for $5,000. He had been a vet scratch a couple of times and FOBs were worried about him. Efforts to purchase the horse privately from his connections failed, so with the help of Maggi Moss, money was raised and Cat was claimed and finally retired. The only running he has to do now is out in the pasture, when the gallant old gelding feels like showing his buddies what an awesome racehorse he was."

—BEV STRAUSS,
MidAtlantic Horse Rescue

"Barbaro was the first horse since Secretariat that made me go 'wow' after he raced. So much so that after the Derby I had to look up his pedigree because I was convinced that he had to be related to Big Red, even though I already knew his background. He brought me back to being a fan of horse racing. Finding TWR/ABR allowed me to remember why I loved horses and racing so much when I was younger, and made me realize there were lots of people out there like me. Because of Barbaro, I realized the horror of horse slaughter existed and have worked to make it end. I support rescues and programs that I never knew existed before, and I've made friends I never would have otherwise had an opportunity to know." —LindaVA

"My love for Barbaro has inspired me to fundraise for horse rescues and to sponsor several horses from different rescues. Because of the Jacksons, my eyes have been opened to the painful truth about horse slaughter. This awareness motivates me to talk to people and hopefully open their eyes as well." —Jamie Gillispie

"I was there that day at Pimlico and watched as the nightmare unfolded; the early break from the gate, and then I watched as he went by me and suddenly seemed to be backing up and my mind screamed, 'Barbaro, the Triple Crown, you can't catch up.' Barbaro knew he was in trouble, but he stood patiently and waited for help to come, like a gentleman and the champion he was, and it was this moment that the inspiration started for me. To this day, I ask him for help; to give me a sign when I have a dilemma. He always does.

"He inspired me to buy a horse (wish I had done it a long time ago). To promote and contribute to laminitis research. To spread the word about horse slaughter and the transport conditions of horses to slaughter. To help rescue horses in need. To keep a scrapbook of the great things that have happened in honor Barbaro. To be a better person."—Ellen Z

"'What lies behind us and what lies before us are small matters compared to what lies within us.' The meaning of that saying lies at the heart of how Barbaro inspired me. Here was this magnificent horse, at the height of his athleticism, at the top of the racing world, faster than them all, brilliant in every way, and in one moment it was all over. Suddenly, Barbaro found himself in a strangely diminished world. His physical boundaries were now those of a small place in an intensive care unit at New Bolton. No more exercise rides in the morning, no more brilliant races, no more fun times in the fields with Eduardo. It is difficult to imagine such a transition without a sadness, a depression. And yet each and every day, come what may—surgery, pain, or anything else—Barbaro showed the same heart, the same courage, the same grit that he showed every time he showed up at the racetrack. He faced his diminished world with the attitude implicit in another favorite saying of mine, 'just when the caterpillar thought the world was over, it became a butterfly.' The world, the life, that Barbaro had known was, in many ways, over, so what did he do, he went on. He would be the best at this world. And that is how Barbaro inspired me. He reminded me that no matter what life throws at you, it is how you face it that matters. Barbaro faced his challenge brilliantly, and the memory of it inspires me every single day." —gaia551

"I had never been a racing fan until the year Barbaro ran in the Kentucky Derby. I was hooked. He inspired me to learn as much about thoroughbred

BARBARO'S MEMORIAL AT CHURCHILL DOWNS

For the Barbaro Memorial unveiling at Churchill Downs, we wanted to organize a weekend celebration for FOBs. We identified our individual strengths and selected projects that matched up with those strengths. I took on the task of organizing the FOB Dinner. Being familiar with Louisville, I knew I wanted to have my fellow FOBs enjoy the city's beautiful skyline during our event, and selected a restaurant just across the river in Jeffersonville, Indiana—one that provided that gorgeous view. Space planning, menu, contract review, and myriad other details were handled during a visit to the venue a few weeks before the dinner, and 130 reservations were accepted via e-mail and phone calls.

FOB Kim and husband Mick, along with FOB MJ and husband Walt from Milwaukee, stepped up to organize and conduct our raffle and door prize drawings during the dinner, proceeds from which benefited horse rescues and laminitis research. FOB Gloria passed around a literal tin cup during the dinner. This initiative was in honor of the beloved Tin Cup Chalice, who had lost his life in a freak accident at Finger Lakes just a week before. Money was raised in his memory for the Finger Lakes Thoroughbred Adoption Program.

FOB Julia from Ohio created centerpieces for the FOB Dinner, as well as two bouquets of red roses that flanked the podium at the Barbaro Memorial unveiling. Each rose was tagged with the name of an FOB who had contributed, proceeds benefited horse rescues. FOB Jamie from Tennessee sold the first edition of the FOB ribbons—yet another fundraiser. And on it went, so many contributing to make the weekend one of the most memorable of our lives.

Each individual event or project was integral to the overall celebration—and the entire weekend worked like a charm, with everyone doing what they do best.

—FOB SALLY BONNEAU,
Indianapolis, IN

BARBARO MEMORIAL BENCH AT NEW BOLTON CENTER

Reaction to my proposal for a memorial bench at New Bolton Center (NBC) was "pure FOB": enthusiastic and generous. Donations poured in prior to the bench being approved by Dr. Corinne Sweeney of New Bolton Center. The bench, a tan blend of exposed aggregate featuring an engraved bronze plaque, would serve as a tangible reminder of the strikingly handsome dark bay colt whose dazzling 2006 Kentucky Derby and tragic misstep at Pimlico catapulted Barbaro from tragic to mythic hero status. 140 FOBs participated in the project, donations exceeding manufacturing and transportation costs three-fold.

The area highlighting the bench was chosen to meet the logistical requirements of NBC employees, patients' families, and the general public. Kathy Freeborn, an NBC employee, created an oasis of repose in the newly christened Barbaro Memorial Garden nestled between two wings of the facility. Another NBC employee, Carol Sheets, provided immeasurable assistance in what was a long-distance endeavor.

The Barbaro Memorial Bench was dedicated under a blazing sun against a sapphire sky on a stunningly beautiful morning in May. Special guests included Dean Joan Hendricks, Dr. Dean W. Richardson, Dr. Corinne Sweeney, Carol Sheets, Kathy Freeborn, and several NBC employees, including a handful of Barbaro's nurses. A check for $3,000 earmarked for Laminitis Research was presented to Dr. Corinne Sweeney with a copy of the Dedication and List of Contributors framed in Barbaro's blue-green racing silks. The Seabiscuit quote at the bottom of the dedication speaks to Barbaro's spirit, will to persevere against the odds, and overall brilliance.

"The main issue in life is not the victory but the fight; the essential thing is not to have won but to have fought well."

—FOB SUSAN HOPKINS,
Chair, Barbaro Memorial Bench at New Bolton Center

racing as I could. (And, I have.) When he got hurt he inspired me to keep going through difficult times, instead of giving up. He reminds me daily, since I had my stroke, to keep trying. Even in tiny increments, it's still improvement and I'm moving forward. He never lost his spirit to live. His body lost its ability to live and no one could change that. The most important thing of all is that he inspired me to learn about all the horses who, for whatever reason, can no longer race and who need new homes, and new careers. We've saved many thoroughbreds that are now in wonderful places where no one would have ever thought they would be. That is the Barbaro legacy at work." —*Faye Weldon*

"Barbaro inspired me because I will never forget that first day I saw him at Churchill Downs. He was 'drop dead gorgeous' and just looked like an athlete. I said to my sister (we always talk on the phone during the Derby), 'Who is that?' She said, 'That's Barbaro, his trainer was in a plane crash.' She had watched all morning while I was at the barn. His win was amazing, and then such utter disbelief and sadness at the Preakness. Then getting to know the Jacksons, more of Michael Matz, Dr. Dean, it was the whole package. The Jacksons were so generous with their support of Barbaro's recovery. I had never known any history like this of a racehorse. Through New Bolton Center, I found TWR. As a horse owner for ten years, I didn't know slaughter existed. I was always kind to horses, fed skinny ones (even if they weren't mine), bought two OTTBs well before Barbaro's time, but have now gone on to volunteering at local rescues in my area, also spreading awareness of the fate of some thoroughbreds when their racing days are over. I have personally contacted racehorse trainers about horses that aren't winning that perhaps should retire and have another career. Now I'm much more vocal about ending horse slaughter, wild horse round-up, etc." —*Kathy*

"The FOBs, through the ABR site, are both a reflection of, and have been a significant force towards, much greater awareness of the horse slaughter problem in this country, and of horse welfare issues more generally. In particular, they reflect and have promoted awareness of a new demographic for equine welfare issues and especially racehorse welfare issues.

"The rescue discussion board permitted direct participation in the rescue of horses by many individuals who, prior to their following of Barbaro's injury and battle with laminitis through the main site, had not previously been aware of the tremendous resource needs of horse rescue organizations or of the diverse set of welfare issues facing the U.S. equine population.

"FOBs have played both a pivotal educational and support role in assisting the cause of horse rescue. The ABR site has been a tremendous information clearinghouse for horses in need and for equine policy issues demanding attention.

"The FOBs have provided great friendship and support to me personally, and to the horses rescued by Southern California Thoroughbred Rescue."

—CAROLINE BETTS,
President and Founder,
Southern California Thoroughbred Rescue

INSPIRED BY BARBARO TO CHANGE FROM WITHIN

"I was at the Preakness that fateful day and so intent on his condition I didn't even know who won the Preakness until much later; in fact, I never saw any of the race as all I could concentrate on was the condition of Barbaro. I had been in an auto accident in which I had broken my foot, ankle, and heel, and needed surgery.

"I had been putting off a second surgery, as the first one was bad enough. But watching our brave Barbaro fight for his life and never giving up convinced me that if he could go through all he was going through, then I could be as brave as he was and do what had to be done.

"I got to walk on my foot again after many painful months, but if not for his courage I would probably still be unable to walk on it today." —*lobieb*

> "ABR is a wonderful site for FOBs who can only contribute smaller amounts of money to network these smaller amounts into actually saving horses from slaughter together with other FOBs who can provide—or arrange—a home for these horses."
>
> —LIN_TX

"Barbaro inspired me because I saw a reflection of myself in him. He was strong, athletic, and 'on top of the world' one moment, and it was all gone in an instant. As I struggle with severe knee arthritis, during those eight months Barbaro fought for his life, I felt a very close bond to him, and when I felt pain while standing (often), I felt Barbaro and I were in this fight together. I was there for him (in spirit) and he was there for me. He felt like a brother to me." —*Kent*

"Barbaro inspired in me a deep sense of gratitude. I became more grateful for my life as I watched him with his daily renewed sense of curiosity and wonder. He seemed grateful and appreciative for all the care that was given him." —*MacRaith1*

"What he has inspired me to do is find the good in a sad and often cruel world. Now that I have shared the FOB experience, I am compelled, from the depths of my heart, to promote Barbaro's many-faceted legacy of Life...and Love. I do what I can, in my way, with daily consideration of this mission. He has changed my life." —*Otherlyn*

"Barbaro inspired me to fight and live. It was a tough fight but I kept fighting because of him. He gave me the will to survive at the worst time of my life. I owe my life to Barbaro. Thank you, Barbaro, for giving me this site to release my sorrow and my grief during the darkest moments of my life." —*Geralyn*

BARBARO'S INSPIRATION IS MUCH BROADER

It was noted earlier that a critical component of being a Fan of Barbaro is some affiliation with TimWoolleyRacing.com or AlexBrownRacing.com. There are clearly many others who were inspired by Barbaro but have not participated in those websites.

Mrs. J. Maxwell "Betty" Moran is the "anonymous" donor who started the Barbaro Fund. Mrs. Moran contacted New Bolton Center on the Monday following Barbaro's surgery in order to establish the fund to honor Barbaro and to support New Bolton Center. The fund was established with a $500,000 donation, and the Jacksons soon matched that gift. Betty Moran explained why she decided to establish the Barbaro Fund: "I made the gift because I am 'in it' for the horse—to improve the care and the well-being of horses. I wanted it to help horses that had come to New Bolton Center to get the best of care. I would do anything for New Bolton Center."

Barbaro was inspirational to young children who were encouraged by his grace and brilliance, and wanted to support him through his time at New Bolton Center. This was illustrated by many class projects that provided support for Barbaro. Dava Rice, who teaches second grade at Southside Elementary in Cynthiana, Kentucky, runs a Kentucky Derby project each year for her students.

"Each year we decide which horse is our favorite for the Derby," said Rice. "In 2006, Barbaro was an overwhelming favorite. His impressive ability to win races, and the handsome white heart on his forehead, had won the hearts of my whole classroom."

"The Monday after the Derby, the chatter around the classroom was full of excitement—their horse had won the Kentucky Derby," she continued. "Two weeks later the chatter was of a different sort. The tone of their voices held a noticeable concern. We stopped all plans for the day and just talked. My class decided they needed to do something to let Barbaro know they cared. Immediately art paper was folded into the shape of cards and the students were hard at work with pencils, crayons, and markers writing sincere messages and recreating pictures of Barbaro. The next day the cards were on their way to New Bolton Center with many hopes and prayers for their hero, Barbaro."

"The week of the Preakness was our last week of school. My 'kids' moved on to third grade, but they didn't forget Barbaro," she added. "Many of them followed his progress. Barbaro still finds his way into the hearts of my kids, not because of the odds he had on the racetrack, but the many times he beat the odds of life."

Dava continued, "Even though the kids I have now were very young when he won the Derby, Barbaro still affects them. Awareness is one of those ways. This year we raised over $800 for a nearby horse rescue, Our Mims Retirement Haven, which is operated by Jeanne Mirabito. The whole school was involved. We decorated wooden horses and sold them at a silent auction. The second-grade classrooms then went for a visit to the Our Mims facility. It was an awesome day. I have heard from several parents of my kids during the summer, they have gone as a family to visit with Jeanne's 'ladies.' I attribute all of that to the awareness brought about by Barbaro and the hearts he touched. It goes far beyond him being a champion."

Barbaro was inspirational to a college student who wanted to put the lessons he was learning to good use. Mike Ince was studying web design. Mike is also a horse racing fan. Shortly after the Preakness, he set up GetWellBarbaro.com, a site that allowed fans to not only get the latest news on Barbaro, but to post their own content and view other tributes to Barbaro. While the site served some of the same purposes as TimWoolleyRacing.com, it also illustrates how Barbaro stimulated a passion for a budding web designer to get involved and make a difference.

Three funds have been established to honor Barbaro and raise money for horse welfare issues. FOBs have been generous in their support of these funds.

The Barbaro Fund at New Bolton Center was established by an anonymous benefactor (Mrs. Moran) who donated $500,000. It supports ongoing patient care at New Bolton Center as well as capital improvement projects. As of 6/30/10, this Fund accrued $1.4 million.

The Laminitis Fund, also established at New Bolton Center, helps to further research in laminitis in order to help find a cure and better manage the disease. As of 6/30/10, this Fund accrued $1.9 million.

NTRA's Barbaro Memorial Fund supports equine research and educational programs. As of 6/30/10, nearly $400,000 has been disbursed from the Fund via the Grayson-Jockey Club Research Foundation.

Mike remembered, "I have always been an animal lover and became a horse racing fan as a teenager. My first bet was on Alphabet Soup, who defeated Cigar. I was hooked on the sport.

"It was painful to watch the Preakness and its aftermath. I was already familiar with Barbaro and his achievements heading into the race. At the time, I was in the midst of my college education, and was focused on the web and graphic design aspects of my degree. It just seemed like a great idea to create a platform where people could express their get well wishes for Barbaro, utilizing what I had learned thus far. Thousands of people kept up with the site and a few hundred e-mailed me for various reasons, whether it was to simply say thank you, or to ask for my address because they wanted to send me photos, newspaper clippings, or anything that could help contribute to the site. The entire experience lasted over nine months and while it didn't have the happy ending we all were cheering for, I was able to learn and meet some very interesting people. More importantly, it was incredible to see firsthand how many people were praying everyday for his recovery."

Mike continued: "I never met Barbaro, or ever saw him in person, but, rest assured, I learned from this magnificent horse. I learned that the heart of a champion does not necessarily have to be within a human. The heart of a champion comes from someone or something that no matter what, keeps fighting. The heart of a champion can bring people and even complete strangers together. Simply because they recognize such effort, beauty, grace, and, above all, that willingness to compete, no matter the circumstances."

Barbaro was inspirational to a Kellogg employee who wanted to create a fundraiser that would support horse welfare. Sharon Clark worked with Mrs. Jackson and New Bolton Center to design four sets of wristbands that would raise money for the Barbaro Fund. Many of the wristbands were sold to Fans of Barbaro. Sharon raised $10,000 in this endeavor, but with a matching gift from her company, was able to contribute $20,000 to the Barbaro Fund. Sharon remarked emphatically, "The experience was awesome!!!"

Barbaro was inspirational to a young lady, Lynden Godsoe, who was twelve at the time of the Preakness accident. Lynden, along with her mother, went to New Bolton Center shortly after the Preakness accident to try to see her hero. Lynden recalled, "If I remember anything from going to see Barbaro, it was all the signs and flowers next to the white fence. It was a very comforting feeling of hope and love for the horse that filled us with hopes and dreams in the first place." While they were unable to visit Barbaro, Lynden remained inspired. She is the artist behind the illustrations for this book.

Barbaro was also inspirational to many horsemen throughout the industry. They were wowed by his sensational Derby performance and wanted to see more. They were devastated by the Preakness events, much as if they had lost their own horse.

Barbaro also inspired the general public at large. Many gifts were sent to Barbaro at New Bolton Center. Royalty were among his admirers; Barbaro received holy water from the River Jordan from HRH Princess Haya.

Personally, Barbaro inspired me to undertake my own unique journey.

11

My Own Journey

In the summer of 2007, I had to make a decision. It had been six months since Barbaro had passed away, and the activity on the TimWoolleyRacing.com site was continuing to increase. Most of the discussion had now shifted to horse racing and horse welfare issues. Now I wondered if I should try to manage this community full time, manage the community as a side project while I continued my teaching and consulting work, or close the community altogether. I have had plenty of opportunities in life, but I had never really focused all of my energies on a single pursuit, one that would marry my core interests of horses, marketing, and the Internet. I therefore decided to take this opportunity and focus full time on the Fans of Barbaro phenomenon, to better support the work that they were doing.

I then pondered a second decision. I could remain at Fair Hill and ride a few horses in the mornings (I thought that this was important not only from a cash flow standpoint, but also to retain credibility within the horse racing community) while managing this project for the rest of the day. Or I could leave Fair Hill, a place I had worked at on and off for twenty years, and travel around to learn about horse racing and horse welfare issues at a local level in many different parts of North America. The latter would also help me develop a strong network—and, it would be an adventure!

I made the decision to travel, and spent a little more than two years on the road. I worked at Penn National (PA), Presque Isle Downs (PA), Keeneland (KY), Churchill Downs (KY), Sam Houston Race Park (TX), Woodbine (Toronto, Canada), and Oaklawn Park (AR). I worked for trainers Murray Rojas (Penn National), Tim Kreiser (Penn National), Clovis Crane (Presque Isle Downs),

Chuck Lawrence (Presque Isle Downs), Liz Merryman (Presque Isle Downs), Eddie Kenneally (Keeneland and Churchill Downs), and Steve Asmussen (Sam Houston Race Park, Woodbine for two meets, and Oaklawn Park).

I left Fair Hill, assuming that horse slaughter was wrong and happy to manage a site that was engaged in discussing the horse slaughter issue. I returned to Fair Hill more than two years later, with a thorough understanding of the issue. I had written articles, visited auctions to understand kill buyer behavior, organized and participated in lobbying events in Washington D.C., and had become a leader on the complicated topic of horse slaughter. I also developed a much better understanding of how horse racing operates in North America after working at seven different racetracks for seven different trainers. I saw firsthand the resources available for horses once their racing careers are over, which is another focus of Fans of Barbaro.

Me galloping

HORSE SLAUGHTER

Christine Picavet is an equine artist. Christine also used to be an exercise rider, at one time riding horses for Hall of Fame trainer Charlie Whittingham. Christine knew both Exceller and Ferdinand and has vivid memories of both champions.

"Exceller was an elegant horse who was by one of my favorite stallions, Vaguely Noble," said Picavet. "I had the pleasure of riding Exceller after he arrived from France and into the barn of Hall of Fame trainer, Charles Whittingham. He was playful but gentle to be around. Exceller was easy to ride and also brave because he kept on winning despite some injuries towards the end of his racing career."

"I painted Exceller for his owner, Nelson Bunker Hunt," she continued. "My watercolor was featured on the cover of the *Blood-Horse*—December 4, 1978 issue. I found out that Exceller had been slaughtered in Sweden from Mike Mullaney, who worked for the *Daily Racing Form* and was writing a story about my artwork. I was so shocked by the news that I could not complete the interview for a couple of days."

Sadly, her experience with Exceller was doomed to be repeated.

Ferdinand winning the 1986 Derby

"I was also very fond of, and impressed by, Ferdinand," said Picavet. "I visited him at his barn frequently and followed his exploits. He was tall, gorgeous, and very kind, despite being by Nijinsky. Kindness must have come from his dam, 1987 Broodmare of the Year Banja Luka. I had the pleasure of being the regular rider of Ferdinand's older stakes-winning half sister, Donna Inez. She was so tiny and dainty compared to 'Ferdi,' but just as kind."

The artist added, "I had the honor of painting Ferdinand, winning the Hollywood Gold Cup over Alysheba, as a commission from owner Howard B. Keck for Charles Whittingham's seventieth birthday."

Ferdinand won the 1986 Kentucky Derby. It was the first Kentucky Derby win for Whittingham. His jockey, Willie Shoemaker, became the oldest jockey to win the Kentucky Derby with this victory. It was a terrific win for the old guard of horse racing. The following year, Ferdinand won the Breeders' Cup Classic to cap off a season that earned him Horse of the Year honors. In the Breeders' Cup Classic, Ferdinand defeated the reigning Kentucky Derby winner, Alysheba. Ferdinand was a Kentucky Derby winner who defeated another Derby winner.

In 1994, after a poor stud career in the United States, Ferdinand was exported to Japan to stand at stud. In 2002, still unsuccessful as a stallion, Ferdinand was disposed of—presumably sold for his meat.

Exceller won major stakes races in Europe and North America, and completed the unique feat of defeating two Triple Crown winners in one race (Seattle Slew and Affirmed in the 1978 Jockey Club Gold Cup). Exceller was also trained by Charlie Whittingham. In April 1997, he was sold for slaughter in Sweden at the request of his owner at the time. His caregiver, Ann Pagmer, had to make an appointment at the slaughter house, and take him over there herself. It was, no doubt, a harrowing experience for both.

The news of the stories that Exceller and Ferdinand had been slaughtered was part of the inspiration for a small group of horsemen to become directly involved in the horse slaughter issue and lobby Congress for the passage of anti-slaughter legislation. In 2006, owners Debby Oxley and Staci Hancock worked with Congressman Ed Whitfield and his wife Connie to develop a marketing campaign designed to exploit the timing of the Triple Crown. The anti-slaughter campaign included sending a letter imploring passage of the anti-slaughter bill, signed by the connections of recent Kentucky Derby winners, along with a red rose, which is synonymous with the Kentucky Derby. These packages were sent to all congressional representatives in order to encourage them to push for the current bill to be released from committee so it could be considered for a floor vote. As part of the process of obtaining signatures for the letter, Staci Hancock contacted Gretchen Jackson. It was this conversation that triggered Mrs. Jackson's involvement in the horse slaughter issue, resulting in the support of the issue from Fans of Barbaro, and in turn, my focus on the topic of horse slaughter.

While I was galloping at Sam Houston Race Park for Steve Asmussen during the winter of 2007–2008, I met with Julie Caramante, a Houston-based horse advocate. From this initial meeting was born the Americans Against Horse Slaughter two-day lobbying event, held in Washington D.C. in March 2008. It was the largest lobbying event in the short history of the horse slaughter movement. More than a hundred advocates attended, many of whom were FOBs lobbying their government for the first time.

I remained in the employ of Steve Asmussen when I moved to Woodbine, in Toronto, Canada, in the spring of 2008, and spent much of that year, and the following, attending the OLEX kill auction in Kitchener, Ontario, each Tuesday. My purpose for attending this auction was to gain a better understanding of the types of horses that the kill buyers purchased for slaughter, and the prices that they would pay. I was also able to provide some reporting of my visits, creating a little more transparency to this aspect of the horse industry. I had previously spent some time attending the New Holland Auction in Pennsylvania, which is also attended by kill buyers.

THE ISSUE

My understanding of horse slaughter has evolved over time. Prior to getting directly involved in the issue in 2006, I think I was like many horsemen. I knew that horse slaughter existed, and I assumed that it was necessary and hoped that it was humane. I would hear, from time to time, from animal rights interests that said it was wrong and inhumane, but they were the same people who were also trying to end the sport within which I worked. They used emotionally-charged rhetoric that I assumed exaggerated circumstances, much like they did when targeting the sport of horse racing. Essentially, their viewpoint did not carry much credibility. Horsemen were more likely to listen to those who advocated for the need for horse slaughter, which included some of our own industry leadership and veterinary organizations.

My initial experiences in running this project and learning more about horse slaughter convinced me to change my viewpoint swiftly. Horse slaughter is wrong; it is inhumane and unnecessary. Horses deserve much better after the service that they have provided us over many millennia. While that viewpoint still forms a basis for my understanding of the issue, prior to attending the Americans Against Horse Slaughter lobbying event in March 2008, I determined I needed to have a better understanding of the entire issue. I conducted more research. After the March 2008 event, I headed up to Toronto, Canada. Part of the reason why I chose to go to Canada was because it is where a number of U.S. horses were being exported for slaughter. Since Steve Asmussen was setting up his first string at Woodbine, it was a great opportunity for me. I dedicated a lot of time that summer to doing more research and understanding horse slaughter from the bottom up.

I now believe that I understand the issue, and recognize the way in which we can end horse slaughter. It would require two key efforts. First, horsemen need to want to end horse slaughter, and secondly, the argument for ending horse slaughter needs to center on whether a horse is a food animal or a non-food animal.

MY RATIONALE

Horse slaughter has received much more coverage in recent years, first because of the deaths of Exceller and Ferdinand, and later, due to the groundswell of interest from Fans of Barbaro, which supported ongoing anti-slaughter efforts.

Legislation has been developed in Washington D.C. for more than ten years now, pioneered by the Animal Welfare Institute (AWI) in 2001. Unfortunately, there really have been no major successes at the federal level, with

THE PATH TO SLAUGHTER AT A HORSE AUCTION

I was coming off the racetrack this morning at Woodbine, and Nancy, assistant trainer for Roger Attfield, hollered at me, "Alex, if you need space to stash a horse for a few months, I have a spot for you." It was a gesture triggered no doubt by the knowledge that I attend a "livestock" horse auction once a week about an hour west of Woodbine. Tuesday was that day.

I attend auctions primarily to study the behavior of the kill buyer, whose main client is a slaughterhouse, and to provide more transparency to this aspect of the horse industry. Occasionally, I buy a horse.

While there is currently no horse slaughter in the United States, auctions like this exist all over North America. They are part of the clearinghouse for animals that eventually wind up on dinner tables around the world. But, as I have come to learn, not just any horse will do for slaughter. Kill buyers prefer healthy horses of medium size. Consequently, kill buyers often end up bidding against those looking for a horse for their daughter or their farm. As for the horses that receive no bids, they are sometimes picked up by rescue farms, or are euthanized.

With about sixty horses for sale, Tuesday's auction was similar in size to those I have attended on recent Tuesdays. In recent weeks, two to three kill buyers have attended. This week, only the main kill buyer attended. Because of that, he was able to buy horses almost at will. He bought about forty horses (most were Standardbreds, owing to the many trotting tracks in Ontario), paying from as low as fifteen cents a pound to as high as forty-nine cents a pound. He bought three of the five thoroughbreds for sale.

The odd thing about his most expensive horse is that it is not the type of horse he typically buys for kill, at that price. I have come to learn the types of horses and conditions of horses that are ideal for kill. This was a big black Percheron. At twenty-five cents, it would have made sense. The best conclusion I could draw is that this horse was bought for someone else. He did pay forty-three cents a pound for another horse, a gorgeous and healthy looking one. That price made sense and is what I would consider his top price for a meat horse. In recent weeks, the top price paid had been about three or four cents higher. On Tuesday, we had the same number of horses, fewer bidders, and therefore lower prices all around. The median price was down about five cents a pound.

What becomes clear at these auctions is that kill buyers pay a premium for healthy looking horses. On Tuesday, the kill buyer paid as low as fifteen cents a pound for a couple of underweight horses. And there were other horses, which were worse off, that the kill buyer simply did not bid on. The point is that kill buyers are not simply buying up horses that have no other demand. They are bidding on healthy horses, paying more for those horses as they outbid private buyers and other dealers. A healthy horse bound for slaughter will provide a better-quality meat, and more of it, to the meatpacking company I assume.

Last year I bought a horse, Kiss My Hoof, for $300 from a kill buyer. He was perhaps the slowest racehorse in Ontario. Beaten about fifty lengths in his final start.

A week later, I watched Magic Flute go to slaughter. Magic Flute was a winner three times in six starts in Canada. He was second in the other three starts.

—*NEW YORK TIMES,*
May 22, 2009

By the pound

bills either getting held up in various committees, or going to the floor for a vote when it became too late in the year for anything to happen. At the state level there have been successes, and the last U.S.-based slaughter plants, in Illinois and Texas, were shuttered in 2007. Sadly, our horses are now simply shipped across the borders in greater numbers to Canada and Mexico for slaughter. Approximately the same number of horses are being slaughtered on a yearly basis; the location of slaughter has simply shifted.

Many of the arguments proposed to end horse slaughter are emotional ones, and as such, are debatable. The anti-slaughter movement will state that horse slaughter is inhumane, and will point to YouTube video evidence which supports this. The pro-slaughter side will argue that not only is slaughter humane—they prefer to label it "horse processing"—but it is also necessary to rid us of excess horses that would simply be left to starve, which in itself is inhumane. Anti-slaughter advocates will argue that there are no excess horses; slaughter is a demand-driven business. We slaughter only the numbers demanded by our customers in European and Asian markets. Kill buyers and slaughterhouses simply represent one target audience within the horse industry. Anti-slaughter advocates will also note that abuse and

neglect occurs whether slaughter numbers increase or decrease. One number does not affect the other. They will also argue that replacing one evil (abuse and neglect) with another (slaughter) is not acceptable. Essentially, they believe in responsible ownership of the horse, which includes planning for a humane end of life.

As a horseman, I came to believe that horse slaughter is inhumane; but then again we really do not like death, and any kind of animal slaughter is going to be visually repugnant. Try watching cattle being slaughtered on YouTube. Is it a double standard to object to horse slaughter, yet not object to other livestock slaughter? Anti-slaughter advocates will note that there is a distinction. Horses are flight animals and have not been bred specifically for the slaughter pipeline, and therefore are less docile. Because they are flight animals, they sense and react to fear more readily. They are harder to kill because their longer necks make the kill process less accurate. It seems a sensible argument, but one left open to debate. Do we really know that cows do not sense fear?

If it is the case that all slaughter is inhumane, then only those who have a vegan agenda can truly argue against the inhumanity of horse slaughter. And the pro-slaughter people will argue that the anti-slaughter movement is just that—a vegan-led agenda that wants to end all livestock slaughter. Clearly, this is a complicated issue, but trying to end horse slaughter solely based on the humanity of the practice will always be a challenge.

This book has addressed the horse's role in human history, and highlighted specific horses that have proven truly inspirational. The deaths of champions such as Ferdinand and Exceller are proof that racetrack success does not guarantee a horse a fate better than slaughter.

No other animal has played such an important role for humans, and no other animal has proven so inspirational. Should this then safeguard our horses from slaughter? Does this provide a necessary distinction for horses from other livestock? Not so, if you ask those who are pro-slaughter. Livestock is livestock and should be treated as such. The debate remains an emotional one.

There is, however, one argument that is neither emotional nor debatable.

Is the horse a food animal?

THE HORSE

Where in this wide world can man find nobility without pride,
Friendship without envy, or beauty without vanity?

Here, where grace is served with muscle
And strength by gentleness confined

He serves without servility; he has fought without enmity.

There is nothing so powerful, nothing less violent.

There is nothing so quick, nothing more patient.
England's past has been borne on his back.

All our history is in his industry.
We are his heirs, he our inheritance.

RONALD DUNCAN, 1954

Read at the end of each Horse of the Year show, London, U.K.

Is the horse bred for the food chain, or is it bred for other purposes? For the most part (there are a few exceptions), the horse is bred for recreational, sport, and work purposes. As a result, a horse will receive drugs over its lifetime that may not be allowable for animals intended for the food chain. One such drug is phenylbutazone (bute). Horses are administered bute much like humans take aspirin. Both the Food and Drug Agency (FDA) and the Canadian Food Inspection Agency (CFIA) have banned bute from horses for slaughter. The CFIA rules are in place to appease the European Union, which is a major customer of our horse meat. Essentially, a horse that has received bute *at any time in its life* is not viable for slaughter.

We know that racehorses are administered bute, while in training, for a variety of reasons. In 2009, 99 percent of starters in California (7,391 out of 7,443) were pre-raced on bute (according to the *Daily Racing Form*). California is one of only a few states to publish the pre-race information, but it can be considered a reasonable proxy for other racing jurisdictions in the United States. Given that pre-racing is only one event during which a horse might receive bute, it is fair to assume that pretty much every racehorse in the United States has received the drug at some point in its life. Racehorses are simply not eligible for slaughter under current rules; this argument is neither debatable nor emotional.

Racehorses are not the only equines that are given bute; it is a fair assumption that most sport, recreational, and work horses have received the drug at some point in their lives. There is no safeguard in place ensuring the meat producers that this is not the case. From a food safety standpoint, it is important to retain the distinction between a food animal and a non-food animal. The horse appears to be the only animal in a gray area.

Beginning in July 2010, in response to growing pressure from the European Union, a horse shipped to slaughter from North America has to be accompanied by an Equine Identification Document (EID). This form illustrates proof that the horse has been drug free for the prior six months. The form is signed by the prior owner, as the horse is being sold at auction, or directly to the kill buyer. Horses without these forms do not sell for the same price to kill buyers, who would then need to hold the horses for up to six months in order to satisfy this new requirement. This reflects the European Union's concern that horse meat coming from North America is drug free; however, the form does not make allowances for permanently banned drugs like bute.

This is an ongoing issue, but it seems clear that the European Union is becoming more concerned with the viability of horse meat coming from North America, where liberal use of drugs is more acceptable in horse sports. It is clear that most of our horses are not eligible for slaughter under current rules.

RACETRACKS RESPOND

A number of racetracks have responded to the horse slaughter issue. Perhaps due to public pressure, or because of genuine concern for their horses, many now have a "zero tolerance" policy with regard to horse slaughter. Horsemen who are discovered sending their horses to slaughter are punished by losing their ability to house or run horses at the racetrack.

It has been a sad reality that a number of our racehorses, once they have finished running, are simply shipped off to the slaughterhouse via kill auctions and kill buyers. These kill buyers, or horse traders, would build relationships with a few of the horsemen on the backsides of the racetracks and would use those relationships to help them fill their quotas needed for their slaughterhouse contracts.

This issue becomes a greater concern when a race meet ends and horses have to move from the backside of the racetrack as it closes down. Some horses will be shipped to other racetracks to continue racing, a few will be given time off, and others will be put up for sale or given away, as the cost to keep them in the short term becomes prohibitive. During the end of the 2009 Fort Erie and Woodbine meets, there was speculation that a significant number of horses were being purchased by meat dealers to be shipped to slaughter. Nothing was ever proven; if the rumors were true, the horses were very likely slaughtered before the evidence could be discovered. What was very interesting, however, was the reaction of both racetracks to the situation. Alarmed, they did everything within their power to prosecute the issue, along with the Ontario Racing Commission. I was involved in some of those discussions while I was at Woodbine. During that time, I also observed a truck and stock trailer on the backside at Woodbine that appeared suspicious. When its driver was paged over the backside's PA system and asked to meet with the racing officials, he immediately exited the backside.

Times have changed, and tracks are beginning to react more responsibly for the welfare of their horses.

· ·

Clever Allemont's Story

The rescue of Clever Allemont was a classic case of the effectiveness of the Fans of Barbaro network. Clever Allemont was a very good horse in his early races. In 1985, he won the Southwest Stakes and the Rebel Stakes at Oaklawn Park to remain undefeated. He was on the Triple Crown trail, and had been a heavy favorite for the Arkansas Derby, but did not win.

Clever Allemont ran as an older handicap horse to some success. He then went on to be a stallion of only modest accomplishment at various locations, including Illinois, Washington, and Kansas. His whereabouts then became unknown.

In 2009, he re-emerged in a horse broker's lot in Kansas; slaughter was a possible next step. A rescue organization posted his situation on the ABR discussion board and a quick succession of events took place that guaranteed a lifetime home for Clever Allemont at Old Friends in Kentucky.

Visiting Clever Allemont, as I traveled from Oaklawn Park to Woodbine in the spring of 2009 was one of the highlights of my two-year journey.

· ·

RETIREMENT PROGRAMS

Some racetracks have created programs that serve as a safe haven between the racetrack and private adopters of our retired racehorses. Woodbine has the Long Run Thoroughbred Society, which is the oldest such program at a racetrack in North America, established in 2000. It is well supported by the racetrack and is very popular among the horsemen on the backside at Woodbine. When traveling back and forth to Woodbine, I would stop and visit the Finger Lakes Thoroughbred Adoption Program, which not only helps find homes for racehorses from the Finger Lakes Race Track (similar to Long Run), but also directly rehabilitates those horses at their on-site location. While I was at Sam Houston Race Park, I attended a fundraiser for Lonestar Outreach to Place Ex-Racers (LOPE), which works with thoroughbreds and quarter horses in Texas. More and more, these types of programs are gaining in popularity and enable second careers for our stars. Other racetracks have similar programs, or work with organizations such as CANTER to help market their horses to the general public.

There are also programs that are independent of the racetracks, but work with, and receive some support from, the tracks. CANTER is the largest such organization, and works with racetracks across North America. CANTER serves as an advertising platform for the horses in some instances; in other racing jurisdictions, they also have facilities where they can rehabilitate horses. Akindale Thoroughbred Rescue, MidAtlantic Horse Rescue, New Vocations Racehorse Adoption Program, Southern California Thoroughbred Rescue, Thoroughbred Retirement Foundation, and Tranquility Farm are other programs that work with horsemen to rehabilitate horses for second careers or offer permanent homes.

Old Friends is a bit of a different beast. It is a sanctuary for horses, rather than a rehabilitation center. I have visited Old Friends on a number of occasions as I traveled through, and worked in, Kentucky. Old Friends also has a number of horses that have been retired with the help of Fans of Barbaro, including Tour of the Cat, Clever Allemont, and Cappucino Kid.

Rescue and rehabilitation programs are not the only means of transfer of racehorses to second careers. Many horsemen at the tracks have their own relationships with individuals that focus on different equine disciplines outside of the tracks. Sometimes the exercise riders and the grooms will take on a horse and rehab it for another career—or simply for themselves.

The following two examples are of horses that went directly from their racing careers to their new owners. I chose these two examples simply because I have ridden both of these horses while they were pursuing their second careers.

Ashkal Way is a Grade 1 stakes winner. In short, he could really run. He is, however, a gelding, and thus does not have any breeding value now his racing career is over. ESPN's Jeannine Edwards now has "Ash," and is developing him into an accomplished dressage horse. Ash is a great example of a horse that seems to excel at whatever he does. Of course, when I rode Ash, he nearly dropped me. He can be a little spooky!

Judge Beautiful is not a Grade 1 stakes winner. In fact, she was not a very good racehorse at all. She ran 39 times, winning only three races. In her last five starts, she was beaten a combined 150 lengths. Yet "JB" is a great example of a horse that was simply involved in the wrong discipline. She is now a show jumper, in the very capable hands of Priscilla Godsoe. Her specialty is the Puissance (jumping a single large wall), which she has also done while Priscilla rides her bareback. Sometimes it is just a case of finding the right discipline for a horse, in order to let the horse develop and thrive. JB is a great example of that.

It is a sad reality but, due to soundness issues, and the use of drugs to mask those issues during racing, some of our racehorses are not able to do much beyond being a "pasture pet" once their racing careers have ended. But that is not always the case, and those able to pursue another career can make great athletes.

Jumping bareback

RETIRING WAR HORSES

I was working at the inaugural meet at Presque Isle Downs in the fall of 2007, and I was mucking out stalls for trainer Liz Merryman when a horse shipped in to a stall opposite Liz's horses. I befriended the horse's trainer (part of why I was traveling was to learn and make connections) and learned a lot about Top Bunk. He had earned more than $500,000, but was now entering the twilight of his career. He was running in a $10,000 claiming race, and his current trainer had only recently acquired him, having claimed him for $12,000 two starts prior. If he won his race at Presque Isle Downs and was claimed, his connections would have profited well from their short association with the horse. This is a large part of the reality of the claiming business—claim a horse, run it two or three times, hope you win a race, and then drop him in (run for a lower level claiming price) so he is claimed before he can no longer race competitively. As it turned out Top Bunk did win, but he was not claimed. His owner entertained the idea of trying to sell him after the race, but was unable to reach a deal he liked. About four days later, Top Bunk shipped out to another racetrack, off for another race where he would again be on offer for sale. He was a cool horse.

Several months later, in the spring of 2008, I had arrived at Woodbine. There was a discussion on our website about a horse that Fans of Barbaro wanted to claim and retire. I had followed the discussion without getting involved, nor really giving it much thought, until the name of the horse was revealed. It was my buddy, Top Bunk. Now I was interested. Top Bunk now had different connections, having been claimed away from the guys who had him for the Presque Isle race for a $6,000 claim price at Hawthorne Park (Illinois). Top Bunk was now entered for a claiming price of $4,000, continuing his slide down the claiming system toward obscurity. Several questions were raised. Could we claim him? Could we raise the money? Should he be claimed? What are the racetrack policies toward something like this? Surely, not just anyone can go ahead and claim a horse. These were all good questions that required serious thought.

Top Bunk was favorite for the $4,000 claiming race, but he ran poorly, finishing fifth of seven starters, beaten by eleven lengths. Unfortunately, our attempt to claim him was thwarted, apparently by a claim slip that was filled out incorrectly. We purchased him for an additional $1,000 over the claim price shortly after the race. Top Bunk was now retired.

This whole incident got me thinking. How many horses are there running in North America that were once good, and were now toiling in low-level claiming races? Top Bunk had made more than $500,000 in his career. I used that as a measure of a good horse; it was arbitrary, of course, but I needed to start from somewhere. I also used the idea that if the horse was now running in a claiming race for $5,000 or less, then the horse was now not as good as he or she once was. There is usually a reason why a fast horse begins to run slowly.

I turned to the *Daily Racing Form* to see if it could produce a report for me, based on the two criteria, earners of more than $500,000, that had started at least once for a claiming price of $5,000 or less. This was the advent of the "Top Bunk List," a list of horses we can track that had been good horses but were perhaps not doing so well now. We could then reach out to the owners of the horses, assess the horses' conditions, and offer to buy them, to claim them if necessary, or whatever may be required to ensure a safe landing for horses that have certainly earned a comfortable retirement.

The Top Bunk List typically has about ten to twelve horses on it at any given time. Approximately twenty horses have successfully retired since the inception of the list—some with the help of Fans of Barbaro, some by their last connections, and some by their original breeders. Sadly, a few horses have also been lost, including Mighty Beau (broke down at Penn National in December 2008, earner of $645,000), Sky Diamond (broke down at Monmouth Park in August 2008, earner of more than $500,000), and Speed Whiz (who died a few weeks after his last race).

Lights on Broadway was successfully retired from the list, but his story illustrates how precarious a situation some of these stars are in.

Lights on Broadway was a Texas champion in 2001. "Lights" had made more than $550,000 in his career, winning 15 races from 83 starts. When we started the Top Bunk List project, he had last run at Fonner Park, Nebraska, on March 16, 2008,

for $2,500 and finished sixth. The meet was over. There was no sign of the horse.

Nearly four months later, on July 2, Lights worked three-eighths of a mile at Fair Meadows in Tulsa, Oklahoma. When I saw that he had a workout, I was not sure if I was excited or relieved. We began to work on figuring out how to contact his trainer and see if we could buy the horse and retire him. It turned out that his new trainer was a quarter horse trainer and none of our thoroughbred contacts had a means to contact him. An Internet search resolved the issue and we made the contact. Lights had been on a kill truck! Fortunately for him, the driver of the truck pointed him out to the quarter horse trainer, who then made the purchase. He was a lovely horse and the new trainer and his family really liked him. They got him ready and ran him twice at the Fair meet at Anthony Downs, Kansas, for a $2,500 claiming price. Lights finished second the first time and fourth a week later. After one work and two races, we were anxious to help retire the Texas champion. It was an easy sell among the members of the Texas racing community, who were equally anxious to have their champion return home. A purchase price was negotiated, and Lights was sold and sent to Donna and Dallas Keen to be retrained for another career.

Lights on Broadway's story illustrates how harsh the claiming system can be for horses that have some talent. It is also a story of a little bit of luck.

THE JOURNEY

An old quote advises us that a journey of a thousand miles begins with a single step. When I took that first step on my own journey, I was not sure what to expect. Two years later, when I returned home, I had a deeper understanding of many issues in the equine world. I also became familiar with the culture of the various racetracks throughout North America, and met countless amazing horses and people. Leaving them behind was the hardest part of the journey. While it would be impossible to describe all of the people I met along the way, I will highlight a few.

I started at Penn National, freelancing for Murray Rojas. Paige, another rider, introduced me to other horsemen on the backside, which enabled me to freelance for Tim Kreiser after I was finished at Rojas's barn. In the three weeks I was at Penn

National I fell off three horses for Kreiser; more spills than I experienced for the next two years!

I met Jimmy at Presque Isle. Having been a professor in Canada, Jimmy was now following his passion, and had served as a shedrow foreman for Ken McPeek along the way. Jimmy gave me some quick lessons in understanding how the racetracks worked, and some of the connections to horse dealers and kill buyers, off the tracks. Jimmy also introduced me to many interesting people along the way, including Mark, who brought Top Bunk to Presque Isle. I remained friends with both Jimmy and Mark throughout my journey. Mark came to Woodbine in 2008 with a two-year-old filly for an allowance race. She won. I started galloping the filly for Mark, on a freelance basis, after I was finished with my morning gallops for Steve Asmussen. The filly, Hooh Why, ran well for the remainder of the meet at Woodbine, and went on to win the Grade 1 Ashland Stakes at Keeneland the following spring, beating two-year-old champion Stardom Bound. The filly returned to Woodbine in 2009, and we renewed our partnership.

At Presque Isle, I also met Darren, one of the head assistant trainers for Steve Asmussen. I asked Darren for a job in Texas. Darren agreed, assuming he would never hear from me again. I worked for Darren, both directly and indirectly, for more than two years during my time working for Steve Asmussen. It was David who suggested that I work for Steve Asmussen in Texas. David was a friend from the old days at Fair Hill. He was, at that time, one of the stewards at Presque Isle. I also ran across another friend from the old Fair Hill days, Gerry, who had shipped a horse in for trainer Eddie Kenneally to run in a stakes race at Presque Isle. I agreed to hot walk the horse after it raced. I don't remember how she ran, but Gerry offered me a job working for Eddie Kenneally for the upcoming fall meet at Keeneland.

Working at Keeneland was a terrific experience for me. Just spending a month in Lexington has to be the dream of many people who love our sport of horse racing. Eddie was great to work for, and offered me a job at Churchill Downs, which I had to accept, even if it was only for a couple of weeks. Eddie also offered me a job for the winter in Florida, which I had to decline because I was determined to head to Texas for a different circuit of racing. The highlight of my working at Churchill

Downs was nearly running over Curlin going to the track one early morning, soon after he had won the Breeders' Cup Classic!

From Louisville, I drove down to Texas, and checked into a motel that would be my residence for the next four months. I called Darren on my way down to let him know I was coming. He told me that Tony, another Asmussen assistant, would be ready for me when I got to the barn; thus began my more-than-two-year association with the Steve Asmussen operation.

I only knew two people in Houston before I arrived: David, the Presque Isle steward who had returned to his full-time steward's role at Sam Houston Race Park; and Jacqui, who used to be a groom at Fair Hill and now lived on a ranch in the suburbs of Houston.

I left Texas with a few more friends, including Paul, who was originally from Stoke, U.K., and was one of the leading jockeys at the Texas meet. He had ridden more than a thousand winners before he rode his first graded stakes win—at the end of that meet. As Paul was a Minnesota Vikings fan, we enjoyed watching football together over the winter. I also befriended "Masterlock" Scott, who had a unique way of riding his horses (hence the nickname I gave him). Scott also had a unique way of dictating a conversation, usually relating to how much a twelve-pack of Pepsi costs at his local supermarket. Another friend, "Superstar" Erik, was planning a career as a jockey. He had turned down an athletic scholarship to a university to become a jockey. His brother and father were both jockeys; his father worked for Cash Asmussen at Sam Houston Race Park. I also met Eddie, who had actually had a stint working at Fair Hill for trainer Barclay Tagg.

Perhaps one of the most interesting experiences I had during my travels was attending match races with Angela while still in Texas. I had heard many stories about match racing, and wanted to see it for myself. Much later, while I was at the Oaklawn Park meet in the winter of 2008–2009, Mandy, an exercise rider and pony girl, told me about her experience in a match race; she rode against a chicken. The rules were "live weight." You can only imagine how a horse runs for a chicken!

After Tony had left Houston to run Steve's string in New Mexico, Darren took over the Texas horses. In the spring, Darren asked me if I wanted to go to Woodbine for the summer. My swift answer was yes. The most attractive aspect about the move was the change in living situation. I was leaving a motel that was located adjacent to a highway that would often host drag races in the early hours of the mornings, to move to a penthouse suite overlooking the Woodbine complex. I also wanted to go to Canada, because that is where many U.S.-based slaughter-bound horses are being shipped.

Because I spent two long meets at Woodbine, separated by a short winter meet at Oaklawn Park, this is where I really got to know more people, and really enjoy my time.

The backstretch Horsemen's Benevolent & Protective Association (HBPA) office was managed by Corrine. Part of my daily routine was to stop by the office to read the *Daily Racing Form* and hang out and chat with Corrine. As I was not the only one, it was a good way to meet more people and develop more friendships.

As I was still actively managing AlexBrownRacing.com during my travels, Internet access was critical for me. When our penthouse suite lost access, I began to use the Jake Howard Center (the Jake), which was a facility on the backside at Woodbine managed by the racetrack chaplain, Shawn. After chatting with Shawn, I offered to teach an Internet class for those on the backside who had never used a computer. The Jake had a few computers wired into the Internet. Teaching those classes was probably the richest experience I had on the backsides of the racetracks where I worked. It allowed me to meet others on the backside I would not have ordinarily met, and enabled me to understand computer usability as I otherwise would never have been able to understand. Some of the students came to the first session and did not come back. Others completed the three-session course we designed, bought their own laptop, and now have access to information, and a means of communication, that they did not have before. Thanks to folks such as Clarence, Denis, and Monica, I enjoyed teaching again, and learning more about their lives at Woodbine.

At Woodbine, I also worked with Mark, who hailed from India. He had been a leading jockey in his own country. He now spends his summers at Woodbine, and the winters working in Dubai. We would hang out a little outside of work while we were both at Woodbine.

While Darren was the assistant at the beginning of the meet in 2008, I also worked for Steve, and later, Hank. I have become good friends with Hank, and recently attended his wedding to Katie. Another rider, Dominic, came up from the U.S. to work for us for a little while. He would ultimately be required by Steve Asmussen to gallop Rachel Alexandra. I had the honor of meeting Rachel myself, during the 2008-2009 winter meet at Oaklawn Park.

At Woodbine, we shared a shedrow with another trainer, David Cotey. During the 2008 meet, he had a nice two-year-old that kept beating our own two-year-olds. The horse, Mine That Bird, then went on to win the 2009 Kentucky Derby. Watching that race, in the track kitchen, with Paul and Tony, who worked for David Cotey, was a memory I wrote about for the *New York Times'* "The Rail."

"We paddock schooled three horses today at Woodbine, then ran one in the ninth race. She ran a nice second. A very gutsy race. After things settled down, I headed over to the track kitchen to watch the Kentucky Derby. I was with Hank, our assistant. There was a crowd gathering, getting ready for the big race. Hank and I were joined by Paul, a groom for David Cotey. We share a barn with him. Tony, who also grooms for David, was there, too.

"We settled in with general chitchat: Who do you like? Track looks bad. Did you bet? The usual pre-race discourse.

"The gates opened. It was hard to hear the commentary above the general buzz of the kitchen. Who's in front? Who's that who looks good in third? Mine That Bird was called well last down the backside. They turned for home. Pioneerof the Nile loomed, cruising. Then he looked to come up a little short. Horses were fanning wide. Then someone sprinted up the rail. Who is it? Who? Borel with Mine that Bird.

"And he drew away impressively. The kitchen exploded. One guy had '10 across.' No one cared who was second or third. It was just a very neat scene.

"A friend just called. She broke Mine That Bird. Just very cool all around."
—*NEW YORK TIMES*,
"The Rail," May 2009

Hanging out in Champions Bar during the races was a favorite occupation of mine, but was also expensive. Danny was a regular acquaintance at Champions. Danny is the agent for jockey Jimmy McAleney who was our jockey for the first meet we were there. Both became good friends, as did Anita, assistant for trainer Terry Jordan, for whom I also freelanced for a little while during the 2008 meet. One horse I rode for them would literally run off with me for the entire mile-and-a-quarter gallop. They decided to put a lighter rider back on him, with the logic that if he was going to run off anyway, why carry more weight? It made sense. That lighter rider was Mike, who went on to become a jockey and a friend. Mike also did some quarter horse racing at Ajax, which was fun to watch. He has also helped with retiring some horses.

Mike would occasionally attend the OLEX auction with me, which is about an hour west of Woodbine. At the auction, I befriended Ellie, another horse advocate. Ellie was very helpful in getting me to understand how OLEX worked, and who the key buyers were. Together we rescued a very slow racehorse.

I also went to OLEX once with April. We arrived too late for the sale, but April was pretty happy about that. April hosted me during the early part of the second year I was at Woodbine. She galloped for us for a little while before starting her regular job with Malcolm Pierce; she also runs a farm where she helps rehab a few racehorses for second careers.

Alison was my tour guide. Alison galloped horses for one of the leading trainers on the backside, and would take me on a trip once a week. We found some very cool towns within an hour of Woodbine; they had pubs and fish and chip shops. Finally, Gemini and Paul (whose father brought Teleprompter over for the Arlington Million a few years ago) hosted me on their island on Lake Huron, at their house to watch the 2008 Breeders' Cup, and on many other occasions.

Of course, the real pleasure of the journey was being able to ride horses every day, and getting paid for doing something I enjoy. A few horses truly stood out for me. The most accomplished was one that I have already mentioned—Hooh Why. The most visually impressive horse I rode was Storm Treasure. He ran in Barbaro's Kentucky Derby. After training and racing with us at Woodbine in 2008, he went to the Breeders' Cup and finished a fast-closing third in the Turf Sprint race. I only rode Golden Hare once at Sam Houston Race Park, but I have to mention him. He won thirteen races in 2007, and was the horse with the most wins for that year! Of all the horses I rode though, my favorite, by far, is Salty Langfuhn. A high-priced claimer, Salty was a joy to ride. He stands out because he is big and a little sway-backed, and has charisma in bucket loads. Because Salty had run at Woodbine for a number of years, and he looked rather odd, many people on the backside knew him when they saw him. Oftentimes when I galloped past someone, the rider would turn to me and shout affectionately, "There goes Salty!" Every time he ran, you knew he was going to try as hard as he could—*every time*. I still follow Salty's career from afar, and hope that one day we will get to hang out again. I am working on it.

My journey across North America was a ton of work, and lots of fun. Along the way, I did develop a deeper knowledge of horse welfare and horse retirement, while supporting the work of Fans of Barbaro, who were becoming more engaged in the issues. All because of a horse named Barbaro.

Laminitis

FROM CAUSE TO COMPASSION TO CURE?

The Barbaro saga created a sharp focus on the issue of laminitis. Barbaro ultimately succumbed to complications related to laminitis when he was euthanized on January 29, 2007. At that point, Barbaro's front two feet had been afflicted, and he no longer had a good leg on which to stand.

Barbaro first contracted laminitis in his left hind foot in July 2006. The coffin bone had rotated and sunk, and as a result, nearly the entire hoof wall became detached from the coffin bone. The laminitis was most likely the result of Barbaro shifting his weight off his right hind leg, which at the time was experiencing soreness due to a bent screw in the reconstructed pastern, and resulting infection from the surgical area. Barbaro survived this episode, although Dr. Richardson described the laminitis at that time as "as bad a case of laminitis as you can get."

Barbaro's chances of survival at that point were described as poor. A mere two weeks earlier, Dr. Richardson had thought that Barbaro was going to make it—such is the rapid onset of the disease.

After Barbaro had successfully undergone his initial surgery the day after the Preakness Stakes, and Dr. Richardson had described his chances of survival as "a coin toss," three complications were noted as concerns:

1. The risk that the metal implant and screws would fatigue before the bones healed;
2. Infection from the surgical area; and
3. Laminitis, which Dr. Richardson later described as "the most feared complication."

> "If you asked me two weeks ago, I really thought we were going to make it … today I am not as confident."
> —DR. DEAN RICHARDSON,
> July 2006 press conference when it was announced that
> Barbaro had laminitis in his left hind foot

Laminitis is an ever-present threat after any type of orthopedic limb surgery, as a horse has the potential to shift weight away from the injured leg onto the opposite leg. Additional weight-bearing on the foot is one condition that makes a horse prone to laminitis in that foot. In this case, the most significant means of prevention of laminitis is to strengthen the injured leg as quickly as possible, and to attempt to normalize the function of the leg while the healing takes place. In essence, the goal is to allow the injured leg to bear weight in the same manner as a normal leg. Preemptive actions are also undertaken; in Barbaro's case, this included placing a special shoe on the left hind foot to help distribute his weight over a wider surface.

"When Barbaro won the Kentucky Derby in such great fashion we were thrilled. We had a soft spot for Michael Matz. We grew up knowing him from the showing world, and had made his great show jumper Jet Run. When Barbaro was injured in the Preakness we were so sad. We really thought he was going to go all the way.

"In the past, we had done some work with New Bolton Center. Our president, Tony Fleischmann, was determined to do something about the situation. We worked with New Bolton Center and the Jacksons; we made a model and donated $10 per model to be distributed between the Laminitis Fund and the Barbaro Fund at New Bolton Center. We raised about $240,000, which is the single largest charitable donation Breyer has made."

—KATHLEEN FALLON,
Marketing communications director, Breyer

The unfortunate reality after surgeries such as Barbaro's is—as well as everything appeared to be going—there is always a fear that laminitis would set in. Because of this, Dr. Richardson was always guarded in his updates on Barbaro, regardless of how well Barbaro seemed to be doing. And for the first seven weeks Barbaro appeared to be doing very well.

"Good things take a long, long time to occur and bad things happen very quickly, even more so with laminitis," acknowledged Dr. Richardson in the July 2006 press conference.

Unfortunately, Richardson's cause for concern was a valid one, as the onset of laminitis in Barbaro's case was rapid and devastating. Barbaro's recovery from this initial bout of laminitis was always going to be precarious. He had to grow back 90 percent of his hoof wall after having it removed during a hoof wall resection. The cells inside of 90 percent of the hoof wall were detached from their blood supply and had therefore died. Leaving the dead tissue would hinder the growth of living tissue. The growth of the new hoof wall would take six months in the best-case

scenario, but there was no guarantee that the growth would occur in an acceptable fashion.

Ultimately, the growing back of Barbaro's hoof wall was not as it needed to be. In January 2007 Barbaro suffered from an infection in his right hind foot because of shifting weight off his left hind foot. Ironically, this was proof that the newly constructed right hind leg was actually strong enough to bear the additional weight. With both hind feet compromised, the greatest fear was that the front feet would become inflicted with laminitis, and they did. As a result, options had run out and Barbaro was euthanized.

WHAT IS LAMINITIS?

Laminae are the thin, intricately folded, interlocking sheets of tissue that connect the coffin bone (the last bone of the foot) to the hoof wall (outside of the foot). A major purpose of the laminae is to transfer weight from the skeleton to the hoof wall. The laminae also help reduce the compressive forces, preventing the hoof wall from crushing blood vessels, nerves, and other vital tissues, against the coffin bone. They act somewhat like the shock absorbers of a car, keeping the car from sinking too low or bouncing too high. Laminae are also known as the lamellae; both terms mean the same thing.

Laminitis is the inflammation of the laminae. Severe cases of laminitis, known as "founder," result in the rotation of the coffin bone away from the hoof wall, or the "sinking" of the coffin bone, or both, as was the case with Barbaro's initial bout of laminitis. Mild cases of laminitis do not involve any movement of the coffin bone, and are more manageable.

"A horse walks on its middle digit, the nail of its middle finger," explained Dr. Richardson to the media during the July 2006 press conference at New Bolton Center. "Essentially, the bone inside of the hoof has to be attached to that nail. The bone is attached by tissue called laminae. If that tissue becomes damaged and separates, then you lose the connection between the bone and the hoof. If the horse loses the connection between the bone and the hoof it's exquisitely painful for the horse."

There are three phases to the onset of laminitis—the developmental phase, the acute phase, and the chronic phase. The developmental, or initial phase, is when laminitis is developing without any outward signs of the disease. This phase lasts from twenty-four to forty-eight hours. In the next phase, the acute phase, the laminitis is detectable, either by the walking gait of the horse, the stance of the horse, which shifts weight away from the afflicted foot, or by a more rapid "bounding" pulse in the afflicted hoof. The horse will exhibit discomfort during this phase, which lasts anywhere from hours to a few days.

The disease will then move to either a sub-acute phase, in which there is no movement of the coffin bone, or the chronic phase, where there is movement of the coffin bone, resulting in founder.

One of the problems with laminitis, as mentioned previously, is the abrupt onset of the disease. Because the disease is undetectable in the developmental phase, and the progression is so rapid, it is difficult to take actions early enough to prevent the disease from moving to the chronic phase if that is the course it is set to take, as was the case with Barbaro.

• •

"There are so many causes of laminitis; nobody seems to be sure what to do about it. The research has been sadly lagging. The Barbaro Fund is spearheading the efforts, but I'm told by several vets that it has hundreds of causes. We recently lost Academy Award and Black Tie Affair to laminitis, and it is just very sad that we have not gotten to the bottom of this terrible condition for all breeds' sake."

—MICHAEL BLOWEN,
Founder, Old Friends

• •

While we know that certain conditions predispose a horse to laminitis, we do not yet understand the true mechanics of the disease itself. As such, there remains debate, among horsemen, veterinarians, and farriers in terms of the best ways to treat the condition.

Various circumstances and conditions make a horse susceptible to developing laminitis. An injury that results in shifting weight off one leg onto another, as was most likely the cause for Barbaro's case, is one situation that increases the likelihood of laminitis. This is also known as Supporting Limb laminitis. Other categories of conditions are septic (colic, colitis, pneumonia, cellulitis, retained fetal membranes), metabolic (pasture, insulin resistance, Cushing's disease, corticosteroid administration) and mechanical (often referred to as Road Founder).

Laminitis is the second largest killer of horses, accounting for approximately 15 percent of deaths; only colic causes more equine deaths. While a horse does not die from the disease itself, laminitis can create excruciating pain for the horse, resulting in euthanasia.

Laminitis can affect horses of all disciplines and breeds. Event horses, show horses, and polo ponies are all susceptible to the disease, as are Arabians, Standardbreds, and Shetland ponies. The following page highlights some of horse racing's premier athletes, who eventually succumbed to laminitis, despite receiving the best quality veterinary care. Even Secretariat—considered by many to be the greatest racehorse of all time—was not able to successfully battle this dreaded disease.

Fran Jurga, editor of *Hoofcare and Lameness Magazine*, has this to say about the disease: "Beware of anyone who tells you they 'know' anything about laminitis because no one knows that much, even the few people who know a lot.

"Some people have only seen pasture-associated laminitis. They've never seen a horse brought in from the racetrack in the middle of the night with a drug-related laminitis, or a colitis-related laminitis. Or Potomac Horse Fever. Laminitis is just a word and it gets thrown around. It means different things to different people depending on their exposure in the horse world. Sort of like colic. Most horses get colicky and are fine the next day. But others…

RACEHORSES THAT SUCCUMBED TO LAMINITIS

- Secretariat: won the Triple Crown in 1973 and is considered one of the greatest racehorses of all time

- Affirmed: won the Triple Crown in 1978, dueling with Alydar

- Sunday Silence: beat Easy Goer in the Kentucky Derby, Preakness, and Breeders' Cup Classic in 1989

- Kip Deville: won the 2007 Breeders' Cup Mile

- Bayakoa: won the Breeders' Cup Distaff in 1989 and 1990

- Singspeil: won the 1997 Dubai World Cup

- Black Tie Affair: won the Breeders' Cup Classic in 1991 and was named Horse of the Year

- Arcangues: won the 1993 Breeders' Cup Classic

- Foolish Pleasure: won the 1976 Kentucky Derby and ran the match race against the ill-fated Ruffian

- Machiavellian: winner of the 2002 Dubai World Cup, and leading European sire and sire of Street Cry

- Barathea: won the 1994 Breeders' Cup Mile

- Nijinsky II: won the 1970 English Triple Crown

- Fappiano: Grade 1 Stakes winner and sire of sires, including Unbridled

- Gate Dancer: won the 1984 Preakness Stakes

- Flanders: out-dueled Serena's Song in the Breeders' Cup Juvenile Fillies in 1994

- Hyperion: won the Epsom Derby in 1933 and became a very important stallion

- Mom's Command: won the 1995 Eclipse Award as a champion three-year-old filly

- Creme Fraiche: won the 1985 Belmont Stakes

- Outstandingly: won the Breeders' Cup Juvenile Fillies in 1984

- Maria's Mon: sired two Kentucky Derby winners, Monarchos and Super Saver

- In the Wings: won the 1990 Breeders' Cup Turf

- Sunline: named four times Horse of the Year in New Zealand and three times Horse of the Year in Australia, with career earnings of more than $11 million

Secretariat

"I've never had a horse with catastrophic laminitis or fatal colic and if I didn't do what I do as a journalist I'd probably be ho-hum about both subjects."

TREATMENT

The Greek philosopher Aristotle described laminitis as "barley's disease," no doubt because one of the conditions that triggers laminitis is the ingestion of rich feed. Horsemen and horses have been battling laminitis in recorded history for more than two thousand years. Over those millennia, a variety of cures have been suggested. Bleeding from the middle of the leg was the first known treatment, during the Roman times. Castration (as geldings seemed less prone to laminitis) and the removal of the sole of the foot—were other treatments that gained favor early on. However, the reality is that there is not yet a protocol that is universally accepted for either preventing the onset of laminitis when a horse is more prone to suffer the condition or treatment once the disease sets in.

RECOVERY

That said, there are success stories; horses have and do recover from bouts of laminitis. If a horse does not founder, if there is no radiographic evidence of rotation or sinking of the coffin bone, then it has a much better prognosis and in many cases can completely recover and return to competition. The horse will experience discomfort during the acute phase of laminitis (lasting from a few hours to a few days), but once this phase passes, the horse's comfort level should improve and return to normal. If the horse does founder, but the rotation of the coffin bone away from the hoof wall is less than five degrees, again the horse is more likely to recover and can return to some form of competition. The goal in this situation is to try to reestablish the orientation of the coffin bone to the ground, without having to be too aggressive in the trimming of the foot in order to do so. Cases of significant rotation, or the sinking of the coffin bone (where the entire suspensory system fails and the foot collapses) are also recoverable, but horses that survive this will not be able to perform at a competitive level. The goal in such cases is to provide the horse a comfortable quality of life going forward.

Once a horse has suffered a bout of laminitis, it is more likely to be at risk of suffering further episodes. It is not known whether this is because the horse was originally predisposed to develop the disease, or that the previous bout of laminitis weakened the integrity of the foot, or a combination of both.

RESEARCH

Laminitis research has been stymied for several reasons. Given the grisly nature of the disease, it is difficult to find horses to work on, as their suffering typically requires rapid euthanasia. Additionally, as the disease also has no human or rodent equivalent, there are no directly transferable lessons from research undertaken in human medicine (which obviously receives a much higher priority from a funding standpoint). All hooved animals can suffer from laminitis, but the disease is more crippling, and potentially catastrophic in the larger domesticated species (cattle and horses). While there has been research conducted on cows, where lameness has been identified as a major issue affecting productivity and cow comfort, distinctions between the two animals make the disease and treatments different. For example, cattle are cloven-footed and tend to lie down more often than horses do.

Despite the setbacks in research, there is cause for optimism going forward as momentum for understanding this problem is gaining steam. There is now more room for collaboration, via conferences and other vehicles, in the research community. In essence, more knowledge sharing is taking place, which is vital in order to maximize the wealth of knowledge that is available from around the world.

In 2001, the first International Conference for Laminitis Research was established. The year 2011 will mark the sixth such conference, which meets in alternate years. In 2008, the first Laminitis West conference took place in California; the second such event took place in September of 2010. These conferences serve as a platform for researchers, practitioners, and care-givers to exchange ideas and present best practices. The American Association of Equine Practitioners (AAEP) has sponsored a number of laminitis workshops, and the topic is addressed at AAEP meetings.

Research techniques have also evolved since the 1990s that allow scientists to investigate diseases at the molecular level. This type of research, which has proven beneficial in fields such as cancer research for humans, also applies to laminitis research. Without these new tools, we would not be able to make the progress we are currently making. The Horse Genome project, released in 2009, allows equine researchers to utilize the same cutting-edge molecular methods that have been available for years to those conducting biomedical research on human disease and in rodent models of human disease, and is further helping in the laminitis research effort.

The combination of more advanced research techniques, better data, and more cooperation among researchers helps explain why we now think the laminitis puzzle is a solvable problem, something we have struggled with for two thousand years.

"We can solve what is happening, which will help prevent many cases and enable evidence-based treatments for those with laminitis. We cannot completely eradicate laminitis, much like we cannot eradicate organ failure when people get sick."

—DR. HANNAH GALANTINO-HOMER,
Laminitis Institute, Penn Vet

There is also clear evidence that momentum for understanding laminitis has increased since Barbaro was euthanized in January 2007. The Laminitis Fund at New Bolton Center, established in 2006 after Barbaro contracted laminitis, has accrued $1.9 million as of June 2010.

According to Ed Bowen, president of the Grayson-Jockey Club Research Foundation, since 1985, they have provided funding for sixteen laminitis projects, for a total of $9,999,928. Eight of those projects have been funded since 2006, at a cost of $547,000. The Grayson-Jockey Club Foundation works with the National Thoroughbred Racing Association's (NTRA) Barbaro Fund to select projects to support, and monitors those projects on an ongoing basis.

Larger amounts of money, interest, and resources are now targeting laminitis since Barbaro was stricken with the disease. The Laminitis Institute at Penn Vet was established in 2007 thanks to a $1 million gift from philanthropists Marianne and John K. Castle, who had to battle laminitis with their own horse, Spot. Roy and Gretchen Jackson have also provided $3 million to endow a chair at New Bolton Center in Equine Research, which includes a focus on laminitis. Other research centers and universities are also working hard to find a cure for laminitis. The Animal Health Foundation (AHF), founded by Donald Walsh DVM, has been funding researchers who are working to find a cure for laminitis since the 1980s. AHF funds research projects focused on the disease, and hosts its own conferences to allow those it supports to share their findings. Members of the American Association of Equine Practitioners (AAEP), in a 2009 survey, noted that laminitis is the most important disease afflicting horses and the highest priority for further research.

With all the renewed momentum and investment in understanding the disease, progress has been made. Dr. Chris Pollitt's cryotherapy is one example of a therapy that has received acceptance as a means to attempt to stop the progression of laminitis from the developmental phase to the acute phase. Cryotherapy is the application of cold therapy to the hoof by placing the foot, or feet, in crushed ice. A certain degree of coldness must be reached to be effective against laminitis, and the leg must be chilled up to the knee. Of course, the challenge is how one can determine when a horse is in the developmental phase of laminitis, if there are no outward signs of the disease. But we do know there are certain conditions that do increase the likelihood of laminitis; thus, when those conditions are present for a horse, cryotherapy can then be used to attempt to stop the potential progression.

Public awareness of the disease continues through various presentations and exhibits. In July 2009, the National Museum of Racing and Hall of Fame in Saratoga Springs, New York, introduced a special temporary exhibit devoted to equine veterinary medicine, with a significant focus on Barbaro's battle with laminitis. Numerous media outlets, including websites, DVDs, and articles, have focused on laminitis in the years following Barbaro's death.

Despite such initiatives, there is still much more work to be done. This is evidenced by the fact that laminitis continues to claim victims of all breeds, ages, and disciplines. In the summer of 2010 alone, the racing world lost both Kip Deville and Black Tie Affair due to complications of laminitis. The hope is that, with continued research, we can solve what is happening in the not-too-distant future.

A Horse that Stirred a Nation

There is no doubt that Barbaro's short life has made a difference in the world. It has created a heightened awareness for the need to solve the puzzle of laminitis. It has made a difference for horse welfare more generally, and has affected the ways in which horse racing supports its stars, the horses. Barbaro has shifted the needle—we are now more aware of the shortcomings of horse racing, and are making strides to fix them. Barbaro has also made people think harder about their own lives, and be grateful for what they have.

But how will Barbaro be remembered in the years to come, by new generations of fans who did not witness firsthand his spectacular Kentucky Derby win, his Preakness breakdown, and his eight-month fight for his life?

To answer this question, I returned to a few of those who follow horse racing, and also spoke with those more closely connected with Barbaro. We explored whether he will be honored by the sport itself; will Barbaro ultimately be inducted into the Hall of Fame? A more tangible representation of Barbaro will be his memorial at Churchill Downs. I have examined how that supports his legacy, and have noted how other racetracks honored Barbaro.

"I believe Barbaro will be remembered as a brilliant racehorse who had his career cut short," said *Daily Racing Form*'s Jay Privman. "We'll always wonder what might have been. And if no one wins the Triple Crown in upcoming years, I think many will look at him even more fondly as a racehorse, because we never found out if he could sweep the Triple Crown. He surely was dominant in the Derby, far more so than Big Brown or Smarty Jones."

"I also think his legacy will be intertwined with medical advances," he continued. "It seems that much was learned about the care and treatment of his serious injury during his post-operative stage. We've made so much progress in equine care in the past twenty years that I would have to think the lessons learned from Barbaro, and the money raised in his name will go a long way toward greater advances in equine health care."

....

"He was a very special horse. On every surface, grass, sloppy track, it did not matter. He destroyed the field in the Derby. He showed his class on the track. He demonstrated his courage after his injury. He was just so special."

—EDGAR PRADO,
Summer 2010

....

While Privman addresses the advances in equine care because of Barbaro, I think he addresses a key point in terms of the question of "what might have been." We have not had a Triple Crown winner for more than thirty years. Some have come close like Real Quiet (1998) and Smarty Jones (2004), but they were defeated. They could not accomplish the feat. What we do not know about Barbaro is whether he could have captured the elusive Triple Crown.

Steve Haskin's concern, that Barbaro's fight for survival will be better

MEMORIES OF BARBARO

How will history remember Barbaro? An inspiration—a call to action—from the hidden world of horse racing he brought light into darkness. For the first time issues could be discussed in a healing context, for the horse and the horse racing industry. The nobility of his breeding and his training and care—and his career, short as it was—were all about excellence, faith, and teamwork. A great racehorse does not come out of nowhere, there are no short cuts. One could see the scaffolding of his rise very clearly, and the intentionality of his owners and trainers—all on the same page, always, the horse first.

He came as a surprise to a somewhat tawdry and worn-out profession and lifted it all up as the best the horse racing world could give—in his connections, his trainers, his handlers—a legacy of extraordinary talent that opened humans to the great potential of the human-horse connection. We are all connected. He was bred in perfect balance, an extraordinary racehorse, an animal from another world, otherworldly—a commotion of dark brown, fluid muscled beauty and motion, elegant, vibrant, keenly intelligent, and very opinionated.

During his fight to survive from his catastrophic injury, he showed tenacious courage, total trust in his exceptional handlers, and the heart of a champion that would not give up. He above all showed humans that there might well be a profound connection between himself and his connections and with those he met during his short life on earth.

He opened hearts to the possibility that his nation, his sport, reflected more than darkness but showed high values; put the horse first as his owners did. He is a great reminder of what is really important: opening the door for many great rescues and campaigns to save thoroughbreds not suited for the track; great devotion and compassion for the horse, craft, and skill. He pointed a way to fix the things not right in the industry that needed a voice; a singular voice of power for the hidden world; of the backstretch; the invisible that makes the visible possible; and athleticism that was given in unselfish and remarkable ways. He showed the world we are all connected.

His layered beauty and unconditional love for running free in the wind, like a romp in the field, transports my heart to ancient Greek wisdom. They understood tragedy and the need to transform their losses and sorrows to a more luminous landscape that in turn would prove instructive and inspirational. They understood the beauty and intelligence of nature and of the animal kingdom—that life was a series of encounters with the divine, that which is larger than us. He opened these doors and windows into our souls and hearts. The tragic loss of such a talent and sentient animal informed many of what greatness looks and feels like.

Those who don't read history are doomed to repeat its ills, so with all this beauty and power seen and felt, we could be inspired to take the high road in his honor and live a great life, live our best life—we sure saw it in him.

—FOB MARTITA GOSHEN

remembered than his sheer brilliance on the racetrack, is shared by many.

"Barbaro will be remembered for his indomitable spirit and courage off the track and his exceptional brilliance on the track," said Haskin. "His will to survive and the battles he fought will forever be embedded in the hearts of not only racing fans, but sports fans and animal lovers. Not even Secretariat received the national exposure Barbaro did during those gut-wrenching eight months following his injury. It is unfortunate, however, that those months will be a greater part of his legacy than his breathtaking victory in the Kentucky Derby and his unblemished record."

Barbaro's exercise rider, Peter Brette, concurs. "I know he was a brilliant racehorse. Unfortunately I think he will be remembered more for being a fighter, than a brilliant racehorse," said Brette. "Some people will say that his Derby win was a fluke, but it wasn't. He was only just getting going. We had not seen the best of him yet."

There is no doubt that many learned about Barbaro through his struggle and fight at New Bolton Center, and he spent a longer time at New Bolton Center than he did as a racehorse. But those who did start to follow him at New Bolton Center discovered the brilliance he had displayed on the racetrack.

Dorothy Ours, author of *Man o' War: A Legend Like Lightning*, suggested how we will choose our own way of remembering Barbaro.

"Over decades and centuries, history distills a subject into a few general impressions: a quick ID," she explained. "For example, most of us may not know much about Napoleon Bonaparte and his military campaigns, but we hear 'Napoleon' and picture a small man with a big hat sticking one hand in his coat. Over time, a similar distillation will happen with Barbaro. Racing aficionados will study details of his life and career. But in the world at large, only a few images will stick: gloriously alone near the Derby finish line, holding up his broken leg at Pimlico, showing remarkable spirit at New Bolton despite the bulky leg cast. Because many people outside the horse world will recognize Barbaro's fight for life even if they missed his Derby performance, they will picture the injury or the cast. And everyone will remember the end."

"There's no escaping this: History will say, 'Racehorse who died young....' Our own responses will complete the image," Ours continues. "I hope that generations of research and rescue springing from Barbaro complete his historical quick ID: '... and saved countless other horses.'"

INDUSTRY HONORS

In terms of industry honors, and how they will help preserve the memory of Barbaro, we might be left wanting. Barbaro did not win an Eclipse Award, and it is quite possible he may not be inducted into the Hall of Fame.

In year-end Eclipse Award honors for 2006, Barbaro was nominated for both the Three-Year-Old Colt category and the Horse of the Year category. He was runner up in both, behind Bernardini in the Three-Year-Old category (210 votes to 56 votes), and behind Invasor, but ahead of Bernardini, in the Horse of the Year voting (Invasor: 228, Barbaro: 21, Bernardini: 16).

After Bernardini won the Preakness Stakes, he went on to win three more races (the Jim Dandy (Grade 2), the Travers Stakes (Grade 1), and the Jockey Club Gold Cup (Grade 1)) before finishing second to Invasor in the Breeders' Cup Classic (Grade 1). In total, Bernardini won six races in 2006, racing from January to November. Voters determined, as a whole, that Bernardini had a better record than Barbaro, who had four wins for the year. Not everyone agreed with the outcome, but certainly the Eclipse Awards does seem to reward those that race throughout the year. The Jacksons did win an Eclipse Award, in a tie with Darley Stable, as owners of the year. Edgar Prado won the Eclipse Award for best jockey, and Michael Matz finished third in the voting for trainer of the year. Team Barbaro also received a special Eclipse Award.

What is less clear is whether Barbaro's accomplishments will be enough for him to gain the highest honor within the horse racing industry—a spot in the National Thoroughbred Racing Hall of Fame in Saratoga Springs, New York. Typically, horses that have been nominated have performed at the highest level over a long period of time. We know Barbaro was robbed of the opportunity to have a long career, which may work against him when the discussion turns to the Hall of Fame.

"Hall of Fame—at this point, I wouldn't think so, based on his limited career," said Steve Haskin. "But times have changed, as has our perception of a horse's legacy. Because of the limited careers of Smarty Jones and Afleet Alex, I think by the time Barbaro becomes eligible he might be considered strongly, depending on whether those other two make it in. If they do, then there is no reason to think he won't, especially considering what he did for racing, veterinary medicine, and for thoroughbreds in general."

Haskin noted that other recent top caliber three-year-olds also have not had long careers, not because they suffered a catastrophic injury, but because they were retired to stud. The *Philadephia Daily News*'s Dick Jerardi concurs and expands on the issue.

"Probably no, because he only started six times before the Preakness," said Jerardi. "He had major wins in the Florida Derby and the Kentucky Derby, yet he might have been one of the greatest grass horses of all time. But as things are judged now, his resume is not long enough. Only Point Given, of the top three-year-olds from the 2000s, has been elected to the Hall of Fame. He was a decent two-year-old, won two out of three legs of the Triple Crown, the Haskell and the Travers."

"Perhaps now because our best horses are retired after their three-year-old career, the way we consider Hall of Fame nominees will change," Jerardi continued. "It's kind of like in college basketball. If a college player plays a few years in college, he is looked down on by the pros. He was not good enough to leave college early. Now if a horse is racing as a five-year-old, he was not good enough to retire to stud. I think if the evaluation process changes, and Barbaro can get on the ballot, then he has a chance of getting in. As things stand now, he likely won't, and nor will many of our modern day stars. Maybe in ten years, fifteen years, or twenty years from now, things will be looked at in a different light."

"I don't know what he didn't have, that you could criticize him for. He was like the perfect horse, flawless. He was easy to train, willing, attractive, athletic, and well-mannered. I don't know what flaw he had.

"His biggest problem was when we put tack on him, you had to do it quickly. He got impatient; when he was ready to go he wanted to go. But he could not have been more of a gentleman. He shipped well. In Kentucky, the media was all over Brother Derek, Barbaro was out grazing at Churchill Downs. Cars were going by, he could not care. I cannot say enough about him, and what it was like to train a Derby winner. It's not difficult; despite the trainer he was still a Derby winner."

—MICHAEL MATZ,
Summer 2010

Daily Racing Form's Jay Hovdey thinks that Barbaro may not make it to the Hall of Fame, but also wonders if it is truly important in Barbaro's case.

"In stark terms, Barbaro's chances for ever being elected to the Thoroughbred Racing Hall of Fame are not promising, especially since his career was so brief and he spent part of it racing on grass, which never has been a mainstream path to enshrinement," said Hovdey. "Beyond that, to my knowledge there is no Hall of Fame horse that got there because of what happened to him after a racing career had come to an end. If that were the case, Ferdinand would have been in the Hall of Fame the moment it was revealed that he had been slaughtered and eaten in Japan. And he was a Horse of the Year who won both the Kentucky Derby and the Breeders' Cup Classic."

"More importantly, I think whether or not Barbaro is ever elected to the Thoroughbred Racing Hall of Fame is beside the point," continued Hovdey. "Because of his tragic injury and sad end, Barbaro transcended the traditional measures by which Hall of Famers are judged. There are any number of outstanding

Thoroughbreds about which could be said the same thing, including Ruffian, Landaluce, Roving Boy, Lamb Chop, and Go for Wand. Some are in the Hall of Fame, some are not. We think of them no differently. Like those before him, Barbaro became an iconic brand, whose name when uttered brings to mind not simply a fast, classy young racehorse who died too young, but also a symbol of fragility and loss in the face of great power and beauty."

Hovdey may be right. It might matter little whether Barbaro makes it to the Hall of Fame, in terms of how people will remember Barbaro in the future. But perhaps it is a lost opportunity for the industry itself to showcase one of its stars that has transcended our sport.

MEMORIAL AT CHURCHILL DOWNS

Perhaps the most significant influence regarding Barbaro's legacy and how he will be remembered for years to come will be his memorial at Churchill Downs. It is also the one aspect that the Jacksons had most control over in terms of how they want to shape the memory of Barbaro for future generations of racing fans.

Barbaro's Memorial at Churchill Downs is arguably one of the most significant memorials to any horse in North America, in terms of location and design. Many regard Man o' War's Memorial at the Kentucky Horse Park as the standard to which all other horse memorials are measured, much like they regard Man o' War the standard of greatness against which all others are compared.

Barbaro is the first horse to be buried on the property of Churchill Downs, which officially opened in 1875. Four other Kentucky Derby winners are buried on the property of the Kentucky Derby Museum: Broker's Tip (1933), Swaps (1955), Carry Back (1961), and Sunny's Halo (1983). Eight Belles, who finished second to Big Brown in 2008 before fatally injuring herself, is also buried at the Kentucky Derby Museum. While the museum is adjacent to Churchill Downs, these horses are not buried on the Churchill Downs property. The decision, by Churchill Downs, to be the final resting place for Barbaro, set a precedent. This is a strong signal that the home of America's most important race reveres Barbaro

and what he accomplished on the first Saturday in May 2006.

The Barbaro sculpture is not the only statue at Churchill Downs. There is also a likeness of the jockey Pat Day and a memorial for the 1875 Kentucky Derby winner, Aristides. But Barbaro's statue is outside of the grounds, freely accessible to the public all year round, and as such, is clearly the most visible memorial on the grounds. In fact, it is so visible that it risks getting as much attention as the Twin Spires, the iconic symbol of the racetrack.

Memorial at Churchill Downs

I'M HOME AT LAST

It is here in Kentucky I entered life

born in a stall, in a barn at first light

days in the grass my mother nearby

it was here I raced and caught your eye

I've come full circle, back to the start

for here is my home, and here is my heart

Poem written by
GRETCHEN JACKSON
read at the Barbaro Memorial unveiling, April 2009

"The Man o' War Memorial and the Barbaro Memorial have become key vehicles in passing on these horses' legacies to the next generation. Because of their size and vitality, these statues capture the transcendental power that attracts us to horses to begin with.

"The memorials have become physical links to these great horses. They are now gathering places where people look up in awe and feel compelled to share their feelings and memories and stories, adding to the oral history.

"Just by its constant public presence, the Barbaro Memorial at Churchill Downs will allow his story to endure far beyond that of other great runners. Many of those, like Man o' War, get to pass on their legacy through their offspring, but for Barbaro, this is the final snapshot."

—ANNE PETERS,
Thoroughbred Heritage

The location is not only a significant honor bestowed on Barbaro by Churchill Downs, but also it is quite simply a very public location. Each year the world focuses on our sport for one day, the first Saturday in May. Those attending the Kentucky Derby will be reminded of Barbaro, and those viewing the Derby on various media around the world will, more than likely, also see glimpses of his memorial. Quite simply, Barbaro's memorial is in a very public place, and as such, he will remain a constant presence, a reminder of the greatness he achieved at the nation's most storied racetrack.

Sculptor Alexa King undertook the monumental task of executing the goals of the project for the Jacksons. Gretchen Jackson told King, during their first meeting, that she wanted the statue to show Barbaro's joy for running. She also wanted the statue to portray Barbaro on the top of his game—powerful and beautiful. It was critical to show Barbaro at full stretch, with all four feet off the ground, "flying." It required groundbreaking engineering to complete that aspect of the design.

The inscription on the statue, in concert with the design of the memorial, further reflects how the Jacksons would like Barbaro to be remembered. It is a quote by Olympic champion Eric Liddell, in the movie *Chariots of Fire*, which reads: "I believe God made me for a purpose but He also made me fast. And when I run, I feel His pleasure." Mrs. Jackson had this to say about the choice of the quote: "When we heard Liddell's quote, we thought it surely must have been written with Barbaro in mind. The speed and the joy of running, the otherworldliness; all this was Barbaro." Eric Liddell's story, portrayed in the award-winning film *Chariots of Fire*, is a story of true inspiration. Liddell was a remarkable athlete with deeply religious convictions, who determined to use his athletic talents to serve his greater purpose.

This statue will serve as the most significant tangible representation for future generations to learn about Barbaro: as a racehorse. And they will be learning about Barbaro at the home of his most famous victory, Churchill Downs.

The memorial will also help overcome our own industry's lack of recognition for Barbaro through traditional honors. King notes, "In Barbaro there is no doubt we witnessed a great racehorse. It is unfortunate he did not win year-end honors with an Eclipse Award. It is also likely, given the brevity of his career, that he will not make it into the Hall of Fame. But with this memorial, there he is, right there. It is an enduring representation of a great racehorse, at the home of America's greatest horse race, that he won with ease."

The statue was unveiled a week before the 2009 Kentucky Derby. The day after Mine That Bird won that Derby, co-owner Mark Allen and trainer Chip Woolley, stood by the Memorial and handed out the four hundred roses from the garland of roses Mine That Bird had won the day before. Chip Woolley remembered, "To lose a great horse like Barbaro, and to see his impact on our industry, it was a tribute to Barbaro. We were very fortunate to be there and to win the Derby; it was our opportunity to give something back, a true piece of the Derby.

"At first there were just a few people, but then word got out. People got stirred up, people were crying. It became a whole lot more than I thought it would be at the time. It was just a gesture to Barbaro and his owners."

OTHER RACETRACKS HONOR BARBARO

Delaware Park, where Barbaro won his first race, and Pimlico Race Course, home of his ill-fated Preakness, both named races after Barbaro, to honor his legacy. Pimlico's Barbaro Stakes replaced the Sir Barton Stakes, named after the first Triple Crown winner. Sadly, this race has been lost, perhaps temporarily, due to the downturn in racing in Maryland. The Barbaro Stakes at Delaware Park, which replaced the Grade 3 Leonard Richards Stakes, is held each summer, and will serve as a reminder of the horse each year.

AND FINALLY

Dr. Dean Richardson spent a lot of time with Barbaro over the eight months of his stay at New Bolton Center.

"To be honest, I am still waiting for there to be enough detachment from Barbaro that I could predict how he will be remembered," said Richardson. "When I really think about it, I hope that he will be remembered as an extraordinary athlete cut down in his prime that was fortunate enough to have owners who truly cared for his well-being and were open-minded enough to try to save him. I hope his struggle helped people both appreciate horses more and more fully understand the available options for treatment."

"The reality, however, is that I think of him on such a personal basis that the most honest thing to say is simply that I miss him," he added. "I wish so much that we could have saved him to become a comfortable horse. He deserved more than he got."

As the author of this book, and someone who was privileged to have known Barbaro, I have my own feelings about how this amazing horse should be remembered. It is my sincere hope that, in some small way, this book helps shape how history remembers Barbaro: as a champion on the track, a champion in life, and, as Michael Matz described him, "a perfect horse, he was flawless."

Afterword

Every time someone talks to me about Barbaro, I am right back to 2005 and the first time I truly saw Barbaro. Oh, yes, sure, I'd seen him before, but this was the first time I had seen him looking so elegant, grand, and confident. He was in superb athletic condition to run his first race at Delaware Park. I had goose bumps all over, waiting and watching in the paddock that October afternoon. Yes, there was something about Barbaro that was special. He won that day, cruising over the grass and giving us all an indication of what was to come.

Barbaro led us through the best of times. Simply stated—it was a goal achieved. The Kentucky Derby is every racehorse owner and trainer's dream. It was our dream also. We spent the days leading up to the Derby participating in all the pre-Derby events. Then there was the huge, unbelievable win, with Barbaro's feet above the track just flying, and a look that said it was all for the fun of it. How he galloped out after the race!

The good, elated times—the indescribable euphoria—did not last that long. We were thrust into a sickening, horrendous moment when Barbaro broke down right before our eyes. We raced to be at his side and to demand he be given a chance.

I did not have to worry about protecting Barbaro, as usual he spoke for himself. He wanted to live. We tried. We all did our best for a horse that might have been even tougher as a patient than as an athlete.

For us, it seemed as if the world came to his rescue. What a reaction to his tragedy! People wrote us inspirational letters and cards. Books were sent; children painted pictures for him; folks sent carrots, cookies, and rosaries from all over the world. People hugged us and sent flowers, gifts, love, and precious support. How we appreciated it! We were awed by the affection so many people had for Barbaro. The letters from his fans related remarkable stories of healing and inspiration found in Barbaro's struggle and his will to carry on.

Barbaro's struggle is over now. His race record lives on. His statue races the wind down at Churchill Downs. He and his memory are fresh and indelibly stamped on my heart. How special was this horse? I do not know how to measure this, or what instrument to use. Surely, there is not one big enough.

GRETCHEN JACKSON, SEPTEMBER 2010